INSTRUCTOR'S MANUAL
WITH TEST ITEM FILE

DATABASE PROCESSING

INSTRUCTOR'S MANUAL

DATABASE PROCESSING

Seventh Edition

David M. Kroenke

Prentice Hall
Upper Saddle River, New Jersey 07458

Acquisitions editor: *David Alexander*
Assistant editor: *Lori Cerreto*
Project editor: *Joseph F. Tomasso*
Manufacturer: *Bawden Printing*

Printed in the United States of America

10 9 8 7 6 5 4 3 2

ISBN 0-13-085819-6

Prentice-Hall International (UK) Limited, *London*
Prentice-Hall of Australia Pty. Limited, *Sydney*
Prentice-Hall Canada Inc., *Toronto*
Prentice-Hall Hispanoamericana, S.A., *Mexico*
Prentice-Hall of India Private Limited, *New Delhi*
Prentice-Hall of Japan, Inc., *Tokyo*
Prentice-Hall (Singapore) Pte Ltd
Editora Prentice-Hall do Brasil, Ltda., *Rio de Janeiro*

Table of Contents

Instructor's Manual

Test Item File

Introduction

The database class has always been fun and interesting to teach. Recently, with the advent of the Web, it has become even more exciting and relevant to the needs of the students. The three chapters on databases using Internet technology (Chapters 11-13) were as enjoyable to write as any I have written in all the years I've been working on this book. I believe you'll find this section fun to teach as well. However, in the face of these new and exciting developments, I do think it is important to remember the importance of the fundamentals — in particular data modeling and database design.

I believe that teaching data modeling skills is the most important part of this class. **Once they have a design**, students can read a book on Access or SQL Server or ORACLE or *something or other for Dummies* to learn how to use a product to create a database. This course is, however, the single, most effective place for students to learn data modeling and database design skills. It may be the only place where anyone even tries!

Over the years I have found that launching immediately into data modeling confuses the students. Until they see and work with a small database, they do not understand how data modeling fits into the larger picture. Hence, I think it is important to set the stage, as is done in Chapters 1 and 2, before beginning the modeling and design topics.

Following this line of reasoning, I believe the general threads of this course are, in order:

- Establish perspective by showing what a database is, how one is used, and what the components are

- Teach data modeling and database design

- Learn how to process a database via SQL and application programs

- Present technology and products for publishing databases using Internet technology

- Discuss other topics as time allows and local student needs require

This is a lot of material to teach. If the students have already used Access or another personal DBMS in other courses, then you can save time by abbreviating the first item. On the other hand, if this is the students' first exposure to database processing, then the first four items will probably fill all the class time and the last item, other topics, may need to be assigned as special projects or independent reading, if at all.

Data Modeling

Two different data modeling tools are taught in *Database Processing.* Chapter 3 explains the basic features and concepts of the entity-relationship model and applies that model to two small case applications. Chapter 6 then shows how to transform entity-relationship designs into normalized database designs. Chapter 4 teaches the features and concepts of the semantic object model, and Chapter 7 then teaches database design using semantic objects.

The entity-relationship model is well known and the inclusion of a large amount of material on it will be of no surprise. You may be surprised to find two chapters on the semantic object model. This model, which is an integration of the semantic data model (Hammer and McLeod) with the design philosophies of object-oriented programming, has, I believe, important advantages over the entity-relationship model. For one, it is easier for users to understand. It also leads, more naturally, to normalized database designs. Additionally, semantic objects can be used to guide database application design (as shown in Chapter 9). They also provide boundaries for logical units of work. Even more important, it is possible to better model complicated databases with the semantic object model than with the entity-relationship model. Finally, in my experience, it is far easier to learn and to teach the modeling of complicated databases with the semantic object model than with the entity-relationship model.

If time is short, you can skip the material on the semantic object model without loss of continuity. But, given the importance of data modeling, I think that presenting two different approaches is certainly appropriate and helpful to the student.

Wall Data, Inc. has developed a database modeling and design tool called DBApp that uses the semantic object modeling. You can use it to generate Access and SQL Server databases as well as to create ASP pages for database processing on the Web. Your students will gain much more from this modeling technique if they use this tool in conjunction with their study. You and your students can download a free copy of it for use in your course. This copy can also be placed in your lab if that is more effective for you. See Appendix C for more information about this product and its use.

Changes from the Sixth Edition

There are four major changes in this edition. First and most obvious is the inclusion of new material on database processing using Internet technology. As stated in the text, many of the databases that use this technology will operate on corporate intranets and so calling them Internet databases or Web databases is misleading. Even though it's awkward to say, I think we should use the phrase *database processing using Internet technology* instead.

The second major change in this edition is a revamping of the discussion of database application design. Chapter 8 in the sixth edition has been substantially rewritten and appears in this edition as Chapter 9. A big part of that discussion concerns the processing of database views. It is most important that students understand the difference between a database view and a SQL view (the views defined in SQL Server and other DBMS products). A database view can have more than one multi-valued path whereas a SQL view may not. This will become very important as XML becomes the standard for inter-organization data transfer. See the discussion on the teaching of Chapter 9 for more information.

When Microsoft shipped Office 2000, it included a version of its OLAP server with every copy of Office. Overnight, the installed base of OLAP exploded. Because of this, I believe it is very important for students in the class to understand the features and functions of OLAP and how they relate to database processing. This discussion has been added to Chapter 14.

Finally, the fourth change is to consolidate all of the discussions of multi-user processing into Chapter 12. In prior editions, the text presented multi-user technology in the context of its use, but this strategy split the discussion into too many pieces and led to confusion and repetition. Hence, all of the multi-user material is presented in a single chapter. Since all database applications that use Internet technology are multi-user applications, it seemed most logical to add that material to that section and this has been done.

Of course, the normal changes that are made from edition to edition have been made as well. For example, all of the Access 97 examples have been replaced by Access 2000 examples. Additionally, all references to SALSA have been removed since Wall Data no longer supports that product. (Wall Data transformed itself into an Internet company and no longer supports non-Internet technology database products.) Other changes have been made to make the examples more current and relevant.

Learning Internet Technology

While Internet technology is proving to be a great boon to database processing, it does require new knowledge on the part of the instructor. It will not be too difficult to learn what you need for this class, however, and there are many helpful resources available. If you are not already familiar with this technology, I recommend the following tasks and resources:

3

1. Read Chapters 11, 12, and 13 to see what will be presented

2. Visit the excellent Web site that the World Wide Web Consortium (W3C) publishes at www.w3.org. Look for tutorials and links to tutorial sites for learning DHTML and XML.

3. Write simple VBScript or Jscript programs and process them in a browser. Use Figures 11-9 and 11-12 as examples.

4. Install a copy of Access 2000, create some tables and forms and export them to ASP. Examine the ASP code that Access generates to understand how to blend database processing with Web server processing.

5. Install a copy of NT with IIS. Publish ASP pages to a directory and use them. Make changes to the ASP pages and observe the consequences.

6. Obtain the ASP pages used in Chapter 13 from the instructor's portion of our Web site and install them on an IIS server. Make changes to the pages and observe the results.

7. Install IE 5.0 and, using Figure 11-19 as an example, write XSL for materializing XML documents.

8. Visit vendor Web sites such as www.microsoft.com and search for tutorials on DHTML, XML, OLE DB, OLAP, and other technologies.

9. Visit online publications such as www.zdnet.com and search for tutorials as above.

Use of SQL Server 7.0

A free evaluation edition of SQL Server 7.0 is packaged with this text. The license is valid for 120 days after installation. Readings and instructions for students can be found in Appendix B. You could assign its use almost any time, but it might be better to do it during or after Chapter 8 since that chapter introduces the tasks required when setting up an enterprise-class DBMS database. Also, students can create some tables and fill them using the Open Table facility in Enterprise Manager (See Appendix B) while discussing Chapter 8. Then they can use Query Analyzer to create and run SQL statements in conjunction with Chapter 9.

Microsoft says they have worked hard to make this version easy to install on any Windows systems, including Win95, W98, NT, and Win2000. I believe that they succeeded. I have encountered no problems during installation and the product seems to work very well. You might want to work through Appendix B with your own copy of SQL Server 7.0 early on in the course to ensure it works in your environment. I have found no ugly surprises at all; in fact, my only surprise was how easy it was.

In this first course, it is difficult to do more than scratch the surface with SQL Server. There is so much more in the software than can be addressed in this text. If your students are going to continue on into a second database course, you might tell them not to install it in this course and to save their 120 day period for the next course where they can take advantage of more of SQL Server's capabilities.

End of Chapter Exercises and Projects

Chapters include two categories of exercises and a set of projects. The purpose of the Group I questions is review. After reading the chapter, students should be able to answer all of the Group I questions without problem or hesitation. I encourage the students to use those questions when preparing for an exam. The Group II questions require the students to apply or extend the material presented in the chapter. These questions require more thought, time, and work.

Projects require application of chapter material in a problem setting. Three projects run through the first seven chapters. Two of them are introduced in Chapter 1 and concern databases that could be used for e-commerce; one uses Dell for an example and the other uses Amazon.com as an example. The third project, which is introduced at the end of Chapter 3, concerns a non-profit organization, the Metropolitan Housing Authority. These projects are used for the purpose of developing entity-relationship models and for semantic object models, as well as for transforming entity-relationship and semantic object designs into relational designs. I recommend that using one of the cases for in-class discussion of text materials and assigning the other two for student projects.

Answers to all of the project assignments are presented in this instructor's manual. In addition, our Web site at www.prenhall.com/kroenke/ contains all DBApp models of the projects. This site also has the Access 97 and Access 2000 databases discussed in the text. All SQL Server tables discussed in this manual can be found in the SQL Server database "SQL Server Example Database." A backup version of this database is located on our site as well. See SQL Server help "How to restore a database backup" for information on creating a database from this backup file.

Materials for a Course Syllabus

The following materials may be helpful for constructing a course syllabus.

Course Objectives

- Learn the role of databases and database applications in contemporary organizations

- Learn and practice data modeling using the entity-relationship and semantic object models

- Learn and practice developing database designs

- Understand the use of SQL and learn SQL syntax

- Learn emerging Internet technology that is relevant to database processing including the use of XML, ASP scripting, and OLE DB

- Understand the special needs of multi-user database processing and learn techniques for controlling the consequences of concurrent data access

- Learn the need for both database administration and data administration

- Understand the issues involved in enterprise data sharing and learn the nature of data warehouses

- Learn the features and functions of OLAP (OnLine Analytical Processing) and understand its relationship to database processing

- Understand the need for object database management and learn the basics of the SQL3 and ODMG standards

  Plus other objectives that relate to the projects you assign.

Sample Course Outline

The course outline shown below can be used for a class having thirty fifty-minute meetings. To cover this amount of material in thirty lessons, the course must move along quickly. If you have many out-of-class assignments or projects, you may want to cut back on the material in Lessons 27-29. Also, this outline does not include any of the Appendices and you may need to make adjustments for them.

If you have a fifteen-week semester, then cases, lectures on DBMS products, and lab sessions can be added. The breakup of the chapters as shown in the outline below could still be used and the other material added around the assignments shown.

Course Outline for Thirty Fifty-minute Lectures

Class Meeting	Topic	Reading Assignment
1	Introduction	
2	Overview and History of Database Processing	Chapter 1
3	Components of a Database System	Chapter 2
4	Entity-relationship Model I	Chapter 3
5	Entity-relationship Model II	Chapter 3
6	Semantic Object Model I	Chapter 4
7	Semantic Object Model II	Chapter 4
8	Normalization	Chapter 5
9	Normalization	Chapter 5
10	Exam I	
11	Database Design with E-R I	Chapter 6
12	Database Design with E-R II	Chapter 6
13	Database Design with SOM I	Chapter 7
14	Database Design with SOM II	Chapter 7
15	Relational Implementation and Relational Algebra	Chapter 8

16	SQL	Chapter 9
17	Review	
18	Exam II	
19	Database Application Design I	Chapter 9
20	Database Application Design II	Chapter 9
21	Database Processing Using Internet Technology I	Chapter 11
22	Database Processing Using Internet Technology II	Chapter 11
23	Managing Multi-user Databases	Chapter 12
24	Accessing the Database Server I	Chapter 13
25	Accessing the Database Server II	Chapter 13
26	Sharing Enterprise Data	Chapter 14
27	DB2 Implementation	Chapter 15
28	Hierarchical and Network Data Models	Chapter 16
29	Object Oriented Database Processing	Chapter 17
30	Review	

Lecture Preparation Materials

This section presents lecture materials. For each chapter, learning objectives, teaching suggestions and lecture ideas, and answers to all of the questions and projects are presented.

Chapter 1

Introduction

Objectives

- Understand different types of databases and their organizational contexts.
- Compare file processing systems and database processing systems.
- Define the term *database*.
- Learn the historical context of database processing.

Teaching Suggestions

1. Introduce the course by explaining that database processing is the heart of all applications today. The demand for knowledgeable people (both users and technicians) is high, but the supply is low. The knowledge gained in this course will be valuable at job-hunting time. Internet technology has tremendously amplified the need for database knowledge.

2. The goal of the opening sections is to teach the fact that databases vary widely in size, complexity, and organizational scope. On completing this course, the students should be able to develop personal and even some work-group databases on their own, and they should be able to participate as productive members of a team to develop an organizational database. With some work, they should be able to develop simple Internet technology applications as well.

3. When discussing file processing systems, remind students that users of file processing systems are almost always at the mercy of the MIS department to write programs that manipulate stored data and produce needed information. One significant development in database processing, particularly with the more user-friendly relational DBMS products, is that users can sometimes get their own answers from the stored data.

4. Today, few students have had experience with file processing systems. You may need to teach them about file processing before discussing how database processing differs from file processing. The major point of all this is the need to process data by relationship.

5. Check to ensure the students distinguish among a database (the stored data), a DBMS (software that processes a database), and a database application (software that calls on a DBMS to process a database on its

10

behalf). These terms are often misused and the differences among them are surprisingly difficult to teach.

6.   I find the term *DBMS products* easier to pronounce than *DBMSs*.

7.   Possibly the most interesting aspect of the history of database processing is how much it has changed in the past 25 years. With the advent of the Web, with XML, with the soon-to-be-realized emergence of fast data transmission to the home, and with HDTV, we are likely to see a continuation of this dramatic rate of change. The students should expect this; I believe that at least every five years, half of the technology they know will become obsolete.

Answers to Group 1 Questions

1.1   It is important because of the immense need for skilled database designers and implementors. Internet technology has made what was already a hot career path into one that is white hot! Without skilled people, the advantages of database technology will not be realized by organizations that need to use it.

1.2   See row 1 of Figure 1-8.

1.3   See row 2 of Figure 1-8.

1.4   See row 3 of Figure 1-8.

1.5   See row 4 of Figure 1-8. Also see Figure 1-7.

1.6   Users have information needs that must be satisfied by forms, reports, and queries. Database applications are programs that process the database to materialize forms and reports and to process application logic. The DBMS is a program that processes the database, which is a self-describing collection of integrated records.

1.7   The DBMS is gradually taking on more and more of the application programs functions and roles.

1.8   Limitations of file processing systems:
    a.   Data is separated and isolated. Example: student grade records are stored separately from student extracurricular activities records, so it is difficult to check on academic eligibility.
    b.   Data is duplicated. Example: student personal data (home address, parent, health status) is duplicated between records described in (a). If a student moves, both sets of files must be updated.

c. Programs dependent on file formats. Example: fifteen programs exist for producing reports based on data in student grade records. Description of that file appears in every program. When file format changes, all programs must be updated.

d. Complex objects are difficult to represent. Example: student transcript is constructed from data belonging to student, course, and (sometimes) professor. Separate files would be kept on each of these objects, plus one for transcripts (containing duplicated data).

1.9 In a database, data is centralized and integrated. It is not duplicated (except in the special case of distributed databases), because all applications access it through a single DBMS. Application programs do not include database file formats because all data about the structure of the database is stored in the data dictionary, which is accessed only by the DBMS, not by application programs. Complex objects are constructed by the DBMS, usually by extracting related data from various sources and combining it into a cohesive unit. This is all done without the knowledge of the user.

1.10 A database is a self-describing collection of integrated records.

1.11 Metadata is data that describes the structure of the database. Indexes are data structures used to improve direct access and sequential retrieval. Application metadata is data about the structure of forms and reports, as well as other application constructs.

1.12 A database contains records of the condition of a company or other organization. As such it is a representation of that company or organization. A database is a model of the way that the users of the database view the business. It is not a model of reality because reality is too complex (in fact, unknowable); hence a database can only be a model of a human's model. This is important because it is a waste of time for one database designer to claim "My model is a better model of the real world than yours." The real question is which model is a better model of the users' models.

1.13 A stockbroker uses a personal database application to keep track of his clients' names, telephone numbers, and addresses.

1.14 A political fund-raising committee uses a workgroup database to keep track of donors (and potential donors).

1.15 A construction company uses a database to keep track of project costs, labor, materials, and schedule. One database supports each of these different applications.

1.16   Slow and unreliable applications. DBMS developers did not know efficient
        ways to provide DB access; programmers did not know how to use new DB
        technology.

1.17   The relational model is readily understood by users because it stores data
        in tables; relationships among rows are stored in user-visible data.
        Relations can be processed by non-procedural programs. Especially
        useful in DSS applications.

1.18   Relational databases typically require more resources than databases
        based on other models. Thus, applications using a relational database had
        unacceptable response time (at least until faster computer technology was
        developed). Also, programmers had become used to databases that
        processed data a record at a time. With the relational model, data was
        processed a table at a time.

1.19   Sales of generalized file processors started micro DBMS industry. Then,
        true relational DBMS products were developed. Also, mainframe DBMS
        products were brought down to micros. Today, GUI products such as
        Microsoft Access and Lotus Approach give great power while being
        (relatively) easy to use.

1.20   The development and acceptance of LAN technology and products.

1.21   With client server, multiple CPUs conducting DB application processing
        simultaneously on the client computers.

1.22   The database is spread across two or more computers. Security, control,
        coordination, and synchronization are difficult problems in distributed
        database systems.

1.23   To provide persistence for OOP objects. Rarely adopted (as of 1999)
        because the data must be converted to object format and the advantages
        of ODBMS aren't perceived to be great enough to justify the expense (and
        risk) of a conversion.

Answers to Projects

A.   I used Dell's Web site and found a page that listed types of computer
        products. From there I found the categories of laptops and looked for
        those under $2500. From there I used a system configuration page that
        gave me options to select and then repriced my laptop. As an aside, you
        can get a pretty spiffy laptop for $2500!

But, to answer the question, all of those pages could be backed by a database application, though I doubt the top-level ones involving product categories are. I believe the system configuration page would be the one most likely to benefit a database application.

Consider what happens if the system configuration page is not driven by a database application. Whenever the options or prices on a system change, without a database application, someone will need to modify the HTML for the page to implement the new options and prices. This could be a very labor intensive process because many servers support this site. If the system configuration page is supported by a database application, and if it reads available options and prices out of a database, then to change an option or price, Dell personnel need only modify the database's data. The next time a customer accesses the page, the new data will be read from the database — very easy with low labor costs.

B. I used Amazon's web site, and chose Book Search. There are several types of searches available. I found Search by Author, Title, and Subject; Search by ISBN; Search by Subject; Search by Publisher, Date; and Power Search. Since I wanted the most recent one, I chose to Search by Publisher and Date, entered "William Wordsworth" as subject and > 1998 as date. Three books were returned.

This searching capability has to be backed by a database application. There is no other way that Amazon could provide acceptable performance. Looking at the Power Search keywords, it appears that they have written an application that translates user-friendly terms for search criteria into predicates for SQL statements.

It is interesting to consider whether or not they have consolidated title data into one unnormalized table or whether they do joins on Title, Author, and Publisher. Because performance matters so much, and because this data is not heavily updated (a title, once it's in, doesn't change), I suspect that they have created a single (unnormalized) table and built many indexes on it for fast retrieval. Depending on the interests of your students, you might show both a normalized (three table) and unnormalized (one table) version and discuss the advantages and disadvantages of each with your students. Also discuss the use of indexes and how a lower level of update makes them more desirable.

Another interesting feature of this site appears when you select a particular book: "Customers who bought this book also bought . . ." I wonder how they generate that? Do they post-process their orders to determine correlations among book purchases and then show books that exceed some level of correlation? Or, do they just pick a book or two that

14

happen to have keywords in common? Interestingly, when using this site, it's hard to keep in mind that Amazon has commercial interests, and while this site appears in the form of a disinterested library, it is not. They have no requirement that facilities like "customers who bought also bought" be backed by any sort of analysis. It could be book buyers in the back room saying "Let's push title XYZ." They are delivering marketing messages in the garb of a reference librarian. Or am I just being paranoid? Hard to say.

Chapter 2

Components of Database Processing Systems

Objectives

- Learn the major elements of a database
- Understand the functions and features of the major subsystems of a DBMS
- Describe the tasks involved in developing a database and related applications
- Learn the major elements of a database application
- Understand two strategies for developing a database and it applications

Teaching Suggestions

1. The goal of this chapter is to present the major elements of a database and its applications. It is intended to provide a broad-brush overview of the subject before descending into the details of the technology in the next chapter.

2. The chapter distinguishes between a database (the data, indexes, and two types of metadata) and the database applications (forms, queries, reports, menus, and application programs). For some reason, perhaps as a result of the efforts of the marketing departments of DBMS vendors, students have a hard time discriminating between the two. To the user, its all one and the same, but the to the developer, creating a database and creating an application are two different tasks, with two different skill sets required.

3. Not all DBMS products incorporate all the features discussed in this chapter. But all DBMS products must have a DBMS engine, a definition tools subsystem (though it may be primitive), and a processing interface subsystem, and some type of data dictionary subsystem. The application development subsystem with some products is nothing more than a report writer, though with other products (Access and Approach) this subsystem is quite extensive. Quite a few DBMS products lack a data administration subsystem. You might install one of the evaluation copies of SQL Server in the lab and show students some of the differences between it and Access.

4. The discussion of the general development strategies starting on page 41 is important. Major corporations that are concerned with wide-enterprise

data modeling generally employ some type of top-down development -- at least to the point where a data architecture has been created. The need for such a strategy will not be apparent to the students, who will only have been exposed to relatively simple systems.

5. The discussion of data modeling on page 42 is intended to set the stage for the discussions of E-R and SOM in Chapters 3 and 4. The goal is to help the students understand what they're going to be doing before they get into the details of those models.

6. The terminology in the database field is often confusing. The same words often have different meanings depending on context, vendor, or even product. This is just the way it is in disciplines where the technology is fast-moving; students should get used to it. In particular, this chapter uses the words *data model* in two different ways. A *users' data model* is a representation of the users' data requirements; a *data model* is a vocabulary for creating such a representation. Thus there is the entity-relationship data model and there is the semantic object data model. Either of these data models can be used to document the users data requirements in a users' data model. Very confusing, but the context usually make the meaning clear.

Answers to Group I Questions

2.1   User data; metadata (describes the structure of the database); indexes (used to improve performance); and application metadata (describes the structure of the application components.)

2.2   PART (PartNumber, PartDescription, VendorName, VendorPhone), where a vendor provides many parts, but a part comes from just one vendor.

2.3   PART (PartNumber, PartDescription, VendorName)
VENDOR (VendorName, VendorPhone)

2.4   They describe the structure of the database. If metadata is placed in tables, then the DBMS query and reporting facilities can be used to report on the metadata.

2.5. Indexes improve performance for sorting and direct retrieval and can be used to enforce uniqueness in a column. They are desirable when any of the benefits described above are needed in the application. Indexes must be updated whenever the source data involved in the index is changed.

2.6   Application metadata is a description of the application components such as forms, reports, menus, and queries. It differs from metadata, which is a description of the database structure.

2.7   To facilitate the design and the creation of the database and its applications.

2.8   It processes requests generated by the application. For example, it finds rows of tables based on column values and returns a set of rows to the application.

2.9   The DBMS engine is the intermediary between the design tools and the run-time subsystems and the operating system. Access uses one of two different engines; the native engine used with mdb files is called Jet. SQL Server is the engine used with .adp files.

2.10   A schema is a description of the structure of the database's tables, relationships, domains, and business rules.

2.11   Relationships are expressed by placing the key of one table into a second table. For example, for the PART and VENDOR tables in the answer to question 2.3 above, the key of VENDOR, which is VendorName, has been placed in PART.

2.12   A domain is a set of values that a column may have.

2.13   Business rules are restrictions on the business's activities that must be reflected in the database and database applications. Examples: 1) A VendorName cannot exist in PART if it does not already exist in VENDOR. 2) A VendorName (in VENDOR) cannot be removed from the database unless there is no PART row that has that VendorName.

2.14   A foreign key is a key of a table that is different from the table in which the key resides. For example, in the answer to question 2.3, VendorName (in PART) is a foreign key. VendorName (in VENDOR) is not a foreign key.

2.15   A form is used to enable users to create, read, modify, and delete data. A report is a structured presentation of database data. Queries allow the users to answer questions from the data. Menus are structured presentations of allowed user actions.

2.16   The primary difference is that Query by Example requires the user to see and understand the structure of the tables. Query by Form, on the other hand, hides the table structure and requires the users only to fill in form fields. Query by example is a way of expressing a query by picking columns from tables and (indirectly) causing tables to be joined.

Languages that are unique to the DBMS and languages that are standardized.

2.17 Build a data model that identifies the things to be stored in the database and defines their structure and the relationships among them.

2.18 To provide a quick means of expressing requirements for users to review.

2.19 Top-down works from the general to the specific. Data models are created with a global perspective; systems have better interfaces and less re-work is required. The danger is analysis paralysis.

2.20 Bottom-up works from the specific to the general. Applications are developed much faster with less initial study and investment. Danger is that systems will be inconsistent and difficult to integrate; considerable re-work may be required.

2.21 A users' data model is a description of the users' data requirements. A data model (as in the entity-relationship data model) is a vocabulary for describing a users' data model.

Answers to Group II Questions:

2.22 You can find this database in Access 2000 format in our instructor support site at www.prenhall.com/kroenke/. Look for the database named CH2DB1.mdb.

2.24 This question is setting the stage for a discussion to come at the end of Chapter 3. I personally have wasted considerable time in my life arguing with other developers that "my model is a better representation of reality than your model." Unknowingly, I was simply saying, "the way I see the world is better than the way you see the world." This is sheer arrogance; what matters is how the users see their world! A database is not a model of reality; I believe Immanuel Kant was right; reality is forever unknowable by humans. All we have is our model of reality and the best we can do when building a database is to create an accurate portrayal of the users' models. This discussion will be picked up again at the end of Chapter 4.

Chapter 3

The Entity-Relationship Model

Objectives

- Learn the elements of the E-R model
- Show how to apply the E-R model for modeling business situations
- Practice building E-R models
- Understand why data models and databases do not represent the real world; they represent a model of the users' model, instead.

Teaching Suggestions

1. The E-R model has many variants. A good number of those have come about because CASE vendors did not want to support the diamond relationship notation. I stress underlying concepts with the students and tell them to expect E-R diagrams in several varieties.

2. One way to organize a lecture is to teach what entities, are and then to present relationships as one of two kinds: either HAS-A or IS-A. Teach 1:1, 1:N, and N:M as varieties of HAS-A.

3. I believe it's important for students to practice applying this model. Have them model situations on campus or businesses in which they have worked.

4. Watch out for confusion among entities in a relationship having a minimum cardinality of 1, existence dependent entities, and ID-dependent entities. The differences are subtle — especially between the first two. For example, an ORDER must have a SALESPERSON, but need not logically, require one for its existence (the ORDER could be a cash sale in which the salesperson is not recorded). The minimum cardinality of 1 arises from a business rule, not from a logical necessity. Thus ORDER requires a SALESPERSON but is not existence dependent on it. However, consider the relationship of PATIENT and PRESCRIPTION. Here, a PRESCRIPTION cannot logically exist without a PATIENT -- hence not only is the minimum cardinality 1, but also, the PRESCRIPTION is existence dependent on PATIENT. Finally, consider ASSIGNMENT, where the key of ASSIGNMENT contains the key of PROJECT. Here, not only does ASSIGNMENT have a minimum cardinality of 1, and not only is ASSIGNMENT existence dependent on PROJECT, but it is also ID-dependent on PROJECT since its key (name) includes the key (name) of another entity.

5.   I believe that the E-R model is important primarily because it is popular and the students are likely to see it. In my opinion, the semantic object model is almost always a better model; it's more complete, users understand it, and it's easier to develop good database designs from semantic objects.

6.   The E-R model is best at providing a broad overview of relationships. I try to teach that the E-R model can be used to model any kind of entities and relationships. I once used it in a meeting with salespeople when we were trying to understand the relationships of products to distributors to dealers to customers.

7.   The note at the end of the chapter is most important. I think the job of designing databases became much easier when I realized it wasn't my job to model the real world; it's only my job to model the users' model. That perspective also focuses data model evaluations where they belong: on what the users think.

8.   If you assign Projects A or B, encourage the students to take the hints there as suggestions, not as requirements. They should look at the Web site and generate the model that they think is correct. Not all of the entities in the suggestion need be in their design, and there may be other entities not mentioned that should be in their design. At this point, they should think art, not engineering. I believe a correct answer is one that can be reasonably justified. The **correct** answer, in any case, resides in the minds of people at Dell or Amazon, not in their teacher's mind!

Answers to Group I Questions

3.1   An entity is something of importance to the user. Something the user wants to track. VEHICLE.

3.2   An entity class is a group of entities of the same type, i.e. VEHICLE. An entity instance is a particular entity, i.e. VEHICLE 12345.

3.3   An item that describes a characteristic of the entity. VehicleSerialNumber, VehicleType, VehicleLicenseNumber are attributes of VEHICLE.

3.4   An attribute that contains several types of sub-attributes. VehicleOwner could be the composite {FirstName, MiddleInitial, LastName}.

3.5   VehicleSerialNumber.

3.6   An association among entities. VEHICLE has a relationship with OWNER.

3.7 A relationship class is an association among entity classes; a relationship instance is an association among entity instances.

3.8 Degree is the number of entities that participate in a relationship. The relationship ASSIGNMENT associates a CLIENT with an ATTORNEY with a TASK.

3.9 1:1, ATTORNEY to COMPUTER
1:N, VEHICLE to REPAIR
N:M, VEHICLE to OWNER

3.10 Maximum cardinality is the maximum number of instances of an entity that can participate in an instance of a relationship. Minimum is the least number of instances of an entity that can participate in an instance of a relationship.

3.11 Rectangle, diamond, rounded-corner rectangle and rounded-corner diamond, line with diamond back to entity, entity with existence symbol.

3.12-
3.14 See examples in text.

3.15 In this text, any entity that is logically dependent on another entity. See also question. For the Audubon Society, A BIRD-OBSERVATION is a weak-entity on a BIRD.

3.16 Depends on the source. Some say any entity whose presence depends on the presence of another entity in the database; hence any entity in a relationship having a minimum cardinality greater than or equal to one. Others say only ID-Dependent entities. This text says any entity that is logically dependent on another entity.

3.17 An ID-dependent entity is one whose identifier contains the identifier or another entity.

3.18 Define an entity EMPLOYEE and an entity SKILL. Let SKILL have the sole attribute SkillName. The relationship from EMPLOYEE to SKILL is 1:N; a SKILL is required to have an EMPLOYEE, and in fact is a weak entity on EMPLOYEE. An EMPLOYEE may or may not be required to have a SKILL depending on the users' requirements.

3.19 Define entities SALESPERSON and PHONE. Let PHONE have the attributes AreaCode, PhoneNumber. The relationship from SALESPERSON to PHONE is 1:N. A PHONE is required to have a SALESPERSON, but a SALESPERSON may or may not be required to have a PHONE, depending on the users' requirements.

3.20 A subtype entity is a special variety of a supertype entity. Consider the supertype ARTIST with properties SocialNecurityNumber, FName, LName, NetWorth and subtypes MUSICIAN with properties SocialSecurityNumber, Instrument, YearsExperience and PAINTER with properties SocialSecurityNumber, PreferredMedium, PaintingStyle.

3.21 Subtype entities take on the properties of the supertype. In question 3.20, both PAINTER and MUSICIAN inherit the properties of ARTIST.

3.22 A HAS-A relationship is an association among entities of different logical types. A DEPARTMENT HAS-A relationship(s) with EMPLOYEE. An IS-A relationships is an association among entities of the same logical type. PAINTER IS-A ARTIST, and MUSICIAN IS-A ARTIST.

3.23 Business rules are limitations on data modification activity. Other than minimum and maximum cardinality, they are documented apart from entity-relationship diagrams as part of the systems requirements.

3.24 Changes are much cheaper at the data model stage than at later stages. Data modeling is artistic, difficulty, and risky. Construct prototypes that show implications of data model decisions. Ask users if prototypes seem correct. Change data model (and prototype) if not, and ask again.

Answers to Group II Questions

3.25

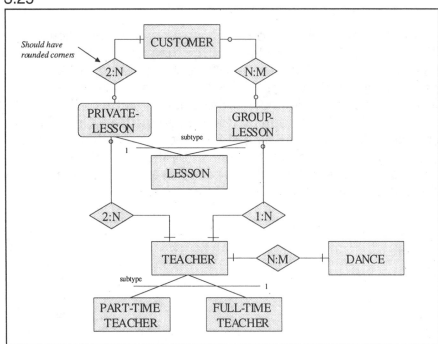

23

3.26

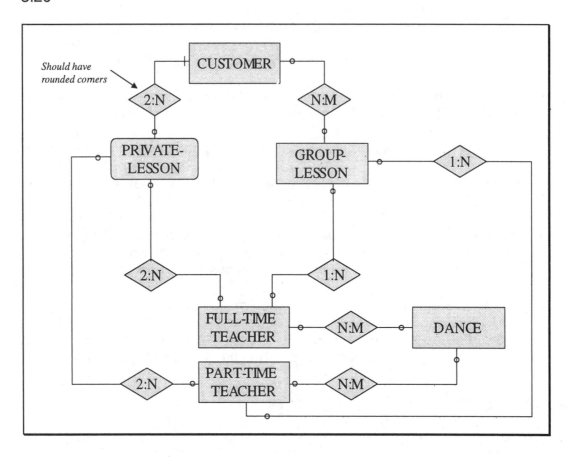

Should have rounded corners

3.27 I don't like either of them. In 3.25, the LESSON supertype adds nothing to the design; the relationships still must arise from the subtype because one of them is weak; also the cardinalities are different. In 3.26, all of the mandatory relationships that were out of TEACHER had to be made optional. If not, the design would imply, for example, that both a FULL-TIME and PART-TIME TEACHER are required to be at a DANCE. One of the two of them are required, but not both. Hence the model was better with the TEACHER supertype. This is a great example, by the way, of the utility of supertypes. A teacher (of some type) is required at a DANCE. Without the supertype, there is no way to show this constraint.

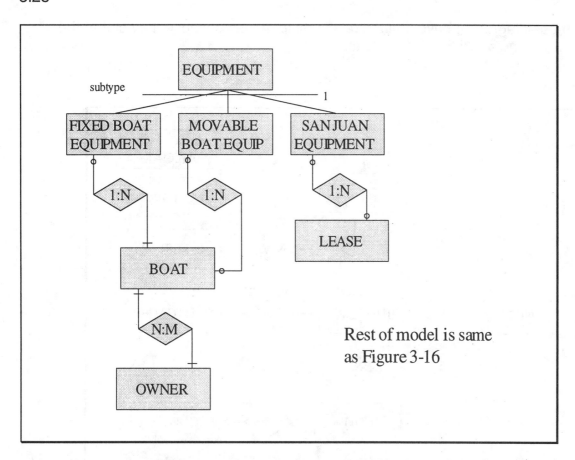

The only significant advantage of this design is that FIXED BOAT EQUIPMENT is required to have a relationship to BOAT. It is tempting to say that this design allows the users to discriminate between equipment owned by San Juan and that owned by the boat (and indirectly OWNER). This distinction could more easily be made by creating an Owner attribute in EQUIPMENT in the design in Figure 3-16. I don't think this design is worth the trouble.

Answers to Projects

In these diagrams I have omitted relationship names because they clutter the diagram and add little to the discussion.

A.

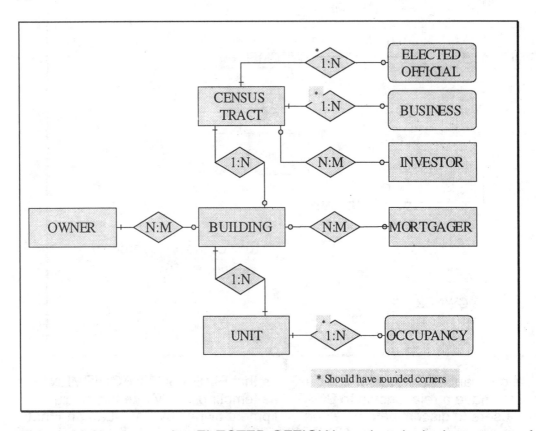

This model assumes that ELECTED OFFICIALs only exist in the context of a census tract. Also, it assumes that there is no need to track such officials indepdent of the tracks in which they have been elected. If these assumptions are not made, then ELECTED OFFICIAL should not be a weak entity and the relationship between it and CENSUS TRACT should be N:M. Similar comments pertain to BUSINESS; businesses are assumed to reside in a single census tract.

Attributes of the entities are as follows:

ENTITY	Attributes
CENSUS TRACT	TractName Boundary Description MedianIncome CrimeData
ELECTED OFFICIAL	Name
BUSINESS	Name

INVESTOR	Name
	AreaCode
	PhoneNumber
	FaxAreaCode
	FaxPhoneNumber
	Street
	City
	State
	Zip
BUILDING	Name
	Street
	City
	State
	Zip
	TotalSquareFootage
	Renovation/Repair Desc
	Handicap Facilities Desc
OWNER	Name
	AreaCode
	PhoneNumber
	FaxAreaCode
	FaxPhoneNumber
	Street
	City
	State
	Zip
MORTGAGER	Name
	AreaCode
	PhoneNumber
	FaxAreaCode
	FaxPhoneNumber
	Street
	City
	State
	Zip
UNIT	Number
	Type
	SquareFootage
	NumberBedrooms
	NumberBaths
	KitchenDining Desc
	Location in Building
	Remarks
	CurrentlyOccupied? (T/F)
OCCUPANCY	From
	To

B.

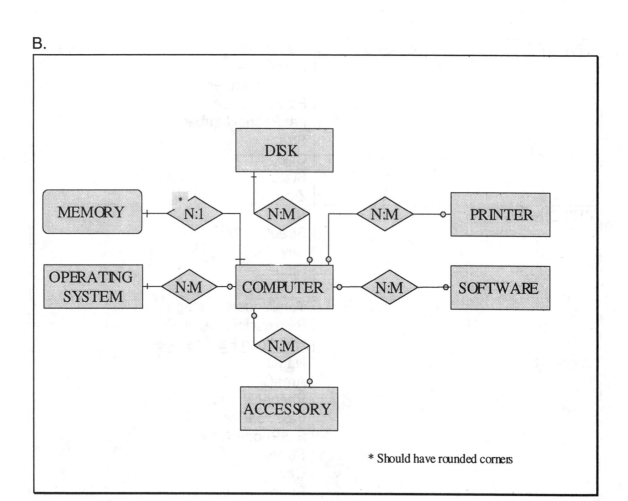

* Should have rounded corners

ENTITY	Attributes
BASE-SYSTEM	ProductNumber BrandName Type Description Processor BaseMemory BasePrice TotalPrice (computed on the fly, not stored?)
DISK	ProductNumber BrandName Type Description
PRINTER	ProductNumber BrandName Type Description
SOFTWARE	ProductNumber

28

	BrandName Type Description
ACCESSORY (including video cards)	ProductNumber BrandName Type Description
OPERATING SYSTEM	ProductNumber BrandName Type Description
MEMORY-OPTION	ProductNumber BrandName Type Description OptionPrice
All N:M relationships	OptionPrice

This model is straightforward except for three characteristics. The first is modeling MEMORY-OPTION as a weak entity. I did this for two reasons. First, because one can argue that various memory options logically depend on the architecture of a particular computer. This is the definition of a weak entity. On the other hand, processor boards are standardized, and so this argument may not be appropriate. This leads to the second reason: to stimulate discussion among the students about the artistic nature of data modeling and to drive home the point that the answer lies in the minds of the marketing department at Dell. No amount of arguing that my students and I do will ever generate the correct answer. The correct answer is at Dell! We need to develop a plausible data model (or several) and check them out with the users.

The second unusual characteristic is to give all N:M relationships the attribute OptionPrice. One can argue that a better design uses weak entities to represent the OptionPrice. The database design that results is the same, so perhaps it doesn't matter.

Third, I chose not to model VIDEO-CARD as a separate entity, but instead included it with ACCESSORY. This is arbitrary on my part; again, the answer depends on how Dell's marketing department wants to show their options. My guess is that if they make a good margin on video cards, they would show them as a separate category; if not, they're probably just an accessory. One message to the students is that **business needs drive database design.**

Finally, note that this model requires computers to have a disk, memory, and an operating system. This, too, may or may not be correct depending on how they view things at Dell.

As an aside, ProductNumber, BrandName, Type, and Description are shared by all entities. This suggest that they might all be subtypes of a generic entity PRODUCT. While this is true, I do not think anything is gained by modeling it that way.

C.

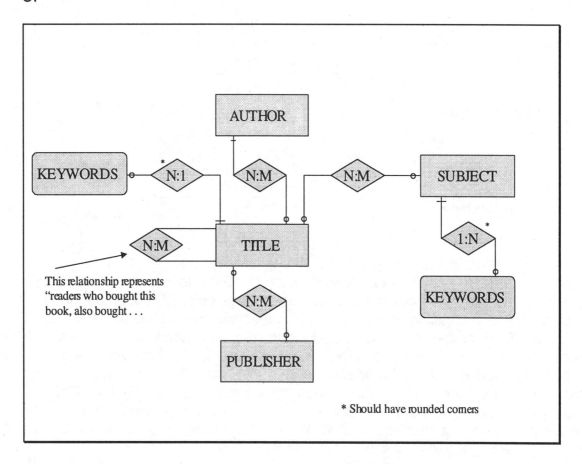

ENTITY	Attributes
TITLE	ISBN Title PublicationDate QuantityOnHand PublisherPrice OurPrice
AUTHOR	FirstName Middle Initial LastName
SUBJECT	Name Description
PUBLISHER	Name

	PhoneAreaCode
	PhoneLocalNumber
	FaxAreaCode
	FaxLocalNumber
	Street
	City
	State
	Zip
	Email
	GrossMargin
KEYWORDS	Keyword

This is a very straightforward design. For the purposes of locating a title, there is no need to include COPY; QuantityOnHand will show how many are available in stock. Name of author is separated into three parts to ease searching. The recursive relationship on TITLE is intended to support the "Readers who bought this title, also bought . . ." I omitted the reviews portion of the Amazon Web site because I didn't think it was relevant to finding a book. One could persuasively argue that this is wrong, however, because reading what others said helps to select among possibilities. If reviews are included, they would have a 1:N relationship to TITLE. I would not add another entity for REVIEWER because they are normally anonymous. REVIEW might have an optional 1:N relationship to AUTHOR and an optional 1:1 relationship to PUBLISHER, if author and publisher reviews are to be represented.

I included GrossMargin in PUBLISHER to bring up the commercial nature of this Web site. Amazon might want to sort the results of a user's query on the basis of the margin they make. This could be done in a gross way by sorting on the books from publishers that give the biggest discount or on a book-by-book basis computing the difference between cost and retail price (not shown in the model). My guess is that if they do this, they do it on publishers discount — and think of the leverage such a strategy would give the book buyers. Again, this is a dangerous Web site because it looks like the friendly, local librarian, but it is not. When I ask a used car salesperson what car I should buy, I expect that his or her answer will be conditioned by margin and inventory and other factors. There is no reason for Amazon to run its business any differently.

Chapter 4

Semantic Object Model

Objectives

- Define the term *semantic object*
- Demonstrate the use of *semantic object diagrams* to build a data model
- Define and illustrate the seven basic types of semantic objects
- Compare the semantic object model to the entity-relationship model

Teaching Suggestions

1. The semantic object data model is straightforward and useful. However, it is new and requires an adjustment in one's mental model. I believe it's worth the effort to learn and teach because I have found it to be much easier to teach data modeling, database design, and applications design using this model. Also, semantic objects can be shown to users; they normally have little difficulty interpreting them. Some of my end-user oriented consulting clients have developed their own semantic object models — without much assistance from me.

2. If at all possible, have the students use the version of DBApp that you can obtain from www.prenhall.com/kroenke/. Appendix C has ideas of how to use it. Note that this product can both produce schemas from models and also create models from existing databases.

3. One of the key differences between semantic objects and entities is that objects show context (the boundaries of an object), they contain multi-valued attributes, and they can contain other objects. This makes the relationships among objects easier to document and to explain to the users.

4. In the context of the Web, students can think of a semantic object as the data that is to appear on a Web page. The links to other objects can be represented as URL links to other pages that show those objects. This, in fact, is done for the ASP pages that are generated by DBApp.

5. Figure 4-2 shows a semantic object diagram, and Figure 4-3 shows an instance of the semantic object. Use these figures to illustrate the

difference. Get the class to suggest some properties for another semantic object, say SOCCER-PLAYER (or whatever sport is popular at your school). With several properties listed (Name, Height, Weight, Birthdate, GraduationYear, Position (multi-valued), Injury (multi-valued), LifetimePointsScored) ask for a semantic object instance. Then ask the class for the name of the semantic object, and the name of the semantic object instance (it is whatever player's name they suggested).

6.   Use the same class-developed semantic object instance to discuss property domains. The physical description is, of course, very computer-oriented (data type, length, position of decimal point, value range and restrictions). But the semantic description of a property is more difficult to define, although it is an important aspect of requirements definition.

7.   Point out that two (or more) attributes that happen to have the same physical description do not necessarily arise from the same domain. Their semantic descriptions differentiate them. Using the soccer player illustration, point out that both Weight and LifetimePointsScored may have the same physical description (positive integer, 3 digits), but they clearly describe different properties.

8.   Walk the students through the development of the semantic object diagrams on pages 80-88. Like dataflow diagrams and flowcharts, early versions are working documents, and are revised as more is learned. Some of the forms are shown with data in them and some are shown blank. This is typical of systems development; both kinds of forms are used.

9.   When semantic object diagrams are complete we summarize all semantic objects and semantic object properties (Figure 4-13). Then we describe every domain (both physical and semantic description) as in Figure 4-14. Using the soccer player example, have the class summarize the semantic object properties and domains, as in Figure 4-14.

Answers to Group I Questions

4.1   These models are tools for representing and expressing the views of users' data structures. They shape the image of the representation that is seen and documented.

4.2   A semantic object is a named collection of properties that sufficiently describes a distinct entity.

4.3   An object class name and an object entity name. STUDENT is an object class name; STUDENT 12345 is an object instance name.

4.4 The properties represent all of the characteristics that the users need to perform their work.

4.5 Something that users recognize as independent and separate. It stands on its own in the users' minds. Each instance of an object is unique and identifiable in its own right. Users have names for them such as Order-number or Employee-number. Everything about that semantic theme will be found in that object.

4.6 Line items are not distinct entities that stand on their own. They are a piece of something that stands on its own, namely, an ORDER.

4.7 Simple attributes, group attributes, and semantic object attributes.

4.8 In the semantic object APARTMENT:
a. NumberOfBedrooms
b. ApartmentName as (BuildingName, ApartmentNumber)
c. Phone jack location (one value for each phone jack in the apartment)
d. Occupant (FirstName, LastName), where more than one person can live in an apartment.
e. BUILDING
f. REPAIR

4.9 The number of values of an attribute that are required. No object will be allowed to exist for which this number is not satisfied. All types have minimum cardinality.

4.10 The maximum number of values an attribute can have in a semantic object. No object will be allowed to exist that has more than this number. All types have maximum cardinality.

4.11 Semantic object attributes are always paired. If OBJECT1 contains an attribute OBJECT2, then OBJECT2 will always contain an attribute OBJECT1. A one-way relationship is logically impossible.

4.12 An attribute that identifies instances of an object. Identifiers can be unique or non-unique. In AUTO, LicenseNumber is a simple attribute identifier. In APARTMENT (BuildingName, ApartmentNumber) is a composite identifier.

4.13 An attribute domain is the set of values that an attribute may have. It has both a physical and a logical (semantic) definition. Types are simple, group, and object. The semantic description is necessary because two domains that look alike are not necessarily the same domain. Dates, for example, look alike but one domain might be ShippingDate and another might be BirthDate.

4.14   A semantic object view is a subset of a semantic object. Consider the object APARTMENT with attributes BuildingName, ApartmentNumber, RentAmount, LastOccupiedDate. One view might have the first three attributes and another might have all four attributes.

Answers to questions 4.15 through 4.20 should be shown in semantic object diagrams.

4.15   SOFTWARE with properties Name, Type, Price, MemoryRequired.

4.16   a. EMPLOYEE with properties Emp#, {ReviewDate, ReviewComments}$_{0.N}$.
       b. EMPLOYEE with properties Emp#, {ReviewDate, ReviewComments}$_{0.N}$, and {SalaryRevisionDate, Salary}$_{0.N}$.
       c. EMPLOYEE with properties Emp#, {ReviewDate, {ReviewerName, ReviewerComments}$_{0.N}$}$_{0.N}$. For this last example, there are multiple reviews on a given date.

4.17   1:1   COMPUTER contains EMPLOYEE
             EMPLOYEE contains COMPUTER
       1:N   PROJECT contains COMPUTERs
             COMPUTER contains only one PROJECT
       M:1   (really same as 1:N, which is the point of this part of the question)
       N:M   COMPUTER contains SOFTWARE-PACKAGEs
             SOFTWARE-PACKAGE contains COMPUTERs

4.18   COMPUTER contains the multi-valued group {SOFTWARE-PACKAGE, Price}$_{0.N}$, where SOFTWARE-PACKAGE is an object and Price is not.

4.19   JOB contains a single value of the object properties ARTIST and CUSTOMER

       CUSTOMER contains many values of JOB
       ARTIST contains many values of JOB.

4.20   SOFTWARE contains the properties Name, Price, Vendor and the subtype objects WORD-PROCESSING-SOFTWARE, SPREADSHEET-SOFTWARE, and DBMS-SOFTWARE. WORD-PROCESSING-SOFTWARE contains the properties Name, Fonts$_{0.N}$. SPREADSHEET-SOFTWARE contains the properties Name, GraphStyles$_{0.N}$. DBMS-SOFTWARE contains the properties Name, MaxTables, MaxColumns, MaxRows.

4.21 AUTO-TYPE has attributres Name, Description and a multi-valued object attribute AUTO-PRODUCED. AUTO-PRODUCED has the composite identifier {AUTO-TYPE, SerialNumber) and DateManufactured attribute.

4.22 Both are tools for understanding and documenting users' data models. Both are concerned with representing the things that are important to the users and the relationships among those things.

4.23 E-R model takes entity as the basic element of interest to the user. Semantic object model takes semantic object as the basic element. Semantic objects show relationships in context of objects containing other objects. E-R model shows relationships as between entities. Usually, an entity is a different name for a table. Entities normally do not have composite attributes nor do they have multi-valued attributes. Entities do not contain other entities.

4.24 An entity is a piece of an object. In Figure 4.34, the entity SALES-ORDER is an artifact of database design. What is shown as a SALES-ORDER is only part of what the user considers a sales order. The full SALES-ORDER contains LineItem, CUSTOMER, SALESPERSON, and ITEM attributes. Entities are unnecessary; databases can be modeled and designed without them.

4.25 See Figures 4.33 and 4.34.

Answers to Group II Questions

4.26 The following model can be found in DBApp (Appendix C) format on www.prenhall.com/kroenke/ as file Ques426.apm.

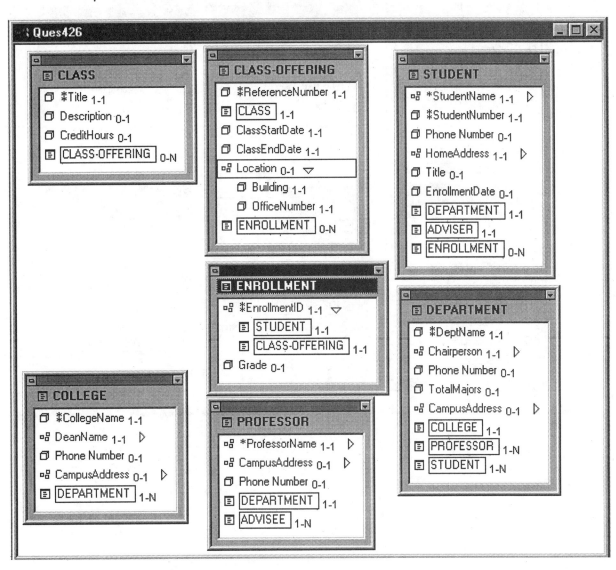

4.27 The following model can be found in DBApp (Appendix C) format on www.prenhall.com/kroenke/ as file Ques427.apm.

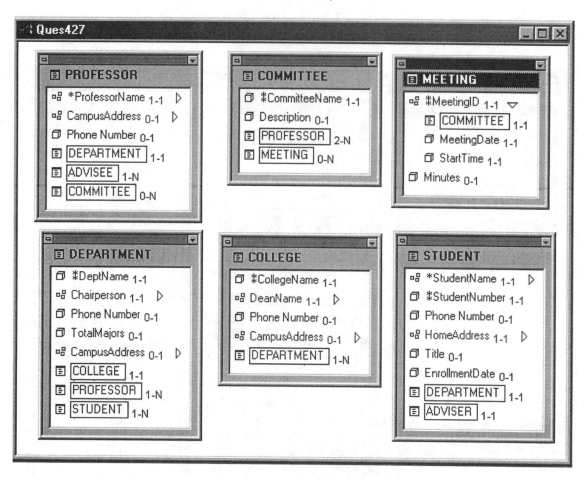

4.27 The following model can be found in DBApp (Appendix C) format on
www.prenhall.com/kroenke/ as file Ques428.apm.

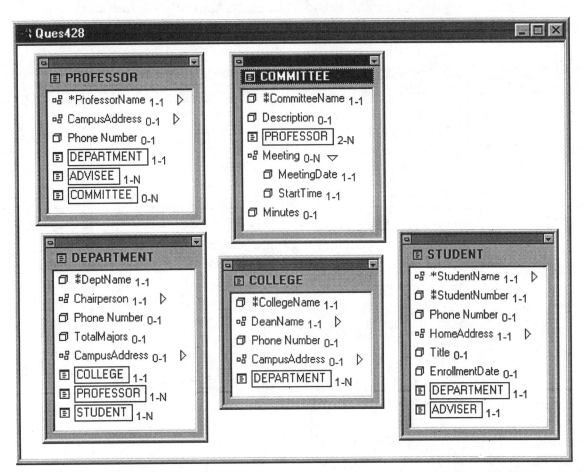

The difference is whether or not the meeting data should have an existence
independent of COMMITTEE. Here, if a COMMITTEE instance is deleted, the
meeting data will be deleted automatically. If meeting data is represented in
MEETING, then it has an independent existence. Further, if COMMITTEE is
required in MEETING, then a MEETING object can prohibit a COMMITTEE from
being deleted. These matters are discussed further in Chapter 10, on the subject
of deleting views.

Answers to Projects

A.   The following model can be found in DBApp (Appendix C) format on www.prenhall.com/kroenke/ as file MHA.apm.

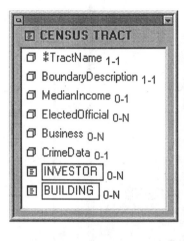

CENSUS TRACT
- #TractName 1-1
- BoundaryDescription 1-1
- MedianIncome 0-1
- ElectedOfficial 0-N
- Business 0-N
- CrimeData 0-1
- INVESTOR 0-N
- BUILDING 0-N

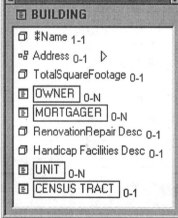

BUILDING
- #Name 1-1
- Address 0-1
- TotalSquareFootage 0-1
- OWNER 0-N
- MORTGAGER 0-N
- RenovationRepair Desc 0-1
- Handicap Facilities Desc 0-1
- UNIT 0-N
- CENSUS TRACT 0-1

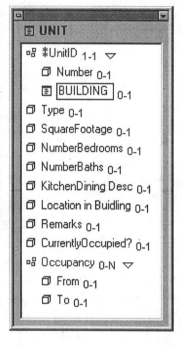

UNIT
- #UnitID 1-1
  - Number 0-1
  - BUILDING 0-1
- Type 0-1
- SquareFootage 0-1
- NumberBedrooms 0-1
- NumberBaths 0-1
- KitchenDining Desc 0-1
- Location in Buidling 0-1
- Remarks 0-1
- CurrentlyOccupied? 0-1
- Occupancy 0-N
  - From 0-1
  - To 0-1

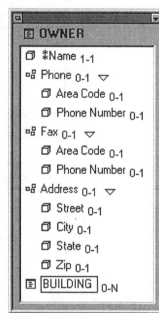

OWNER
- #Name 1-1
- Phone 0-1
  - Area Code 0-1
  - Phone Number 0-1
- Fax 0-1
  - Area Code 0-1
  - Phone Number 0-1
- Address 0-1
  - Street 0-1
  - City 0-1
  - State 0-1
  - Zip 0-1
- BUILDING 0-N

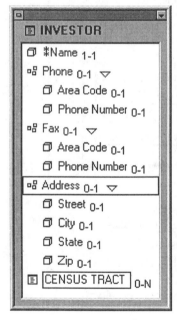

INVESTOR
- #Name 1-1
- Phone 0-1
  - Area Code 0-1
  - Phone Number 0-1
- Fax 0-1
  - Area Code 0-1
  - Phone Number 0-1
- Address 0-1
  - Street 0-1
  - City 0-1
  - State 0-1
  - Zip 0-1
- CENSUS TRACT 0-N

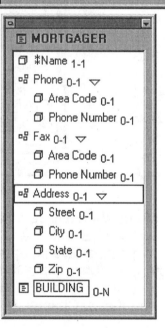

MORTGAGER
- #Name 1-1
- Phone 0-1
  - Area Code 0-1
  - Phone Number 0-1
- Fax 0-1
  - Area Code 0-1
  - Phone Number 0-1
- Address 0-1
  - Street 0-1
  - City 0-1
  - State 0-1
  - Zip 0-1
- BUILDING 0-N

40

B.   The following model can be found in DBApp (Appendix C) format on www.prenhall.com/kroenke/ as file DELL.apm.

This model makes the same assumptions as the E-R model in Chapter 3. Notice how the attributes of relationships in the E-R model are carried as hybrid groups

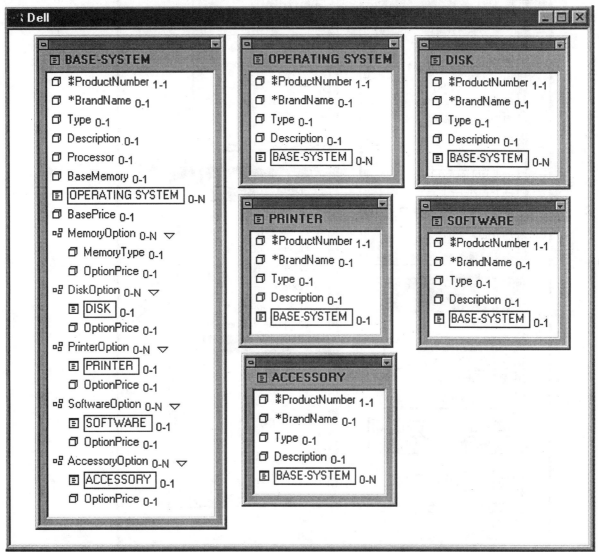

in the semantic object model. See, for example, DiskOption in BASE-SYTEM. Also, the weak entity Memory Option is represented as a multi-value group attribute here.

C. The following model can be found in DBApp (Appendix C) format on www.prenhall.com/kroenke/ as file Amazon.apm.

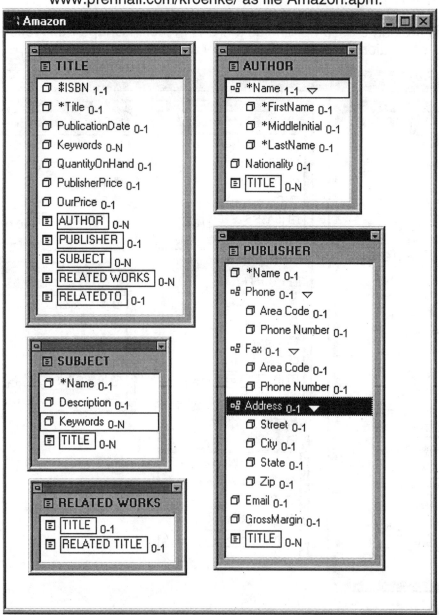

Note the recursive relationship from TITLE to RELATED WORKS. In TITLE, the object link RELATED WORKS is paired with TITLE in the RELATED WORKS object. In TITLE, the object link RELATED TO is paired with RELATED TITLE in the RELATED WORKS object. This is an example of 1:N recursion. The maximum cardinality of the RELATED WORKS object link is N. This means that many instances of the RELATED WORKS object can be connected to it. Each instance of the RELATED WORKS object points back through the RELATED TITLE link to a different title. Create sample data and work through it to make these relationships clear.

Chapter 5

Relational Model and Normalization

Objectives

- Define basic relational terminology
- Understand anomalies and the need for *normalization*
- Define first, second, third, Boyce-Codd, fourth, and domain/key normal forms
- Understand the special importance of domain/key normal form
- To learn how to synthesize relations using functional dependencies

Teaching Suggestions

1. Introduce this chapter by explaining that the primary design goal is to describe the database in terms of appropriately structured relations. Such relations must be as free of modification anomalies as is practicable, given the requirements. The first part of this chapter addresses anomalies we might find in a relation as well as how to get rid of them by changing the design of the relation.

2. Relational terminology is introduced on page 114. Some people use the terms *relation, attribute,* and *tuple* for relational designs and the terms *table, column,* and *row* for relational implementations. I avoid the term *tuple* here because it is so seldom used in practice and sounds pretentious when it is used.

3. To show the students how the relational model relates to data modeling as discussed in Chapter 4, pick a simple object, say, COMPUTER with properties SerialNumber, Type, Model, AcqCost, AcqDate. Explain that, as they will learn in Chapter 7, this simple object maps into a relation COMPUTER with attributes SerialNumber, Type, Model, AcqCost, AcqDate. Thus, non-object, non-repeating properties map directly into attributes. Other mappings will be discussed in Chapter 7.

4. In my opinion, the differences in the various normal forms is not of great importance to undergraduate business students. However, the idea and means of eliminating modification anomalies, and an intuitive understanding of DK/NF and the role it plays in design is vitally important. The bottom line: just as Mrs. Gazernplatz, our eighth grade English teacher said about paragraphs, a relation should have a single theme. If it has two themes, break it up into two relations. If it has three themes,

break it up into three relations. Every time we break up a relation, we create the possibility of referential integrity constraints; hence we always need to check for them.

5.   Point out to students that a functional dependency means that if we know the value of one (or several) data items, then we can *find* the value of another one (or several). They can read a functional dependency such as X--->Y as "If I know the value of X, then I can look up the value of Y" (in a table somewhere).

6.   A key uniquely identifies a row. It can be one attribute or it can be a group of attributes. A relation can have several possible candidate keys. A key is always a determinant. In fact, a key functionally determines the entire row. But a determinant is not necessarily a key.

7.   In the section "The Synthesis of Relations" starting on page 131 we describe another way to design relations that will not suffer from modification anomalies. In this case, we begin with a group of attributes and figure out which ones belong together in the same relation. This approach has been used to create expert systems that construct normalized relations from lists of attributes and their functional dependencies. Such systems have never enjoyed much popularity, however, because it is non-trivial to examine all pairs of all attributes of a complicated database for possible functional dependencies.

8.   Students should be aware that many databases are poorly normalized. Sometimes that was intentional, because of design trade-offs, but sometimes it was because the designers didn't know any better. The goal for the students in this class should be to ensure if they do not normalize data, that they know that they are doing so and are prepared for the consequences. In maintenance projects, the students should expect to find many existing relations that are poorly normalized. It shouldn't be, but it is.

Answers to Group I Questions

5.1   A cell contains one and only one data value; a column must contain data of the same type; no row can be duplicated; the order of the columns is immaterial; the order of the rows is immaterial.

5.2   Relation a two-dimensional table that meets the restrictions in question 5.1; tuple is a row of a relation; attribute is a column of a relation; file is often considered the same as relation; record same as tuple; file same as attribute.

5.3   A functional dependency is a relationship between attributes such that
       given the value of one attribute it is possible to determine the value of the
       other attribute. Example of functional dependency: Name--->Phone#.
       Example of attributes that are not functionally dependent: Age and
       Address.

5.4   No, a particular value of SID can occur many times in the relation. A
       determinant (such as SID) is not necessarily unique within a relation.
       However, a particular value of SID will have only one corresponding value
       of Activity, no matter how many rows they appear in.

5.5   A determinant is an attribute whose value enables us to obtain the
       value(s) of other related attributes. It appears on the left side of a
       functional dependency. Thus, in A--->B, the determinant is A.

5.6   TOWN-RESIDENTS (Name, Age, Citizenship, Voter-eligibility) where
       (Age, Citizenship)--->Voter-eligibility.

5.7   A key is a group of one or more attributes that uniquely identifies a tuple.

5.8   Yes, SID is a determinant. No, multiple values of SID may not occur in a
       relation in which it is the key.

5.9   A deletion anomaly occurs when facts about two themes are lost with one
       deletion. Example: the relation VENDOR-PART (VendorName, Phone,
       Part#), and assume Vendor 123 supplies only one part. When that part is
       deleted, information about the vendor is deleted from the database as
       well.

5.10   An insertion anomaly occurs when insertion of a fact about one theme
       requires a fact about another theme. Example: in VENDOR-PART in the
       answer to question 5.9, suppose engineering is developing a product that
       requires a new part, but the vendor has not been selected. With an
       insertion anomaly you cannot add the part to the database until the vendor
       is also added.

5.11   Each higher normal form includes the one(s) preceding it. A relation in
       3NF is also in 1NF and 2NF.

5.12   A relation is in 2NF if all nonkey attributes are dependent on all of the key.
       This relation is not in 2NF:
              LINE-ITEM (OrderNumber, ItemNumber, Description).
              Key: (OrderNumber, ItemNumber).
              Dependencies: (OrderNumber, ItemNumber)--->Description.
               ItemNumber--->Description.
       These equivalent relations are in 2NF:

LINE-ITEM (OrderNumber, ItemNumber).
STOCK (ItemNumber, Description).

5.13   A relation is in 3NF if it is in 2NF and has no transitive dependencies. This
relation is not in 3NF:
        DOG (Name, Breed, MaxSize)
                Key: Name
        Dependencies: Name--->Breed
                  Breed--->MaxSize
        (transitively)Name--->MaxSize
        These equivalent relations are in 3NF:
        REQUIREMENT (Name, Breed)
        OFFERINGS (Breed, MaxSize)

5.14   A relation is in BCNF if every determinant is a candidate key. Consider
this relation: FAC-OFFICE (FID, Department, Building, Office). Assume
faculty members in the same department have offices in the same
building. The key is FID. FID determines Department, Building, and
Office. But Department (not a candidate key) determines Building. These
relations are in BCNF:

        FACULTY (FID, Department, Office)
        DEPARTMENT-LOCATIONS (Department, Building)

5.15   A multi-valued dependency exists if there are three attributes in a relation
and an attribute is dependent on only one of the other attributes. An
example is: PROF (Name, Hobby, Class-taught). Assume professors
have many hobbies and teach many classes. The key of the relation is
(Name, Hobby, Class-taught). When a professor takes up a new hobby.
all of the class-taught values must be duplicated. Makes no sense.

5.16   Multi-valued dependencies must exist in pairs because a multi-valued
dependency calls for two independent attributes that can have multiple
values.

5.17   A relation is in 4NF if it is in BCNF (every determinant is a candidate key)
and it has no multi-valued dependencies. The following relation is in
BCNF but not 4NF: EMPLOYEE-HISTORY (Name, Project,
PublicServiceActivity). Project can be multi-valued because an employee
could have worked on many projects. PublicServiceActivity can also be
multi-valued. But Project and PublicServiceActivity are unrelated. These
relations are in 4NF:
        EMPLOYEE-WORK-HIST (Name, Project).
        EMPLOYEE-SERVICE-HIST (Name, PublicServiceActivity)

5.18 A relation is in DK/NF if every constraint on the relation is a logical consequence of the definition of keys and domains. DK/NF is important because if a relation is in DK/NF, then there will be no modification anomalies.

5.19 Assumptions:
BuyerName --> BuyerPhone, PlantLocation, City, State, Zip
　　　　　　Zip --> City, State
　　　　　　(Manufacturer, Model, BuyerName) --> AcqDate
Relations:
BUYER (BuyerName, BuyerPhone, PlantLocation, City, State, Zip)
PURCHASE (Manufacturer, Model, BuyerName, AcqDate)

Ignore Zip functional dependency.

5.20 Assumptions:
Number -->　CustomerNumber, ItemNumber, ItemQuantity,
　　　　　　SalespersonNumber, SubTotal, Tax, TotalDue
ItemNumber --> ItemPrice
CustomerNumber -- > CustomerAddress
SalespersonNumber --> SalespersonName

Relations:
INVOICE (Number, CustomerNumber, ItemNumber, ItemQuantity, SalespersonNumber, SubTotal, Tax, TotalDue)
ITEM (ItemNumber, ItemPrice)
CUSTOMER (CustomerNumber, CustomerAddress)
SALESPERSON (SalespersonNumber, SalespersonName)

5.21 CUSTOMER becomes two relations:.
EX-CUSTOMER (CustomerNumber, CustomerName, CustomerAddress, CustomerTaxStatus).
Constraint: CustomerTaxStatus = 1.

NOT-EX-CUSTOMER (CustomerNumber, CustomerName, CustomerAddress, CustomerTaxStatus).
Constraint: Customer-tax-status = 0.

5.22 BASKETBALL-PLAYER (Number, Name, Position, GameDate, PointsScored), with key (Number, GameDate). Not normalized because Number $\rightarrow$ (Name, Position), but (Number, GameDate) $\rightarrow$ PointsScored. People are used to looking at this data in non-normalized format.

5.23 Two reasons are de-normalization and controlled redundancy. De-normalization might be done because people are accustomed to seeing data particular way – the example of Zip $\rightarrow$ (City, State) and the answer to question 5.22 are examples. Controlled normalization usually occurs to improve performance — creating a table that has a subset of the data for query or high-transaction applications. The first is less risky because people expect it — if a player changed her number, everyone would expect to update all of her score data — or would adjust it their minds. The second is unexpected — even unknown by the users.

Answers to Group II Questions

5.24

a. False
b. False
c. True, but only because EmployeeName → Employee Salary. Sometimes this is stated that (ProjectID, EmployeeName) is not a minimal key.
d. True
e. False
f. False
g. (ProjectID, EmployeeName)
h. No. EmployeeSalary is dependent only on EmployeeName
i. 1st but not in 2nd
j. Insertion: to give an employee a salary, we must first assign the employee to a project. Deletion: If project 200c is deleted we lose Parks's salary.
k. No
l. Yes
m. Yes
n. No. (Actually, for the data given, it is a determinant. This is most likely happenstance unless the organization has a rule that only one employee can have a given salary. This seems unlikely. This illustrates the dangers of inferring dependencies from sample data. Ask the users!)
o. No
p. ASSIGNMENT (ProjectID, EmployeeName)
    SALARY (EmployeeName, EmployeeSalary)

5.25
This relation is a mess. Certainly, EmployeeName multi-determines ProjectID. From the hint "TaskID is the name of a *standard* task" it appears that EmployeeName multidetermines TaskID as well. It could be, however, that there is a transitive multidependency: EmployeeName multidetermines ProjectID and Project ID multidetermines TaskID. The answers below follow the hint and assume that ProjectID and TaskID are independent.

a. False
b. True
c. False
d. True

e.	True

f.	True

g.	True, but not minimal (see answer to 5.24c)

h.	False

i.	False

j.	False

k.	Assuming there is not transitive multidependency, EmployeeName is the only determinant.

l.	Assuming note at start, there is no transitive depedency.

m.	Yes, the two unrelated attributes are ProjectID and TaskID. Note, too, that even if TaskID were not in the relation, there would still be a multivalued dependency because of the presence of Phone and TotalHours.

n.	If you delete the second row, you must also delete the fourth row to preserve the multi-valued dependency.

o.	Three: employees and their projects, employees and their tasks, and employees and their personal data (Phone, TotalHours). You could even say four if you split Phone and TotalHours, but that seems too fine, to me.

p.	EMPLOYEE-PROJECT (EmployeeName, ProjectID)
	EMPLOYEE-TASK (EmployeeName, TaskID)
	EMPLOYEE-DATA (EmployeeName, Phone, TotalHours)
	Three; one theme each.

5.26 In this question, EQUIPMENT is like a machine or medical equipment or something similar.

a.	To enforce this constraint, we need EmployeeName to determine EquipmentName. Think of this as a typical normalization problem and say that EmployeeName → EquipmentName in APPOINTMENT. In this case, we split APPOINTMENT into EQUIP-APPT and EMP-EQUIP as follows:

	EQUIP-APPT (Date, Time, EquipmentName) with key (Date, Time, EquipmentName)

	And

	EMP-EQUIP (EmployeeName, EquipmentName) with key (EmployeeName, EquipmentName).

b.	Make the following changes to the design:
	1. Add EmployeeType to EMPLOYEE:
	   EMPLOYEE (EmployeeName, PhoneNumber, EmployeeType)

	2. Define new attribute NightEmp with domain in (EmployeeName of EMPLOYEE, where EmployeeType = 1)

	3. Define new attribute DayTime with domain HH >05 and <21

4. Define new attribute NightTime with domain HH <=21 or <= 05

5. Replace the APPOINTMENT relation by

DAY-APPT (Date, DayTime, EquipmentName, EmployeeName)
NIGHT-APPT (Date, NightTime, EquipmentName, NightEmp)

This design effectively enforces a business rule using domain and key definitions. It probably, however, is not worth the effort because of the problems it will cause when building the rest of the application. It would most likely be a better choice to enforce the rule in application code. This does illustrate, however, a means for using DK/NF to enforce such constraints.

Chapter 6

Database Design Using Entity-Relationship Models

Objectives

- Learn how to transform E-R data models into relational, DBMS-independent designs
- Define and model three special structures: trees, networks, and bills of materials

Teaching Suggestions

1. The goal of this chapter is to learn to transform data models in E-R form and notation into relational, DBMS-independent designs. These designs will later be implemented using a particular DBMS product.

2. While the E-R model as defined by Chen and others included ideas like composite attributes and mutli-valued attributes, those ideas were never really developed. In practice, most people make the tacit assumption that an entity will become a single (usually normalized) relation. In fact, some people teach the idea that an entity should already be normalized. This situation presents a tough decision for us. We can teach what could have been (by assuming that an entity can be one or more normalized relations), or teach what is and will probably be the norm where your students go to work (that an entity is usually a normalized relation by a different name). In writing this chapter, except for the section on multi-value attributes, I took the latter point of view.

3. The chapter breaks into two parts: transformation of E-R and representation of the special structures. Each part should take about one class period.

4. The best way to teach this is with plenty of examples. Also, students seem to learn it the best if they are given plenty of homework assignments and problems to work.

Answers to Group I Questions

6.1   Create a relation for each entity. Create an attribute for each property. Normalize the relation if necessary and appropriate. Represent relationships with foreign keys. 1:1, key of either as the foreign key of the

51

other; 1:N, key of parent in child; N:M, intersection relation having keys of both.

6.2   An entity may contain more than one semantic theme. Normalize to eliminate modification anomalies. Don't normalize if performance considerations indicate otherwise.

6.3   Inter-relation constraints will be generated. Also, if the weak entity is ID-dependent, then the key of the relation upon which it depends will need to be added to the relation.

6.4   In a marina: 1:1, BOAT to SLIP; 1:N, BOAT to RENTAL-CHARGE; N:M, BOAT to OWNER.

6.5   A foreign key is an attribute that is a key of a different relation. SALES-ORDER(OrderNumber, OrderDate, SalespersonNumber, . . .) SalespersonNumber is a foreign key (assuming there is a SALESPERSON table with SalespersonNumber as its key).

6.6   Assume relations: BOAT (LicenseNumber, Type, Length) and SLIP (SlipNumber, Location, Charge). Either (a) place LicenseNumber in SLIP or (b) place SlipNumber in BOAT.

6.7   To go from BOAT (using LicenseNumber) to SLIP: for (a) look up LicenseNumber in SLIP; for (b) use LicenseNumber to get row of BOAT, obtain SlipNumber from BOAT, look up row in SLIP using SlipNumber obtained. To go from SLIP (using SlipNumber) to BOAT: for (a) use SlipNumber to get row of SLIP, obtain LicenseNumber from SLIP, look up row in BOAT using LicenseNumber obtained; for (b) look up SlipNumber in BOAT.

6.8   Because they describe the same thing. Combine if they are the same thing and are not separated for performance or security reasons and are not subtypes.

6.9   A parent is a row on the one side of a 1:N relationship. A child is a row on the many side of a 1:N relationship. Say DEPARTMENT and EMPLOYEE have a 1:N relationship, a row of DEPARTMENT is a parent and rows of EMPLOYEE that pertain to that department are children.

6.10   BOAT to RENTAL-CHARGE is 1:N. Assume BOAT (LicenseNumber, Type, Length) and RENTAL-CHARGE (ChargeNumber, ChargeDate, ChargeAmount). Place LicenseNumber in RENTAL-CHARGE.

6.11   Given a value of LicenseNumber, look up all rows in RENTAL-CHARGE having that value for LicenseNumber. Given ChargeNumber, look up row in RENTAL-CHARGE having that number; obtain the value of the LicenseNumber for the parent, use that value to look up BOAT data.

6.12 Not enough room. Can only have one value per cell in the relational model.

6.13

a. BOAT to SAILs
b. BOAT to FIRE-EXTINGUISHERs
c. BOAT to RENTAL-AGREEMENTs
d. BOAT to REPAIR-BILLs (assumes that every boat has at least one repair bill

6.14 Create an intersection table having the key of BOAT and the key of OWNER.

6.15 Assume LicenseNumber is key of BOAT and ONumber is key of OWNER. Place both keys in intersection table OB. To get all of the owners for a boat, start with LicenseNumber, look up all rows in OB having that LicenseNumber. For each row found, obtain value of ONumber. For each of these values, look up the appropriate row in OWNER. To get all of the boats for an owner, start with ONumber, look up all rows in OB having that ONumber. For each row found, obtain value of LicenseNumber. For each of these values, look up the appropriate row in BOAT.

6.16 Because there is only room for one value per cell in a relation.

6.17 A relation that represents the intersection of two entities having an M:N relationship. Each row of the table represents one line in a diagram connecting related entities.

6.18 1:1, 1:N, N:M. Consider MEMBER, an entity representing the people who belong to an athletic club. SPOUSE is 1:1 recursive; REFERRED-BY is 1:N recursive (assuming a new member is referred by only one only one existing member; SPONSORED-BY is N:M recursive assuming several people are required to sponsor a new member.

6.19-6.21
For 1:1, place a new attribute SpouseNumber in MEMBER; for 1:N, place a new attribute ReferredByNumber in MEMBER; for N:M, create a new table SPONSORED-BY with SponsoreeNumber and SponsorNumber as its attributes. Same basic technique.

6.22 A REPAIR has a CAR, MECHANIC, and FACILITY, the relationships from each is one to many (CAR has many REPAIRs). Place the foreign key of CAR, MECHANIC, and FACILITY in REPAIR.

6.23 A MECHANIC works in one and only one FACILITY; a FACILITY has many mechanics. Thus, the relationship from FACILITY to MECHANIC is 1:N, and constrains REPAIR as follows: pick the FACILITY and only a set of MECHANICs are available. Pick a MECHANIC and the FACILITY is given. Represent the constraining binary relationship by placing the key of FACILITY in MECHANIC. The constraint must be enforced by application programs.

6.24 In the example in question 6.22, a MUST NOT constraint would be that a given FACILITY cannot make the REPAIRS on some CARs. For MUST COVER, assume that a REPAIR has many MECHANICS. Now assume that all of the MECHANICs in a given FACILITY MUST WORK on all of the CARs that are repaired in that FACILITY.

6.25 ARTIST supertype; PAINTER, MUSICIAN, DANCER are subtypes. Create one relation for supertype and one for each subtype. All have the same key.

6.26 A tree is a structure of nodes having 1:N relationships such that each node except the root has one parent. The root has no parent.

6.27 BOAT has many REPAIRs; REPAIR has many PARTs. Create a relation for each entity. For each, place the key of the parent in the child.

6.28 BOAT has many REPAIRs; MECHANIC has many REPAIRs; REPAIR has only one BOAT and one MECHANIC. Create a relation for each entity. Place the keys of BOAT and MECHANIC in REPAIR.

6.29 Same as 6.28, but change so that a REPAIR has (potentially) many MECHANICs. Create a relation for BOAT, REPAIR, MECHANIC, and a new, intersection relation, REP-MECH, for the M:N relationship between REPAIR and MECHANIC. The attributes of REP-MECH are the key of REPAIR and the key of MECHANIC.

6.30 A bill of materials is a data structure that shows the components of sub-items and assemblies. A boat consists of hull, masts, rigging, sails, and inner compartment. The hull consists of the body, stern, bow, and keel. The stern consists of the transom, stern walls, and stern floor assembly, etc. Use structure shown in Figure 6-25.

Answers to Group II Questions

6.31 The following is a SQL Server database that was generated by DBApp from the model JDC.apm located on the www.prenhall.com/kroenke/ Web site.

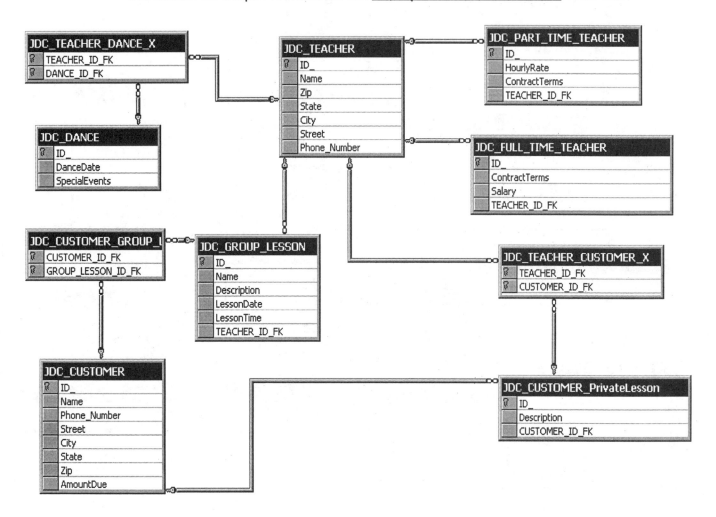

Surrogate keys are used throughout. Column names that end with FK are foreign keys. Table names that end with _X are intersection tables.

6.32 The following is a SQL Server database that was generated by DBApp from the model SJC.apm located on the www.prenhall.com/kroenke/ Web site.

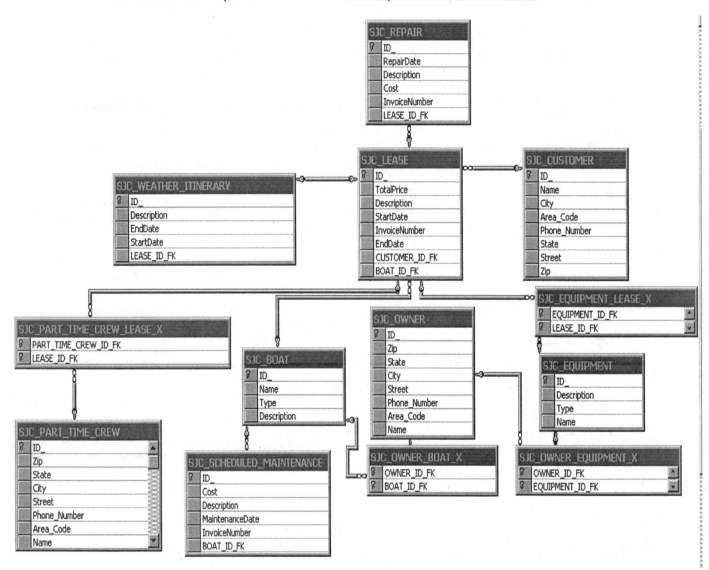

Surrogate keys are used throughout. Column names that end with FK are foreign keys. Table names that end with _X are intersection tables.

6.33 First, domain key normal form concerns the constraints that occur on a single table. So, the constraint in Figure 6-19(a) that SalespersonNumber of OrderNumber 500 must be 20 is not governed by DK/NF because it is an inter-table constraint. A similar comment pertains to Figure 6-19(b). In Figure 6-19(c) however, there are constraints that do concern just one table. In particular, InvoiceNumber multidetermines RepairNumber and RepairNumber multi-determines TaskNumber. So there are both transitive

56

dependencies and multi-value dependencies. The result as far as normalization is concerned is to create an INVOICE-REPAIR table that has (InvoiceNumber, RepairNumber), remove TaskNumber from AUTO-REPAIR (its data is carried in TASK), and thus reduce AUTO-REPAIR to (InvoiceNumber, other nonkeydata . . .). Doing this, however, obviates the reason for creating the schema in the first place: namely, to enforce the MUST COVER constraint. In fact, reflection on the meaning of the term *must cover*, indicates that the purpose of the AUTO-REPAIR relation is to create, intentionally and by design, the insertion and deletion anomalies that DK/NF eliminates. Thus, this is a case where normalization is not only not wanted, it is undesirable! Note, too, that application programs will need to be coded to properly process the modification anomalies.

Answers to Projects

A. The following SQL Server database was generated by DBApp from the file MHAER.apm located on the www.prehnall.com/kroenke/ Web site.

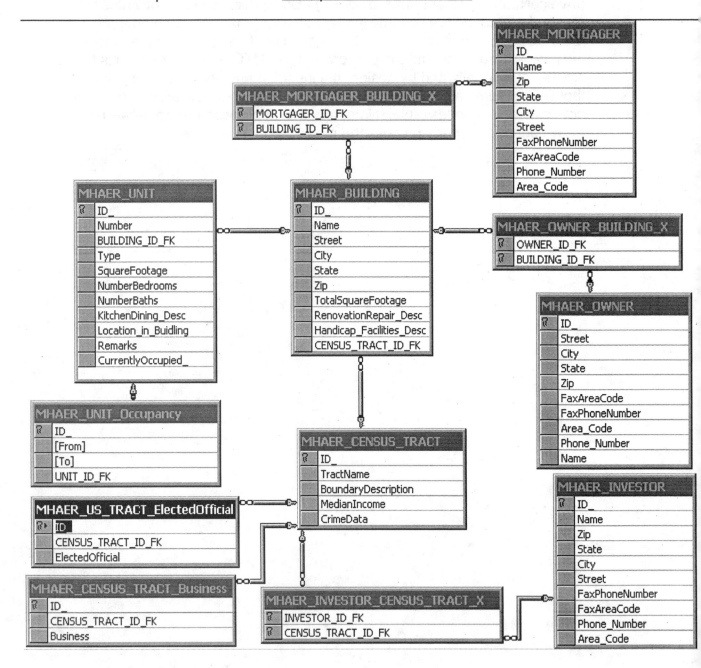

Surrogate keys are used throughout. Column names that end with FK are foreign keys. Table names that end with _X are intersection tables. Except for Zip → City, State, all tables are in DK/NF.

B. The following SQL Server database was generated by DBApp from the file
Dell.apm located on the www.prehnall.com/kroenke/ Web site.

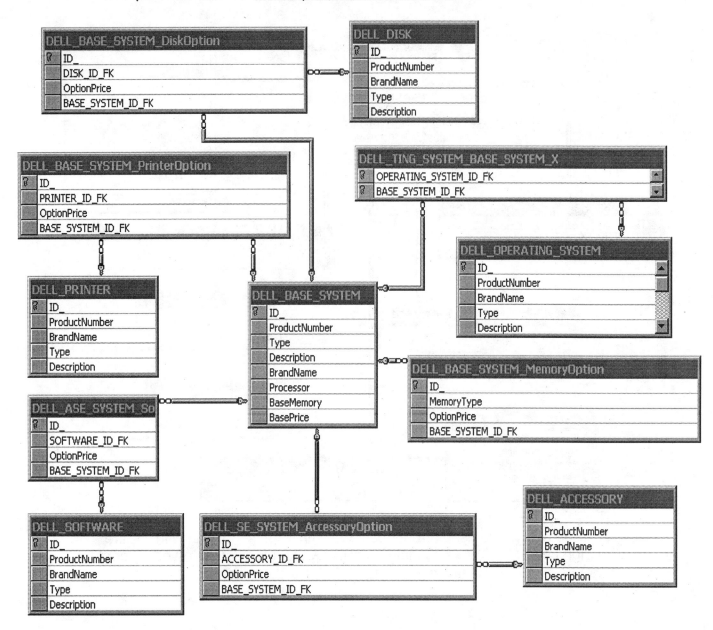

Surrogate keys are used throughout. Column names that end with FK are
foreign keys. Table names that end with _X are intersection tables. Except for
Zip → City, State, all tables are in DK/NF.

C. The following SQL Server database was generated by DBApp from the file Amazon.apm located on the www.prehnall.com/kroenke/ Web site.

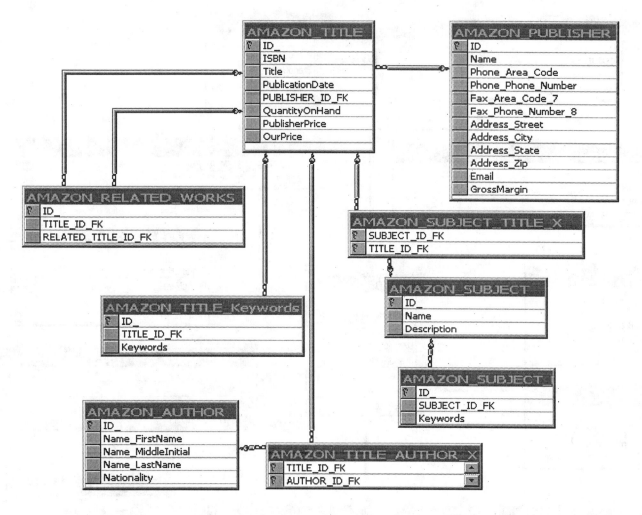

Surrogate keys are used throughout. Column names that end with FK are foreign keys. Table names that end with _X are intersection tables. Except for Zip → City, State, all tables are in DK/NF.

Chapter 7

Database Design Using Semantic Object Models

Objectives

- Learn how to transform the seven types of semantic object into relational, DBMS-independent designs
- Understand the role of encapsulation in hybrid objects
- Practice modeling several real-world objects

Teaching Suggestions

1. The goal of this chapter is to learn to transform data models in semantic object form and notation into relational, DBMS-independent designs. These designs will later be implemented using a particular DBMS product.

2. This is a very important chapter. An understanding of the techniques discussed here is arguably the most important learning in the course.

3. The chapter breaks into two parts: transformation of the seven types of objects and then modeling of three sample objects. Each part can take about a class period -- you might have the students bring a prepared response to question 7.22 to the second class. That is a very interesting problem.

4. You can use Figure 7-13 and the related discussion to teach encapsulation. In cases 1 and 2, an ITEM gives itself to an ORDER. How many times that ITEM appears on that ORDER is not the business of ITEM; it is purely the business of ORDER and that fact is recorded within (encapsulated) ORDER. A similar argument holds for cases 3 and 4.

5. It's worth having the students use DBApp. They can create many models and let DBApp generate the database structures. You can ask them to explain why the program did what it did. Also, as indicated by the projects, the easiest way to generate a SQL Server database is to use DBApp. Take the SOM models in the files with suffix .apm and use them to generate the databases.

Answers to Group I Questions

7.1 MUSICIAN with properties Name, Instrument, SectionChairNumber. Create relation MUSICIAN (<u>Name</u>, Instrument, SectionChairNumber).

7.2 MUSICIAN with properties Name, Instrument, SectionChairNumber, {ConcertDate, ConcertLocation}$_{0,N}$. Create relations MUSICIAN (<u>Name</u>, Instrument, SectionChairNumber) and MUSICIAN-CONCERT (<u>Name, ConcertDate</u>, ConcertLocation).

7.3 1:1 example: MUSICIAN, UNIFORM
Create a relation MUSICIAN and a relation UNIFORM. Place either the key of MUSICIAN IN UNIFORM or the key of UNIFORM in MUSICIAN.

7.4 1:N example: MUSICIAN, INSTRUMENT-OWNED. Create a relation for each object and place the key of MUSICIAN in INSTRUMENT-OWNED.

7.5 M:1 example: N:1 MUSICIAN, BAND. Create a relation for each object and place the key of BAND in MUSICIAN.

7.6 N:M example: MUSICIAN, INSTRUMENT-PLAYED. Create a relation for each object and an intersection relation. Place the key of each of the relations in the intersection relation.

7.7 See answer to question 7.20.

7.8 See answer to question 7.20.

7.9 Consider the association object CONTRACT which contains the non-object properties ContractNumber, Date, TotalPay, and Position, and the object properties BAND and MUSICIAN. Suppose that BAND contains the properties <u>BandName</u>, Conductor and that MUSICIAN contains the properties <u>MusicianName</u>, Phone. Create a relation BAND (<u>BandName</u>, Conductor), a relation MUSICIAN (<u>MusicianName</u>, Phone), and a relation CONTRACT (<u>ContractNumber,</u> Date, TotalPay, Position, BandName, MusicianName).

7.10 Same as 7.9 except that the key of CONTRACT is (BandName, MusicianName).

7.11 ARTIST supertype object contains subtype objects PAINTER, MUSICIAN, and DANCER as subtypes. Each subtype contains properties unique to that subtype and also the supertype object as an object property. Assume an ARTIST can only be one of these types. Create a relation for each object; place ArtistNumber as the key of each relation. Add an attribute to

ARTIST that indicates the type of artist; only allow one type in this attribute.

7.12 Same as 7.11, but all the type attribute to have more than one subtype; an example value of the type indicator is: PAINTER/DANCER.

7.13 - 7.19 Answers depend on forms that are found.

Answers to Group II Questions

7.20 The following objects represent cases 1-4, respectively. They each concern the counting of fish species on a particular river. Case 1 counts a species only once on one river. Case 2 counts a fish many times on a single river. Case 3 counts many fish, but only once per river. Case 4 counts many fish and potentially many times on a river.

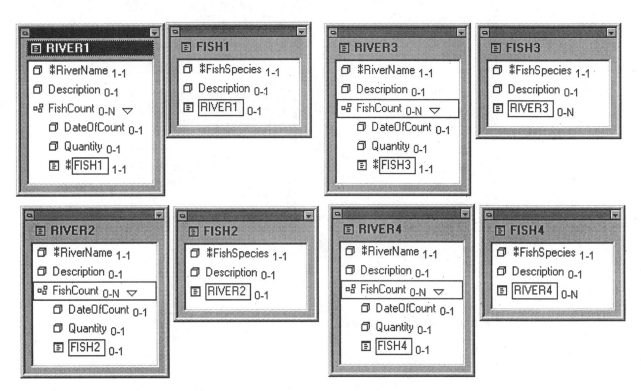

Cases 1, 3, and 4 would be represented with the following three tables:

RIVER (RiverName, Description)
FISH (FishSpecies, Description)
FISHCOUNT(FishCountID, DateOfCount, Quantity, RiverName, FishSpecies)

In case 1, (RiverName, FishSpecies) would be created as a unique index.
In case 3, (DateOfCount, FishSpecies) would be created as a unique index.
In case 4, no special indices would be created.

Case 2 would be presented by the tables:

RIVER (<u>RiverName</u>, Description)
FISH (<u>FishSpecies</u>, Description, *RiverName*)
FISHCOUNT(<u>FishCountID</u>, DateOfCount, Quantity, *RiverName, FishSpecies*)

Where (FishSpecies, RiverName) in FISH would be created as a unique index.

7.21 Add an INGREDIENT object and a SUPPLIER object as follows:

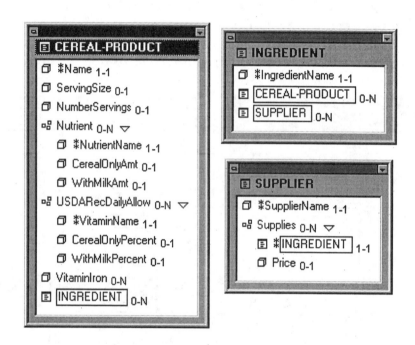

Resulting tables are (in SQL Server):

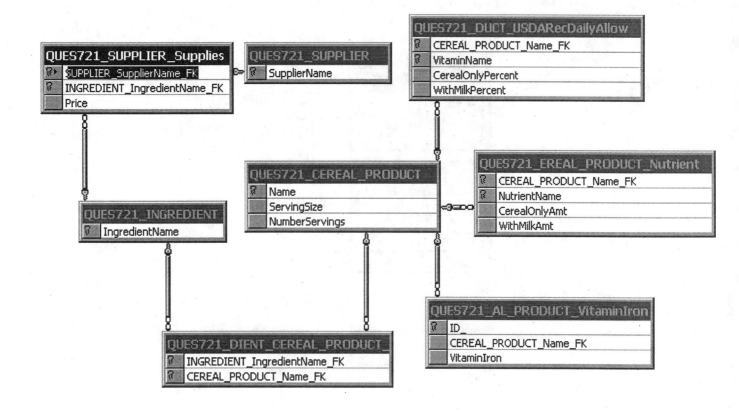

7.22 All three objects are compound objects. The other questions are answered in this model and in the SQL Server database.

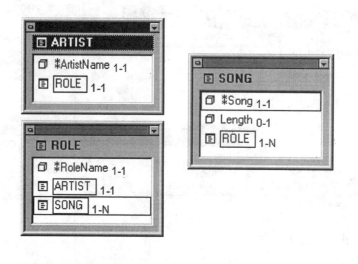

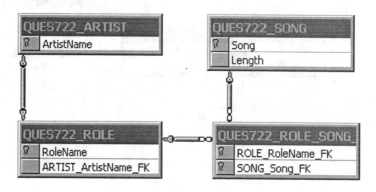

66

Answers to Projects

A. The following SQL Server database was generated by DBApp from the file MHASO.apm located on the www.prehnall.com/kroenke/ Web site.

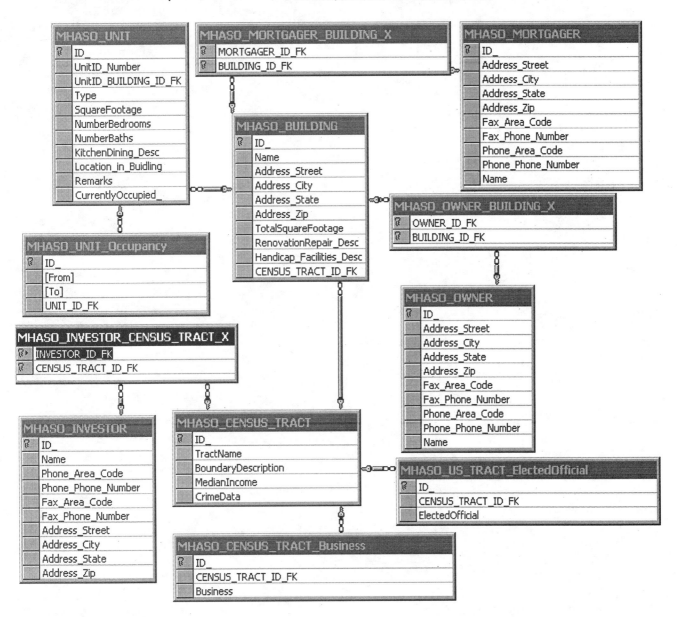

All tables use surrogate keys. Attributes ending in FK are foreign keys. Tables ending in _X are intersection tables.

This is almost the same schema as for Project A of Chapter 6. The only difference is the single valued group names, like Address, have been appended to the names of attributes they contain. See for example, MHASO_OWNER.

B. The answer is the same as given for Project 6 B.

C. The answer is the same as given for Project 6 C.

Chapter 8

Implementing Relational Databases

Objectives

- Review relational terminology
- Describe the tasks to be accomplished in relational data definition
- Survey the types of tools available for relational data manipulation and describe three modes of DML interface
- Describe basic relational algebra operations and illustrate their use in expressing database queries

Teaching Suggestions

1. When discussing the relational model, emphasize the fact that relationships between tables are represented within the data that is visible to the users, not in hidden data structures (like linked lists or indexes). You may want to cover some of the material in Appendix A so that the students can get a feel for these data structures.

2. In general, users do not want to process relations. They want to process objects composed from relations. This means that applications need to create views of data from relations as discussed in Chapter 10. A relation, then, is a building block — akin to a brick. Just as buildings are made of bricks, database applications are constructed from rows in relations.

3. Relational algebra is seldom used in commercial processing. Still, I think it is important to teach it so the students understand the kind of work that the DBMS must perform. For example, the students need to know what a join is so that they understand what they are requiring the DBMS to do when they express a query in SQL that implies a join.

4. If you're going to use SQL Server, this chapter is a good place to introduce it. The discussion in the section on Implementing a Relational Database can be given substance if the students are at the same time creating their own SQL Server database. They can then create several tables and be prepared to use Query Analyzer to run SQL statements in Chapter 9.

Answers to Group I Questions

8.1 Define the structure to the DBMS (text file or graphical creation facility) allocate space (done automatically for personal DBMS, can be considerable work for server or mainframe DBMS products); create data (keyed or mass input, verification important, may write verification programs).

8.2 Relation: a two-dimensional table with no repeating columns and no identical rows. Attribute: column of a relation. Tuple: row of a relation. Domain: set of values an attribute can have.

8.3 Both sets: same as relation, attribute, tuple.

8.4 A relational schemata is the structure of a set of relations with constraints. A relation is the structure of the tables without constraints.

8.5 A key is an attribute or group of attributes that identifies a unique row. A logical key is the same as a key as just defined. A physical key is an attribute that has a data structure defined (usually an index) to improve direct or sequential access. Sometimes physical keys are defined to create uniqueness constraints.

8.6 Improve performance for direct access; improve performance for sorted sequential processing. Used to implement a uniqueness constraint. (Also can be used to improve performance in joins.)

8.7 When the database is to be implemented using a product based on a model other than the relational model. Today that would be an ODBMS, or perhaps DL/I or IMS — see Chapters 16 and 17. No transformation is required when using a relational product because the DBMS-independent design has been expressed in terms of the relational model.

8.8 The data definition language is a means for describing the structure of a database. One can use SQL to define tables and indexes, but this is usually not done.

8.9 Using a graphical facility, as in Access or SQL Server.

8.10 Name each table, define columns in that table, describe the physical format of each column. Specify constraints, define passwords and other control facilities.

8.11 Two objects are processed concurrently. One is ORDER with ORDER and LINE-ITEM tables. The other is CUSTOMER with CUSTOMER and PAYMENT tables. The objects have no data in common. If the organization has two disk drives and channels, it may be best to put ORDER and LINE-ITEM on one and CUSTOMER and PAYMENT on the other. That way, processing of ORDER object does not interfere with the processing of the CUSTOMER object.

8.12   Best: data is on computer-sensible media — it is known to be consistent and free of errors. Worst: data is on hard to read paper forms that were scribbled in number 6 pencil in a rain forest by people who did not speak English. Many forms were lost when a barge overturned in the Amazon with the source documents. Documents contain the only existent data about the location of highly toxic chemicals located in industrial dump sites in areas around Philadelphia, New York, or Boston. Strangely, all of the documents pertaining to Langley, VA, survived intact.

8.13   Relational algebra manipulates relation via operators similar to arithmetic operators. The user must know what is desired and how to extract it. Relational calculus in contrast is non-procedural. Transform-oriented languages are also non-procedural, and are used to transform inputs into desired outputs. Query by Example provides the user with a picture of the structure of the relation. The user then fills in an example of the desired results.

8.14   Use either default form or form custom created using application tools subsystem of DBMS.

8.15   Statement at a time by users at terminals (mainframe) or personal computers. Or use stored queries that were created by SQL experts and stored with the database.

8.16   Call a subroutine library (more difficult) or insert SQL or other data sublanguage commands. Precompiler converts data sublanguage commands into standard language commands.

8.17   SQL is relation at a time oriented; programming languages are row at a time. Treat the result of an SQL command as a pseudofile; this is shown in for ADO in Chapter 13 and for DB2 in Chapter 15.

8.18   In high school algebra variables that are operated on represent numbers. The result is also a number. In relational algebra the operands are relations and the end result is always another relation.

8.19   The result of a series of relational algebra operations is always another relation.

8.20 To be union compatible each relation in the union must have the same number of attributes and attributes in corresponding columns must come from the same domain.

Compatible: INVENTORY (Inumber, Description, Cost)
ORDER (Inumber, Description, Price)

or

EMPLOYEE (Enumber, Name, Dept)
VACATION-SCHEDULE (Number, Name, Dept-to-be-billed)

Non-compatible: INVENTORY (Pnum, Desc, Quantity-in-stock)
ORDER (Item, Desc, Price)

and

INVENTORY (Part, Desc)
ORDER (Pnum, Desc, Supplier)

8.21 COMPANY (Name, Number-employees, Sales)
MANUFACTURER (Name, People, Revenue)

COMPANY

IBM	50000	9000000000
Univac	25000	500000000
Microsoft	2500	1500000000

MANUFACTURER

IBM	50000	9000000000
Univac	25000	500000000

Union of COMPANY and MANUFACTURER

IBM	50000	9000000000
Univac	25000	500000000
Microsoft	2500	1500000000

8.22 Difference of COMPANY and MANUFACTURER:

Microsoft	2500	1500000000

8.23 Intersection of COMPANY and MANUFACTURER:

IBM	50000	9000000000
Univac	25000	500000000

8.24 The product of these two relations will contain 42 tuples. You might caution the students of this fact. Or better, change the question to ask how many tuples will be in the resulting product relation.

8.25

SALESPERSON[Name, Salary]

Abel	120,000
Baker	42,000
Jones	36,000
Murphy	50,000
Zenith	118,000
Kobad	34,000

SALESPERSON[Age, Salary]

63	120,000
38	42,000
26	36,000
42	50,000
59	118,000
27	34,000

SALESPERSON[Age, Salary] would have fewer rows than SALESPERSON if any two people have the same age and salary (which they do not in this example).

8.26 SELECT SALESPERSON WHERE Name = "Baker"

SELECT SALESPERSON WHERE Age < 30

SELECT SALESPERSON WHERE Name = "Jones" AND Age > 30

8.27   SALESPERSON JOIN (Name = Salesperson-name) ORDER

Abel	63	120,000	30	Manchester Lumber	Abel	480
Abel	63	120,000	40	Amalgamated Housing	Abel	2500
Abel	63	120,000	60	Tri-City Builders	Abel	700
Jones	26	36,000	20	Abernathy Construction	Jones	1800
Jones	26	36,000	70	Manchester Lumber	Jones	150
Murphy	42	50,000	50	Abernathy Construction	Murphy	6000
Zenith	59	118,000	90	Abernathy Construction	Zenith	560

This is an equijoin. For a natural join, remove the second column of salesperson
names (next to last column).

8.28
a.   SALESPERSON[Name]
b.   ORDER[Salesperson-name]
c.   SALESPERSON[Name] - ORDER[Salesperson-name]
d.   ORDER WHERE Salesperson-name = 'Abernathy Construction'
e.   SALESPERSON JOIN (Name = Salesperson-name) ORDER WHERE
      Cust-name = 'Abernathy Construction' [Age]
f.   ORDER WHERE Salesperson-name = 'Jones' JOIN [Cust-name = Name]
      CUSTOMER [City]
g.   SALESPERSON LEFT OUTER JOIN (SALESPERSON.Name =
      SalespersonName) ORDER [SALESPERSON.Name, CustName]

Chapter 9

Structured Query Language

Objectives

- Introduce the relational data access language SQL
- Show SQL for querying a single table
- Show SQL subquery and join for querying multiple tables
- Understand the differences between subqueries and joins
- Demonstrate the use of SQL for updating data

Teaching Suggestions

1. The best way to teach SQL is with lots of examples. Show the syntax of SQL commands and then have the students answer sample queries. Use the questions at the end of the chapter as one source of examples.

2. If possible, have the students install SQL Server and execute SQL statements using Query Analyzer. They could duplicate the SQL in this chapter, or, if they have been doing the MHA, Dell, or Amazon.com projects they could develop SQL statements for those case situations.

Answers to Group I Questions

9.1   SELECT   Age, Salary
         FROM   SALESPERSON

9.2   SELECT   DISTINCT Age, Salary
         FROM   SALESPERSON

9.3   SELECT   Name
         FROM   SALESPERSON
         WHERE   AGE < 30

9.4   SELECT   SalespersonName
         FROM   ORDER
         WHERE   CustName = 'Abernathy Construction'

9.5   SELECT   Name
         FROM   SALESPERSON

	WHERE	Salary > 49999 AND Salary < 100000

9.6	SELECT	Name
	FROM	SALESPERSON
	WHERE	Age BETWEEN 49 AND 60

9.7	SELECT	Name
	FROM	SALESPERSON
	WHERE	Age LIKE '5_'

9.8	SELECT	Name
	FROM	CUSTOMER
	WHERE	City LIKE '%S'

9.9	SELECT	SalespersonName, Salary
	FROM	ORDER
	WHERE	CustName NOT IN ['Abernathy Construction']
	ORDER BY	Salary DESC

9.10	SELECT	COUNT(*)
	FROM	ORDER

9.11	SELECT	COUNT (DISTINCT CustName)
	FROM	ORDER

9.12	SELECT	AVG(Age)
	FROM	SALESPERSON

9.13	SELECT	Name
	FROM	SALESPERSON
	WHERE	Age = MAX(Age)
	(not valid for all implementations of SQL)	

9.14	SELECT	SalespersonName, COUNT(*)
	FROM	ORDER
	GROUP BY	SalespersonName

9.15	SELECT	COUNT(*)
	FROM	ORDER
	GROUP BY	SalespersonName
	WHERE	Amount > 500

```
9.16   SELECT      Name, Age
       FROM        SALESPERSON
       WHERE       Name IN
                   (SELECT      SalespersonName
                   FROM         ORDER
                   WHERE        CustName = 'Abernathy Construction')
       ORDER BY    Age DESC


9.17   SELECT      Name, Age
       FROM        SALESPERSON, ORDER
       WHERE       SALESPERSON.Name = ORDER.SalespersonName
           AND     ORDER.CustName = 'Abernathy Construction'
       ORDER BY    Age DESC


9.18   SELECT      Age
       FROM        SALESPERSON
       WHERE       Name IN
                   (SELECT      SalespersonName
                   FROM         ORDER
                   WHERE        CustName IN
                                (SELECT Name
                                FROM CUSTOMER
                                WHERE City = 'Memphis'))


9.19   SELECT      Age
       FROM        SALESPERSON, ORDER, CUSTOMER
       WHERE       SALESPERSON.Name = ORDER.SalespersonName
           AND     ORDER.CustName = CUSTOMER.Name
           AND     City = 'Memphis'


9.20   SELECT      IndustryType, Age
       FROM        SALESPERSON, CUSTOMER, ORDER
       WHERE       SALESPERSON.Name = ORDER.SalespersonName
           AND     ORDER.CustName = CUSTOMER.Name
           AND     CITY = 'Memphis'


9.21   SELECT      SALESPERSON.Name, ORDER.CustName
       FROM        SALESPERSON LEFT JOIN ORDER
           ON      SALESPERSON.Name = ORDER.SalespersonName


9.22   SELECT      SalespersonName
       FROM        ORDER
       GROUP BY    SalespersonName
       HAVING      COUNT(*) > 1
```

```
9.23   SELECT      SALESPERSON.Name, Age
       FROM        SALESPERSON, ORDER
       WHERE       SALESPERSON.Name = ORDER.SalespersonName
       GROUP BY    SalespersonName
       HAVING      COUNT(*) > 1


9.24
       SELECT      Name, Age
       FROM        SALESPERSON
       WHERE       NOT EXISTS
           (SELECT      *
           FROM        ORDER
           WHERE       NOT EXISTS
               (SELECT      *
               FROM        CUSTOMER
               WHERE       SALESPERSON.Name =
                   ORDER.SalespersonName
               AND   ORDER.CustName= CUSTOMER.Name))


9.25   INSERT      INTO        CUSTOMER
                   VALUES      ['Wilson','Dayton','F']

9.26   INSERT      INTO SALESPERSON
                   (Name, Age)
                   VALUES      ['Jacob', 35]

9.27   INSERT      INTO HIGH-ACHIEVER
                   (SELECT      Name, Age
                   FROM        SALESPERSON
                   WHERE       Salary >= 100000)

9.28   DELETE      CUSTOMER
       WHERE       NAME = 'Abernathy Construction'

9.29   DELETE      ORDER
       WHERE       CustName = 'Abernathy Construction')

9.30   UPDATE      SALESPERSON
       SET         Salary = 45000
       WHERE       NAME = 'JONES'

9.31   UPDATE      SALESPERSON
       SET         Salary = Salary * 1.9
```

```
9.32   UPDATE      SALESPERSON
       SET         NAME = 'Parks'
       WHERE       NAME = 'Jones'

       UPDATE      ORDER
       SET         SalespersonName = 'Parks'
       WHERE       SalespersonName = 'Jones'
```

Answers to Group II Questions

These questions and the projects below just scratch the surface of SQL and its application in SQL Server. It's so tempting to assign many more such questions and expand the project on and on, but there is so much to cover in the course that I think the time cost is too high. I used just a sampling here to ensure that students can run SQL Server and execute queries.

Install SQL Server, open Query Analyzer, select Northwind database

List all columns of suppliers

```
SELECT * FROM Suppliers
```

List CompanyName from suppliers with CompanyName starting with New

```
SELECT CompanyName
FROM Suppliers
WHERE CompanyName LIKE 'New%'
```

List all columns from products from suppliers with CompanyName starting with New. Show answer using both a join and a subquery

```
SELECT *
FROM Products
WHERE Products.SupplierID = Suppliers.SupplierID
      AND CompanyName LIKE 'New&'
```

and

```
SELECT ProductName
FROM Products
WHERE Products.SupplierID IN
      (SELECT SupplierID
      FROM Suppliers
      Where CompanyName LIKE 'New%')
```

List the ReorderLevel and count for all products

```
SELECT ReorderLevel, Count(*)
FROM Products
GROUP BY ReorderLevel
```

List the ReorderLevel and count for all levels having more than 1 element

```
SELECT ReorderLevel, Count(*)
FROM Products
GROUP BY ReorderLevel
HAVING Count(*) > 1
```

List the ReorderLevel and count for all levels having more than 1 element for products from suppliers whose names start with New.

```
SELECT ReorderLevel, Count(*)
FROM Products, Suppliers
WHERE Products.SupplierID = Suppliers.SupplierID
AND Suppliers.CompanyName like 'New%'
GROUP BY ReorderLevel
HAVING count(*) >1
```

Answers to Projects

A.   Note in this answer, the table name is UNIT, not APARTMENT, and because the tables were generated by DBApp, the name of the model (here MHAER) is appended to the names of all the tables.

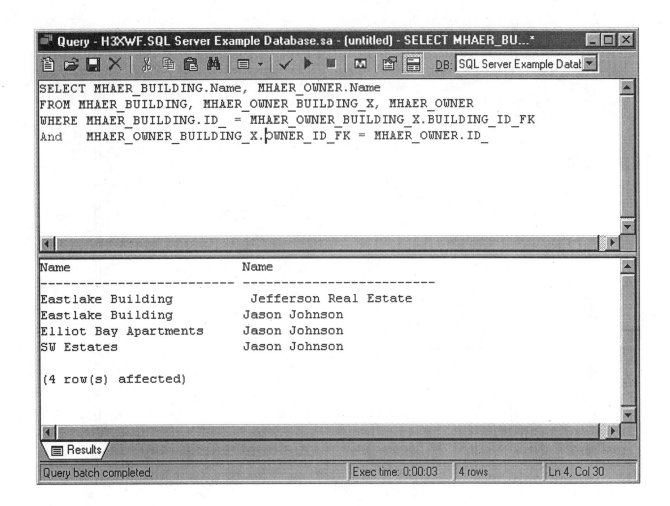

```
SELECT MHAER_BUILDING.Name, MHAER_OWNER.Name
FROM MHAER_BUILDING, MHAER_OWNER_BUILDING_X, MHAER_OWNER
WHERE MHAER_BUILDING.ID_ = MHAER_OWNER_BUILDING_X.BUILDING_ID_FK
And    MHAER_OWNER_BUILDING_X.OWNER_ID_FK = MHAER_OWNER.ID_
```

```
Name                              Name
--------------------------------  --------------------------
Eastlake Building                  Jefferson Real Estate
Eastlake Building                 Jason Johnson
Elliot Bay Apartments             Jason Johnson
SW Estates                        Jason Johnson

(4 row(s) affected)
```

The second query is:

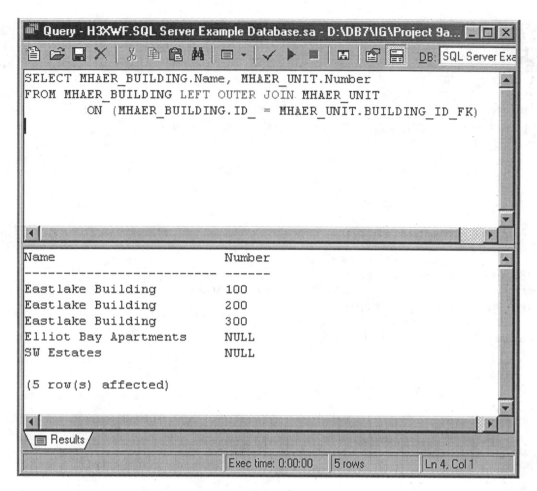

One example of a subquery is:

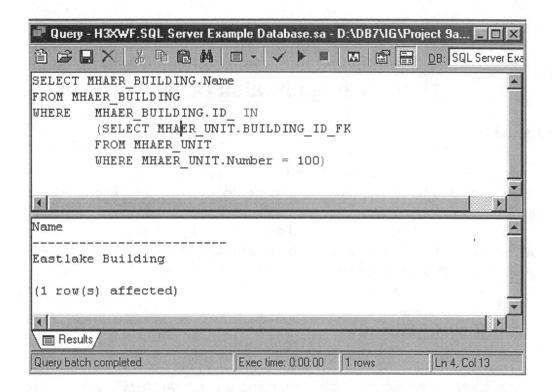

```
SELECT MHAER_BUILDING.Name
FROM MHAER_BUILDING
WHERE    MHAER_BUILDING.ID_ IN
         (SELECT MHAER_UNIT.BUILDING_ID_FK
         FROM MHAER_UNIT
         WHERE MHAER_UNIT.Number = 100)
```

```
Name
-------------------------
Eastlake Building

(1 row(s) affected)
```

B.   The table, key, and query structure is identical to that for the answer to project A. Just change the names of the tables and the names of the columns.

C.   The table, key, and query structure is identical to that for the answer to project A. Just change the names of the tables and the names of the columns.

Chapter 10

Database Application Design

Objectives

- Learn the five basic functions of a database application
- Understand database actions require to create, read, update, and delete database views
- Learn fundamental principles of database view materialization
- Understand the application's role in enforcing constraints
- Understand the application's role in control and security

Teaching Suggestions

1. The relationship of database applications and the DBMS is sometimes confusing. For a simple application using a personal DBMS, the application and the DBMS are nearly indistinguishable. If an application has only a few forms and reports, and all of these are created using DBMS facilities, then the application and the DBMS are the same. On the other hand, for an organizational database processed by say, DB2, all of the elements discussed in this chapter will be provided by application program code completely separate from the DBMS. It's easier to understand all of this by focusing on application functions that must be provided — in some cases by facilities in the DBMS and in other cases by separate application programs.

2. It is important to distinguish between a view (the logical structure of data elements) and a materialization of the view (a form or report). One view can have many materializations. While this distinction has always been important, it has become even more so in light of the three-tier architecture described in Chapter 11 where database views are constructed and processed on the Web server but are materialized on the browser.

3. A database view is a hierarchical structure of attributes from one or more entities or semantic objects. An entity or object can appear more than once in the view. Views can have more than one multi-valued path. In the View Ridge case, a CUSTOMER view has a multi-valued path to TRANSACTION and a second one to ARTIST. (See Figure 10-3e.) No single SQL statement can represent all of this view. Hence, SQL is a poor facility for describing views — even though it has been used for that

purpose for years, because of the lack of anything better. XML (in the next chapter) cures this problem. It is important to make this distinction.

4. The purpose of the discussion of view CRUD is to show students how SQL relates to database applications. Too often I have found that students understand how SQL can be used for interactive query, but do not really understand its role in application processing. In fact, SQL is far more frequently used for view processing as described here than it is an interactive query tool.

5. The principles of form and report design in this chapter overlap those taught in a systems development class. This may be review for some students. The essential point here is to understand how the structure of the view and the nature of its contents dictate certain visual structures and controls. Forms and reports that are hard to use always have some element in which the structure of the view and the structure of the materialization fight with one another.

6. Constraints fall in four major categories: domain, uniqueness, cardinality, and business rule. In general, domain and uniqueness constraints are best enforced by the DBMS (setting aside issues involving Microsoft's Transaction Service for distributed databases which are beyond the scope of this text). Some cardinality constraints are enforced by the database design and some can be enforced by making foreign keys required or unique or both. Others, like 2.3 (min of 2, max of 3) are best enforced by the application or by stored procedures. Business rule constraints can be enforced by stored procedures in the DBMS or by the application. Ensure that students understand why DBMS enforcement is usually better than application enforcement.

7. It is important for the students to understand the limitations of user name and password security provided by most DBMS products. Such security is worthless if users are careless with their identities. In this regard, it is unfortunate that most users cannot watch professional software developers at work. They, of all people, understand the risks of user name and password and they as a class are absolutely paranoid about protecting their passwords. In fact, an etiquette and protocol has evolved in which it is considered rude not to look away when watching another person enter his or her password. When one developer is helping another at the second developers machine, if a password is required, it is understood that the first developer will leave the computer and look away to allow the second to enter his or her password. Asking another developer for his or her password is never done and if it were it would be considered as rude as asking for their PIN or a bank card or even for their bank balance. By the way, a good way to select a personal password is to think of the first line of a favorite song or poem and use the initial letters of

the phrase. Thus, "I Left My Heart in San Francisco" would result in the password ILMHiSF. Easy to remember and very difficult to guess.

8.   Even if user identities are protected, such security is limited to vertical security. Horizontal security must be provided by application code.

Answers to Group I Questions

10.1   CRUD views, materialize views, enforce constraints, provide control and security, execute application logic.

10.2   Create, read, update, and delete.

10.3   A view is a structured list of data items from the entities or semantic objects in the data model.

10.4   A view instance is a view structure for a particular entity or semantic object instance.

10.5   A view is a structure of data. A materialization is presentation of that data in some format — form, report, or API. A materializations include labels, colors, boxes, etc. Report materializations almost always include formulas.

10.6   An entity or object can appear more than once in a view. See ARTIST in the View Ridge Customer view. Any attribute of an entity or object that appears more than once in a view can appear more than once in a view.

10.7   When there is only one multi-valued path through the entities or objects. See Figure 10-3(e). Only CUSTOMER and TRANSACTION or CUSTOMER and ARTIST (via the intersection table) can appear in the view. Here's a trickier one: consider STUDENT with a 1:N relationship to GRADE, and CLASS with a 1:N relationship to GRADE. Create the view STUDENT:GRADE:CLASS. At first it appears there are two multi-valued paths — those between STUDENT and GRADE and between CLASS and GRADE. However, this view transverses from STUDENT to GRADE to CLASS, which has a max card of 1 in that direction.

10.8   When there is more than one multi-valued path.

10.9   One is via TRANSACTION; the other is via the CUSTOMER_ARTIST_INT to ARTIST.

10.10 A record set is the result of the execution of a SQL statement that is wrapped in object structures. Recordset has methods and properties. These are discussed further in Chapter 13.

10.11 Obtain the data values and create in memory and then store new rows of appropriate relations in the database. Set foreign key values to establish relationships within the new data rows as well as to connect the new view data with data that already exists in the database.

10.12 By setting foreign key values. If surrogate keys are used, this will probably require storing new rows, reading back their surrogate keys, and then using new values to connect the new rows.

10.13 Store the row and then read it back. Note, if there is no unique identifier other than the surrogate key, several rows may be returned. The application must check additional attribute values to find the correct one.

10.14 Updating an attribute value; changing a relationship; adding new rows for new multi-valued attributes, such as TRANSACTION for CUSTOMER as discussed in the text.

10.15 Change 1:N relationships by modifying the foreign key value. Change N:M relationships by modifying the key value in the intersection table.

10.16 The difficulty is in knowing how much to delete. In terms of the entity-relationship model, all weak entities are deleted. In terms of the semantic object model, all data in a given object is deleted, but no data in other objects. Deletions are also not allowed if the deletions were to cause a cardinality violation.

10.17 All weak entities that depend on the base entity of the view are deleted.

10.18 All attributes contained within the semantic object are deleted.

10.19 Cascading deletions occur when the deletion of one row causes the deletion of another row. They can be used to enforce the rules in the answer to questions 10.17 and 10.18.

10.20 The structure of the view should be graphically evident in the structure of the form. Using the semantic object model, data from the entry point relation is presented first, followed by data in the order of the semantic object (assuming that order reflect the order of the forms and reports from which the object was derived). Multi-value data occurs in regions with column headings and possibly footings. Data from the entry point relation may need to be split on the form, but otherwise data from a relation is presented in contiguous areas on the form. The same principles can be used for report design.

10.21   Place group boxes around groups; ensure the hierarchy of the view is expressed consistently in the hierarchical structure of the form. Keep related items together. Example: Place Address, City, State, Zip, together in a group on a form. In this way, data that is logically grouped in the user's mind is physically grouped on the form.

10.22   Example: Buttons and other controls should be located in obvious places. Example: suppose a user is creating an order and needs to look up item data. The button for the item look up should be near the item number text field on the form. Then the form will encourage the user to look up in the correct context of the form.

10.23   A drop-down list box is a box superimposed on the existing screen. It enables the user to interrupt normal processing, perform a related task, and return to the original procedure. An option group represents a group of mutually exclusive choices. Only one can be selected. A check box represents a binary selection; more than one check box can be on in a group of check boxes.

10.24   With banded report writers, only one multi-valued path can be readily represented. If a CUSTOMER, for example, has multiple ContactPersons and multiple Payment terms, the two multi-valued groups cannot be readily presented on the report. Sub-reports, calculated values, or other artifice must be employed to show the two multi-valued attributes.

10.25   The values change frequently and stored values are not reliable. Either that, or some facility must be created in the application to automatically update stored computed values when the determinants of the computations change. This is costly and wasteful and is almost never done.

10.26   A request to sort an object refers to a set of objects and not to the named object. Show CUSTOMERs sorted by Zip is a request to create a materialization of a set of CUSTOMERs and not to a single customer. The set, in fact, is a different object.

10.27   If a constraint is enforced by the DBMS, then the constraint will be invoked regardless of the source of the data change: form, application program, import program, or other. If the constraint is placed in application programs, then it must be enforced by every program — and inconsistency is likely.

10.28 Because the DBMS lack facilities to enforce the constraint or because the constraint is particular to a given application.

10.29 InvoiceTotal must be less than 10,000. If InvoiceTotal is stored in the database, then set a rule in the table definition as shown in this chapter. If it is not stored in the database, then trap an event and write code to enforce the constraint as shown in Chapter 2.

10.30 A null value can mean that the value is unknown, that it is inappropriate for this instance, or something else. Make the value required, or, in the case of value-inappropriate nulls, create subtypes.

10.31 Because it creates indexes to make such checking very fast.

10.32 Non-zero settings of minimum cardinality, and maximum cardinality settings other than 1 or N.

10.33 Make the foreign key required.

10.34 A fragment is a child or parent row that does not have a required parent or child. An orphan is child row that does not have a required parent.

10.35 M-M: CUSTOMER has ORDERs (assumes no one becomes a customer until they order)
M-O: REPAIR has LABOR-CHARGEs
O-M: APPOINTMENT has DOCTORs
O-O: SALESPERSON has AUTO

10.36 Because the surrogate key is never seen nor modified by the user.

10.37 See text discussion on pages 260-262.

10.38 See text discussion on pages 260-262.

10.39 See text discussion on pages 260-262.

10.40 Because the only automatic relationship maintenance is cascade modify and cascade delete. These do not cover the cases shown in column one of Figure 10-19(a) nor column three of Figure 10-19(b).

10.41 No data is ever to be deleted for a CUSTOMER who purchased any work for more than $50,000. Trap the delete event in Access. Write code to find the maximum SalesPrice. Examine that value; if it is greater than 50,000 disallow the delete. Show a message box to the user to explain why.

10.42 Horizontal security allows access to all columns of the data, but restricts access to certain rows. Vertical security allows access to all rows of the data, but restricts access to certain columns.

10.43 Horizontal.

10.44 Vertical or both.

10.45 They can be tailored to the context in which the user is operating.

10.46 Short answer: by trapping events and writing application code for those events. Longer answer, if access is a cover over SQL Server, then trap events and fire stored procedures in SQL Server. (The longer answer is not discussed in the text.)

Answers to Group II Questions

```
10.47 SELECT    ARTIST.Name, ARTIST.Nationality,
                TRANSACTION.PurchaseDate, TRANSACTION.SalesPrice,
                CUSTOMER.Name, CUSTOMER.AreaCode,
                CUSTOMER.LocalNumber,
      FROM      CUSTOMER, TRANSACTION, WORK, ARTIST
      WHERE     CUSTOMER.CustomerID = WORK.Customer_ID
          AND   WORK.WorkID = TRANSACTION.WorkID
          AND   ARTIST.Name = "Mark Tobey"
```

Followed by:

```
      SELECT    CUSTOMER.Name
      FROM      CUSTOMER, CUSTOMER_ARTIST_INT
      WHERE     CUSTOMER.CustomerID =
                CUSTOMER_ARTIST_INT.CustomerID
          AND   ARTIST.ArtistID = CUSTOMER_ARTIST_INT.ArtistID
```

10.48
```
      INSERT    INTO ARTIST

                (ARTIST.Name,
                ARTIST.Nationality)
      VALUES    (NewArtist.ARTIST.Name,
                NewArtist.ARTIST.Nationality)
```

To get the new surrogate key value:

```
SELECT      ARTIST.ArtistID, ARTIST.Nationality
FROM        ARTIST
WHERE       ARTIST.Name = NewArtist.Name
```

To get the value for WorkID:

```
SELECT      WORK.WorkID
FROM        WORK, ARTIST
WHERE       WORK.ArtistID = ARTIST.ArtistID
    AND     ARTIST.Name = NewCust.WORK.ARTIST.Name
    AND     WORK.Title = NewCust.WORK.Title
    AND     WORK.Copy = NewCust.WORK.Copy
```

Assume that the returned surrogate key value is stored as
NewCust.WORK.WorkID.

The following SQL can be executed to add the new TRANSACTION row:
```
INSERT      INTO  TRANSACTION
                  (TRANSACTION.WorkID,
                  TRANSACTION.DateAcquired,
                  TRANSACTION.AcquisitionPrice,
                  TRANSACTION.PurchaseDate,
                  TRANSACTION.CustomerID,
                  TRANSACTION.SalesPrice)
            VALUES
                  (NewArtist.WORK.WorkID,
                  NewArtist.TRANSACTION.DateAcquired,
                  NewArtist.TRANSACTION.AcquisitionPrice,
                  NewArtist.TRANSACTION.PurchaseDate,
                  NewArtist.CUSTOMER.CustomerID,
                  NewArtist.TRANSACTION.SalesPrice)
```

Now all that remains is to create rows for the intersection table.

For each NewArtist.CUSTOMER.Name
```
      SELECT      CUSTOMER.CustomerID
      FROM        CUSTOMER
      WHERE       CUSTOMER.Name = NewArtist.CUSTOMER.Name

      INSERT      INTO        CUSTOMER_ARTIST_INT
                              (ArtistID, CustomerID)
                  VALUES      (NewArtist.ARTIST.ArtistID,
                              CUSTOMER.CustomerID)
```
Next NewCust.ARTIST.Name

91

10.49

    A.   UPDATE ARTIST
        SET   ARTIST.ArtistName = "Mark Toby"
        WHERE   ARTIST.ArtistName = "Mark Tobey"

    (Consider here the advantages of surrogate keys. Otherwise, we'd have to cascade this change through WORK and TRANSACTION)

    B.   Assuming have the id of the work in NewTrans.WorkID. Otherwise, have to issue SELECT for the work specified.

        INSERT   INTO TRANSACTION
                (TRANSACTION.WorkID,
                TRANSACTION.DateAcquired,
                TRANSACTION.AcquisitionPrice,
                TRANSACTION.PurchaseDate,
                TRANSACTION.CustomerID,
                TRANSACTION.SalesPrice)
           VALUES
                (NewTrans.WorkID,
                NewTrans.TRANSACTION.DateAcquired,
                NewTrans.TRANSACTION.AcquisitionPrice,
                NewTrans.TRANSACTION.PurchaseDate,
                NewTrans.CUSTOMER.CustomerID,
                NewTrans.TRANSACTION.SalesPrice)

    C.   SELECT   ArtistID
        FROM   ARTIST
        WHERE   ARTIST.ArtistName = "Mark Toby"

    For each NewCust.Name
        SELECT   CUSTOMER.CustomerID
        FROM   CUSTOMER
        WHERE   CUSTOMER.Name = NewCust.Name

        INSERT   INTO   CUSTOMER_ARTIST_INT
                        (ArtistID, CustomerID)
              VALUES   (ArtistID,
                         CUSTOMER.CustomerID)
    Next NewCust.Name

10.50 Execute deletions from the bottom up:

```
DELETE       TRANSACTION
WHERE        TransactionID IN
    (SELECT      WORK.TransactionID
    FROM         WORK
    WHERE        WORK.ArtistID IN
        (SELECT      ARTIST.ArtistID
        FROM         ARTIST
        WHERE        ARTIST.ArtistName = "Mark Toby"))
```

Then,

```
DELETE       WORK
WHERE        WORK.ArtistID IN
        (SELECT      ARTIST.ArtistID
        FROM         ARTIST
        WHERE        ARTIST.ArtistName = "Mark Toby"))
```

Next,

```
DELETE       CUSTOMER_ARTIST_INT
WHERE        CUSTOMER_ARTIST)_INT.ArtistID IN
        (SELECT      ARTIST.ArtistID
        FROM         ARTIST
        WHERE        ARTIST.ArtistName = "Mark Toby")
```

And finally,

```
DELETE       ARTIST
WHERE        ARTIST.ArtistName = "Mark Toby"
```

Answers to Projects

A.   See the ViewRidge.mdb database located on www.prenhall.com/kroenke/

B.   Here are three views from the DBApp model MHA.apm.

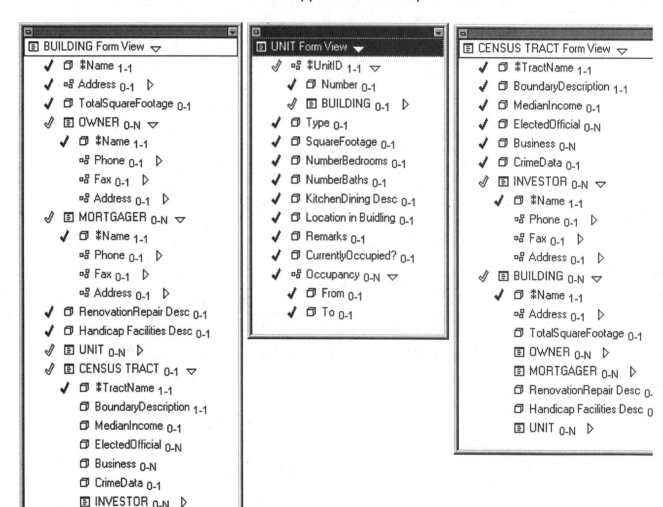

A GUI menu would present the forms and reports of the application. Most likely, the application would be divided into major functions and each of the major functions would have a set of forms and reports. Different users would see different menus. If you're using DBApp, you can use it to generate a possible browser based menu for this application.

With regard to form controls, consider the UNIT view above. Here are the attributes and field types I would use:

Control	Attribute
Textbox	Number Square Footage Kitchen Dining Desc LocationInBuilding Remarks From To
Drop down list	APARTMENT Type NumberBedrooms NumberBaths
Group Box	UnitID Occupancy
Check Box	CurrentlyOccupied?

Chapter 11

Database Applications Using Internet Technology

Objectives

- Understand the historical context of the Internet and learn basic Internet terms
- Learn the three tier architecture and understand the role and purpose of each of the three tiers
- Become familiar with Web-oriented languages
- Understand the nature, characteristics, and advantages of DHTML and XML

- Learn the role of Web servers for database applications

Teaching Suggestions

1. The students will most likely be very interested in this topic. Clearly, database processing using Internet technology represents substantial opportunities for jobs and careers. As of 1999, many medium-sized businesses are not yet using the Web for database publishing, and there are likely numerous opportunities close to home.

2. As stated earlier, I think it is misleading to use phrases like Internet database processing or Web database processing for this general class of applications. Many database applications will use Internet technology on WANs, LANs, and even on a single machine, and so I believe the term database processing using Internet technology is more accurate.

3. I include the following in the category of Internet technology: HTTP, HTML, DHTML, XML, browsers, and in the sense explained in this chapter, the three tier architecture.

4. Most often, the three tiers reside on three or more different machines. They could, however, reside on two or one. I often give demos with a browser, IIS, and SQL Server all running on the same laptop computer. Note, too, that in high volume applications, there are likely to be several or even many computers operating as Web servers. Thus, working from user to DBMS, there might be thousands of user computers running a browser; dozens or even hundreds of Web servers running IIS, the Netscape server or Apache; there most likely will be just one database server, however.

5. In practice, so far at least, it is difficult for Web processing to keep the DBMS very busy. For applications that use IIS and ASP, anyway, I have found the workload on the Web server to be much higher than that on the database server. There are exceptions, of course. Applications that involve the processing of graphic or other BLOB data can bog the DBMS down.

6. Microsoft has stated that ADO is the data access standard now and for the future. It is a cover over OLE DB as explained in Chapter 13.

7. I think students should become proficient with one scripting language — if not in this course, then somewhere along the line before they graduate. JScript will operate on any browser, so learning it is probably better than VBScript. On the other hand, if the students already know VB, learning VBScript will be very easy. If the students are using IIS, and if all of the scripting is on the server, then there is no problem in using VBScript.

8. I believe XML is VERY important to database applications. Because of the clean separation between structure, content, and materialization, and because of its extensibility, XML will be used as the standard way of inter-changing data on the Web. XML has strong endorsements from every major vendor; ORACLE is supposedly developing an XML document storage facility.

   By the way, as of this writing (Spring, 1999), there is a serious disagreement underway within and around W3C concerning the role and purpose of XSL. Some people, largely from the document processing community, want XSL to be used only for the transformation of XML to XML. They want XML flow objects to be used for materialization. Others, primarily Microsoft and other database vendors, see XSL as a way to transforming XML to either XML or a version of HTML. This text presents the latter viewpoint since the popularity of IE 5 will probably overcome the resistance that exists within W3C. This is an issue to watch, however, as the future unfolds . . .

9. ASP processing is included in this chapter to give a better idea of the role of the Web server in view CRUD. Chapter 13 has ASP examples and more discussion, so you might choose to cover this topic only lightly here.

10. Please see the ideas for learning Web technology at the front of this guide for more information about learning resources.

Answers to Group I Questions

11.1   A network is a collection of computers that communicate with one another using a standard protocol. Anyone can sign on to a public network by making the appropriate connections or by paying a fee to an organization that has already made such connections. A private network can only be used by those who are preauthorized to connect to it.

11.2   The Internet is a public network of computers that communicate using TCP/IP.

11.3   Terminal Control Program/ Internet Protocol. It is the standard way that computers communicate over the Internet.

11.4   Email, newsgroups, file transfer, remote terminal access.

11.5   Hypertext Transfer Protocol; a protocol that enables the sharing of documents with embedded links that is based on TCP / IP.

11.6   Hypertext Markup Language; A standard set of codes to format documents and to place links to other documents.

11.7   Standard Graphical Markup Language. A document markup and coding standard that is more comprehensive than HTML.

11.8   A program for viewing and processing HTML documents. The Netscape browser and Microsoft's Internet Explorer.

11.9   Universal Resource Locator. A standard means for locating documents on the Internet.

11.10 Multipurpose Internet Mail Code. The MIME code standard indicates which program can process which types of file attachments to an HTML document.

11.11 Request-oriented because Web servers do not solicit activity. Stateless because the server does not maintain state of a session or transaction. The stateless characteristic is a problem for database applications because several user/database interactions may be required to complete a transaction and the application must be able to know that status of a transaction to resume processing. Web servers include some means to maintain state via session variables or other means as will be shown in Chapter 13.

11.12 An intranet is a private LAN or WAN that communicates using TCP / IP. The Internet is a public network that uses TCP / IP. Intranets are private — used within a corporation, division, or department.

11.13 A firewall is a computer that serves as a security gateway between an intranet and the Internet.

11.14 Three common types of network database applications are static report publishing, query publishing, and application publishing.

11.15 Client; Web server; database server. The client provides the UI for the user and materializes views; the Web server provides HTTP services and CRUDs database views; the database server gets and puts database data.

11.16 There are standardized interfaces and protocols between each of the three tiers; this enables different operating systems to run on each tier and products from different vendors to interact with one another.

11.17 IIS, ISAPI, ASP, Win NT or 2000. IIS is an HTTP server; ISAPI is the interface between IIS and an IIS client. ASP is one ISAPI client that provides a scripting environment and maintains state; Win NT is the operating system. Users can create ASP pages or they can write their own custom programs for processing via ISAPI.

11.18 Apache or Netscape; NSAPI or ISAPI; CGI; Perl; Unix. Apache or Netscape server are HTTP servers for Unix. NSAPI serves the same function of ISAPI; CGI, or the common gateway, interface provides a customer program interface to the HTTP service. Perl is a scripting language most often used by CGI.

11.19 They are all variants of the same scripting language. Netscape owns JavaScript, Microsoft created JScript, and ECMA is the same language expressed as a standard.

11.20 JScript will run in any browser; VBScript will run only in Microsoft browsers. There are many more people who know VB (hence VBScript) than know JScript.

11.21 Practical Extraction and Report Language. Has very strong string manipulation capabilities.

11.22 COM is Microsoft's standard for object programming; OLE is COM with more interfaces supported for embedding; Active X objects are a light-weight versions of OLE objects; ActiveX controls are Active X objects with interfaces that allow them to be used in development environments like Visual Interdev.

11.23 They can be used to provide preprogrammed functionality on the Web server and they can also be downloaded to the browser.

11.24 So that everyone codes their pages with the same symbols that mean the same things. This enables browsers to process pages consistently.

11.25 W3C is the organization that facilitates the development of standards and publishes and supports recommended standards.

11.26 They establish required features and functions and set a target; that target may invalidate features important to the vendor. Standards make products into commodities; vendors extend the standards to have distinct features but then are criticized for being "non-standard".

11.27 Lack of DOM, lack of CSS (consistent style sheets), poor facilities for database data; too much freedom (the last is true with HTML 4, as well).

11.28 DHTML is Microsoft's version of HTML 4.0.

11.29 DOM provides a programming interface to Web pages. With DOM, program code can address elements of the page and dynamically change or otherwise process them.

11.30 CSS enables the page designer to define a style that will be applied to particular tags. When the tag appears, the style is used. In this way, the style of one tag, say, H3, can be modified in one place and the modification will occur in all places in the pages that use H3.

11.31 Remote Data Service. Provides facilities to cache data on the browser and performs formatting, querying, and other limited processing of it without Web server involvement.

11.32 One of them sets up the cache and interacts with the Web server to get and put data. The second is used to present data in the cache in the browser.

11.33 Yes, certainly. SQL is used to declare the data that RDS is to obtain from the server.

11.34 Extensible Markup Language. Clear separation between structure, content, and materialization. Can be extended.

11.35 Elements are used to get a particular formatting and not to declare a semantic. H1, for example, might be used to get strong bold type, rather than to declare the first level of a document. Hence, elements cannot be reliably used to infer document structure.

11.36 DTD is a document type declaration. It defines the structure of an XML document.

11.37 An XML document is type-valid if it conforms to its DTD; it is not-type-valid if either (a) it does not conform to its DTD or (b) it has no DTD.

11.38 The same way as with HTML; styles are given to document elements and are applied when those elements are encountered in the document.

11.39 XSL is a facility for transforming XML documents. It can transform XML to XML; it is also used with IE5 to transform XML documents into HTML documents.

11.40 With XSL, you do not create procedures for processing documents; instead, you state that when a particular element is encountered, that something is to be done — move this to that or show this as that. Documents are changed from one format to another.

11.41 XSL is context-oriented. XSL specifies that when a certain context is encountered, certain transformations are to take place.

11.42 Because it provides a standardized and extensible way for expressing database views. It separates content from materialization. It can be used for database view transfers among computers or users.

11.43 Because if the view involves two or more multi-valued paths, then two or more SQL statements will be required. The method by which this is done is not standardized.

11.44 Maintain state; provide a scripting environment; publish stylesheets and DTDs (the last is really a function of the Web server more than it's a function of ASP).

Answers to Group II Questions

Answers are unknown at this time.

Answers to Project

1. Answer is the same as Figure 11-8. Database server supports Access. Depending on the volume of users, the Web server and the database server might reside on the same machine.

2. Answer is the same as Figure 11-5. Not possible to run Access on Unix so will need a separate NT or Windows machine to work as the database server.

3. DOM allows scripting access to page elements; CSS allows for easier creation and maintenance of page materialization; for answer A.1, can use RDS to work with Access on browser. Risks are that the application might have problems working with Netscape or other non-Microsoft browsers; developers will need to check out the application with many different browsers (older browsers are a strong possibility in this environment).

4. If the developers know JScript, use it. It's portable, will run with any browser, and its features and functions are equivalent to VBScript. If the developers know VBScript, however, and if all script will either run on the server or MHA knows all of its users have IE, then use VBScript. Or could use VBScript on the server and JScript on the browser.

5. Here is a DTD and two sample documents:

```
<?xml version='1.0'?>
<!DOCTYPE apartmentlist [
        <!ELEMENT apartment (apartmentnumber, unitdata, occupancy+)
        <!ELEMENT apartmentnumber (number, buildingname) >
        <!ELEMENT number (#PCData) >
        <!ELEMENT buildingname (#PCDATA)>
        <!ELEMENT unitdata (type, squarefootage, numberbedrooms, remarks) >
        <!ELEMENT type (#PCDATA)>
        <!ELEMENT squarefootage (#PCDATA)>
        <!ELEMENT numberbedrooms (#PCDATA)>
        <!ELEMENT remarks (#PCData) >
        <!ELEMENT occupancy (from, to) >
```

102

```
        <!ELEMENT from (#PCDATA)>
        <!ELEMENT to (#PCDATA)>
]>

<?xml:stylesheet type="text/xsl" href="ApartmentList.xsl" ?>

<apartmentlist>
<apartment>
<apartmentnumber>
<number>123</number>
<buildingname>Westlake Building</buildingname>
</apartmentnumber>
<unitdata>
<type>single occupant</type>
<squarefootage>650</squarefootage>
<numberbedrooms>0</numberbedrooms>
<remarks>clean and bright</remarks>
</unitdata>
<occupancy>
<from> 12/21/98</from>
<to> 1/4/99</to>
</occupancy>
<occupancy>
<from> 2/2/99</from>
<to> 1/4/00</to>
</occupancy>
</apartment>

<apartment>
<apartmentnumber>
<number>445</number>
<buildingname>Westlake Building</buildingname>
</apartmentnumber>
<unitdata>
<type>double occupant</type>
<squarefootage>1060</squarefootage>
<numberbedrooms>1+</numberbedrooms>
<remarks>older but in great building</remarks>
</unitdata>
<occupancy>
<from> 10/22/99</from>
<to> 11/14/00</to>
</occupancy>
</apartment>
</apartmentlist>
```

6. Here is IE 5 XSL for that document:

```
<?xml version="1.0"?>
<HTML xmlns:xsl="http://www.w3.org/TR/WD-xsl">
  <BODY STYLE="font-family:Arial, helvetica, sans-serif; font-size:14pt;
      background-color:teal">
<xsl:for-each select="apartmentlist/apartment ">
        <DIV STYLE="background-color:brown; color:white; padding:4px">
        <SPAN STYLE="font-weight:bold; color:white">
         <xsl:value-of select="apartmentnumber/buildingname"/></SPAN>
        - <xsl:value-of select="apartmentnumber/number"/>
         </DIV>


        <DIV STYLE="margin-left:20px; margin-bottom:1em; font-size:10pt; font-
style:bold; color:yellow">
                Type:  <xsl:value-of select="unitdata/type"/>
                Square Footage:  <xsl:value-of select="unitdata/squarefootage"/>
                Bedrooms:  <xsl:value-of select="unitdata/numberbedrooms"/>



        </DIV>


        <DIV STYLE="margin-left:20px; margin-bottom:1em; font-size:12pt; font-
style:bold">
        <xsl:value-of select="unitdata/remarks"/>
        </DIV>
         <xsl:for-each select="occupancy">
        <DIV STYLE="margin-left:20px; margin-bottom:1em; font-size:10pt; font-
style:bold; color:yellow">
        <xsl:value-of select="from"/> to
        <xsl:value-of select="to"/>
         </DIV>
        </xsl:for-each>


  </xsl:for-each>
  </BODY>
</HTML>
```

7. Here is the way the document looks in IE 5:

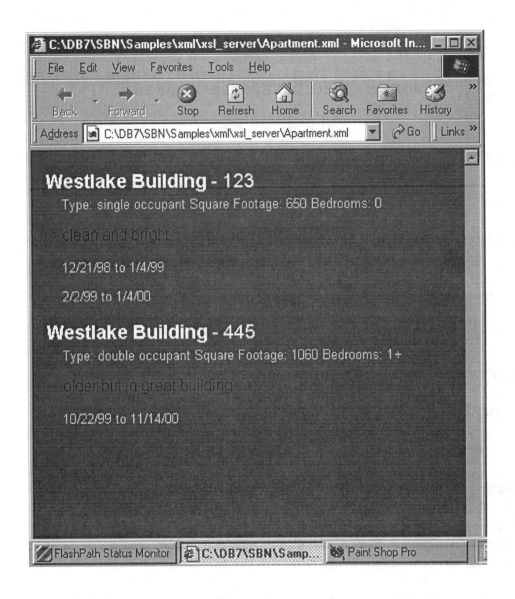

Chapter 12

Managing Multi-user Databases

Objectives

- Learn the importance of multi-user database management

- Understand the need for concurrency control and learn the basic techniques used

- Learn the fundamentals of database reliability

- Learn techniques for database security

- Understand the purpose and importance of database administration

Teaching Suggestions

1. The issues and concerns of multi-user databases are not just Internet-technology issues, but have been issues for mainframe and client-server processing for many years. They are introduced here because they are important for Internet technology applications and because many of the people who work in these applications do not yet understand their importance. Be certain the students understand that the issues are much broader than Internet technology.

2. Concurrency control is important and sometimes seems obscure. We will use the concepts in this chapter, however, in the next chapter. The caution at the end of the concurrency control section is important: "If you do not specify the isolation level of a transaction or do not specify the type of cursors you open, the DBMS will use a default level and types. These defaults may be perfect for your application, but they also may be terrible. Thus, even though these issues can be ignored, the consequences of them cannot be avoided. Learn the capabilities of your DBMS products and use them wisely!"

3. Backup and recovery is an important topic and only the high-level essentials are considered in this chapter. If the students install SQL Server, they can learn much more about the particulars of using a backup log and so forth from the SQL Server documentation and the Books Online material that is installed with it.

4. Students who have experience on the Web will probably relate to the security issues very well. Imagine the exposure of a database to the open Web! In this book, we address DBMS security only. Operating system and network security are not considered. Almost all DBMS products implement security with some version of User id and password. See teaching suggestion number 8 for Chapter 10 for comments on that issue.

5. In this text we distinguish between database administration and data administration. The latter is an organizational activity that typically sits high in the enterprise organization chart and may be concerned with much larger issues than the maintenance of a particular database. We address that function in Chapter 14. This chapter is concerned with database administration, a more pedestrian function that occurs at a much lower level in the organization. Every multi-user database needs a database administrator. The administrator may only have a few tasks to perform and may work on them only a few hours a week, but someone needs to be given the responsibility for ensuring that the database administration tasks are accomplished on a timely basis. This is especially true for Internet technology databases where the users may be far away or even anonymous, and where the consequences of failures and mistakes will be difficult to correct.

Answers to Group I Questions

12.1 Both Amazon and Dell sell and support through databases on their Web sites. If those databases fail or are compromised in some way, then corporate critical applications and functions will halt. This cannot be allowed. Imagine the press that would occur if either of those companies or others like them were unable to process orders for even a day!

12.2 Concurrency control, reliability, security, and database administration.

12.3 No, these ideas and concepts were developed in the 1960s in the context of organizational databases. They were reapplied (relearned!) with client server in the late 1970s and 1980s.

12.4 In some applications, the work of two users is supposed to be completely isolated from each other, say patient records processing for two different patients in a hospital. In other applications, two users work need not be so isolated — someone who wants the latest stock price won't mind if the price is updated as the list is being produced — as long as they know that it may happen.

12.5 The more control that is provided, the more overhead is required to support it, and the slower response time will be.

12.6   An atomic transaction is one in which either all of the database actions are committed to the database or none of them are. Without it, there is a danger that partially processed transactions will be committed to the database.

12.7   With concurrent transactions, two or more users accessing the database using a single CPU on the database server. The CPU executes some instructions from one, then executes some from the other, switching back and forth between them. The actions may appear simultaneous to the two users. For transactions to be processed simultaneously, two or more CPUs are required. With modern server computers, such processing is possible.

12.8   The lost update problem occurs when two transactions attempt to update the same data resource simultaneously. Because each transaction copies the record into its work area, each can effect different changes, then rewrite the record. The problem is that all updates except the last one to be rewritten are lost. Example: at Treble Clef (from Chapter 1) two salespeople rent the same Bflat clarinet.

12.9   Explicit locks are set by the application program; implicit locks are set by the DBMS on behalf of the application or users.

12.10   The size of the resource that is locked. Large grained locks are easy for the DBMS to administer but result in frequent conflicts; small grained locks are more difficult and expensive to administer but result in fewer conflicts.

12.11   Exclusive lock allows no other access; shared lock allows other transactions to read but not update the data.

12.12   The two-phase locking strategy is to obtain locks throughout execution of the transaction, but release them all at once at the end of the transaction. It can prevent the concurrent update problem by holding all resources until they are ready to be committed, preventing other transactions from accessing the same data resources.

12.13   It is a special case of two-phase locking — during the life of the transaction, locks are only acquired (the growing phase). When the transaction is committed, all locks are released. The shrinking phase occurs at one point.

12.14   The boundaries should be defined by the contents of a database view.

12.15   Deadlock occurs when each of two transactions is waiting for a resource the other has locked. Both transactions are placed in the wait state, but neither one can get out of it. A DBMS can either prevent the deadly embrace from occurring (via control over locking) or it can allow it and then detect and break it (by killing one of the transactions, thus releasing its locks and enabling the other transaction to continue).

12.16 The assumption with optimistic locking is that conflict will not occur. No locks are placed until the transaction is completed. At that point, locks are obtained and records are updated only if they have not been changed since last read. With pessimistic locking, the assumption is made that conflict will occur. Records are locked as they're read. When the transaction is complete, all locks are released.

12.17 Generally, optimistic locking is preferred because users are likely to browse away from the application and forget to close it down. If pessimistic were used, records would be locked until the user timed out.

12.18 It's more flexible and adaptable. This is a declarative style of development. Declarations are always easier to change than procedures. If the developer codes the locks in place, then considerable work will need to be done to change the locking strategy. If locking strategy is just declared, then the declarations can readily be changed.

12.19 They mark transaction boundaries. BEGIN starts the transaction, COMMIT commits it, and ABORT terminates it with no permanent database changes.

12.20 The transaction isolation level of a transaction, T1, concerns the visibility of other transaction's changes to T1 activities

12.21 Exclusive use locks the entire database. No other transaction can execute any command against the database. DBA uses this level when reorganizing the database.

12.22 With repeatable read, all of the rows read by a transaction can be reread and the contents will be the same as when they were read the first time. A set of records must remain the same throughout the transaction. In a resource switching application, some resources are held as all the elements required in the switch have been allocated.

12.23 A cursor is a pointer into a recordset.

12.24 Cursor stability means that the transaction obtains a shared lock on the current row of the cursor. This means, among other things, that no other user can delete the current row of the cursor. Order processing on an ITEM.

12.25 No locks are held. The transaction is exposed to changes from any other transaction. Latest stock price quotations.

12.26 One cursor is required for each table or query that is being processed.

12.27 A transaction need only have the degree of protection that it needs. Throughput is increased.

12.28 The cursor can only move forward through the data. A single-pass report writer.

12.29 A snapshot is taken of the table or query at the time it was opened. No changes appear during the processing of the cursor.

12.30 When the cursor is opened, the keys of all rows in the table or query is saved. The transaction can process those rows; if it updates a row that has been deleted by another transaction, the DBMS will create a replacement and fill that replacement with the updated data. Additions by other users will not be visible. Unless the isolation level is dirty read, changes by other users are visible only when committed to the database.

12.31 All updates, insertions, and deletions by other users are visible. Only committed changes are visible unless the isolation level is dirty read.

12.32 The DBMS will pick one for you. Probably bad, unless the DBMS happens to pick choices that work well for your application.

12.33 Reprocessing means reapplying all transactions since the latest database save to that saved copy of the database. Because reprocessing takes as much time as original processing, reprocessing is usually infeasible.

12.34 Rollback means applying before images (before changes were made) to the current database. This takes the database backwards in time. Rollforward means loading the latest database backup then applying all after images (after changes were made) to it. This brings the database forward in time.

12.35 In the event of failure, the log record is correct — otherwise the database could be behind the log and changes that were committed might not be recovered.

12.36 Take current copy of DB, back out changes. Use when DB has not been lost — just some update activity needs to be removed.

12.37 Restore DB from prior save. Apply after images. Use when database has been lost.

12.38 Checkpoints are snapshots of updated parts of a database. They can be taken automatically by the DBMS. In the event of recovery, checkpoints provide a point of synchronization between the log and the database, so they can be used to perform recovery. This is faster than recovering the entire database from a backup and then applying all after images since the backup was taken.

12.39 See Figure 12-13.

12.40 See the discussion of Figure 12-14 and 12-15.

12.41 The DBA addresses management functions for coordinating the design, development, use, protection, and change of the structure of the database. The database would be in danger of being lost or corrupted with bad data.

12.42 See Figure 12-16.

12.43 Configuration control is a process by which changes to the structure of the database are coordinated and controlled. A database can be shared. Developers cannot make changes to DB for one user that may create problems for other users. Must take a community-wide view. Let need for changes be known, let people discuss impact of changes on them, etc.

12.44 See Figure 12-17.

12.45 A data proponent is a key database user who works with the DBA to establish processing rights and responsibilities for particular data items.

12.46 See Figure 12-18.

12.47 A collection of metadata about databases, database applications, Web pages, users, and other application components. A passive repository has to be maintained manually; an active repository is automatically updated as database or application elements are changed.

12.48 A data repository is a key resource for maintaining the database and its applications and for planning changes and extensions to them. Without one maintenance is likely to be costly, slow, and very risky.

Answers to Group II Questions

12.49 and 12.50 Answer depends on what the students find.

12.51 It's relatively simple and straightforward to set up and for the DBMS to enforce. It provides good vertical security, but poor horizontal security. Users might give one another their passwords or otherwise make their passwords public. The chief protection is education of the users and programs that ensure users change their passwords on a regular basis.

12.52 Answer depends on what the students find.

Answers to Project

1. Creating new instances of the Customer View necessitates creating new rows in Customer and possibly transaction, and adding new rows to the intersection table. No data will need to be modified or deleted. Because ARTIST appears twice in the view, I would choose repeatable read to ensure that an ARTIST row does not disappear in the middle of the transaction.

Cursor	Recommended Cursor Type
CUSTOMER	KeySet
TRANSACTION	Forward Only
WORK	Forward Only
CUSTOMER_ARTIST_INT	Forward Only

2. If only modifying data values, I would choose cursor stability isolation level. I just need to know that the row I'm on won't disappear underneath me.

Cursor	Recommended Cursor Type
CUSTOMER	KeySet
TRANSACTION	Forward Only
WORK	Forward Only
CUSTOMER_ARTIST_INT	Forward Only

3. Answer is the same as number 1 above, for the same reasons.

4. To ensure that the application doesn't delete a customer just as he or she is buying art, I would choose repeatable read. Note in the following that we need access to TRANSACTION to find out if a CUSTOMER has purchased art in the past.

112

Cursor	Recommended Cursor Type
CUSTOMER	Forward Only
TRANSACTION	Keyset
CUSTOMER_ARTIST_INT	Keyset

Chapter 13

Accessing the Database Server: ODBC, OLE DB, and ADO

Objectives

- Understand the nature and characteristics of the data environment that surrounds Internet technology database applications

- Learn the purpose, features, and facilities of ODBC

- Understand the nature and goals of OLE DB

- Learn the characteristics and object model of ADO

- Learn how to access databases via ADO using ASP pages

Answers to Group I Questions

13.1   Internet technology applications need to publish database applications that involve dozens of different data types; this includes many different types of DBMS data plus non-database data.

13.2   ODBC is an older standard for processing relational databases or flat files (including spreadsheets). OLE DB is a new standard, based on OLE, for accessing data of any type. ADO is an object cover over OLE DB that can be used by non-object oriented programmers and in scripting languages such as VBScript and JScript.

13.3   That's a tough one — I agree or I wouldn't have written it that way, but that's not to say that I don't have misgivings about it. The rich get richer and I guess that's just a fact of life. Still, it's a well-managed company with strong technology.

13.4   Driver manager, DBMS drivers, and data source.

13.5   The driver manager loads the correct driver for a given call. It is part of Windows.

13.6 A DBMS driver is a program that translates ODBC and possibly SQL calls into commands for a particular DBMS. It is supplied by the DBMS vendor or by an independent software company.

13.7 A single-tier driver processes both ODBC calls and SQL statements. Used with file-server oriented DBMS products

13.8 A multiple-tier driver processes ODBC calls but passes SQL statements to the server DBMS for processing.

13.9 No, nothing.

13.10 Conformance levels are important because they allow products having different levels of capability to participate in the ODBC standard. The standard need not conform to the lowest level, nor need it address only the capabilities of the highest level products.

13.11 See Figure 13-7.

13.12 See Figure 13-8.

13.13 User pertains to a single user on a single machine. File holds the data source data in a file that can be shared among users. System pertains to a particular computer.

13.14 System on the Web server.

13.15 Pick the DBMS driver and a particular database.

13.16 It is the foundation of Microsoft's data access capability. Anyone who wants to consume or provide data via Windows needs to know about OLE DB and use it in their products and programs.

13.17 Vendors can implement only a portion of their product's capabilities to provide an OLE DB interface. It's a smaller bite to take to participate.

13.18 An abstraction is a generalization. When we abstract something, we lose detail, but we gain the ability to work with a broader range of types. A recordset is an abstraction of a relation.

13.19 A rowset is an abstraction of a recordset.

13.20 The properties of an object represent the object's characteristics. The methods of an object represent its behaviors.

13.21 An object class is the structure of an object. An object is a particular instance of the object.

13.22 Data consumers obtain data or services from OLE DB. Data providers deliver data or services to consumers via OLE DB.

13.23 An interface is a packaging of objects that exposes certain properties and methods.

13.24 The implementation is how objects support the interface. Interfaces never change, but implementations are free to do so; no one will know.

13.25 Because users of the object depend on the interface remaining the same. If an interface changed, users of the object would have to change their code as well.

13.26 See Figure 13-10.

13.27 A provision in OLE DB for allowing transactions to process data on multiple data sources that may reside on multiple computers.

13.28 A tabular data provider presents data in rowsets; a service provider is a transformer of data.

13.29 In OLE DB, they are equivalent.

13.30 Basically any: JScript, VBScript, VB, Java, C++, etc.

13.31 See Figure 13-14.

13.32 The connection object establishes a connection with an ODBC data source or with an OLE DB data source. It is the basis of the other objects in ADO.

13.33

```
Dim objConn
Set objConn = Server.CreateObject("ADODB.connection")
objConn.IsolationLevel = 4096 ' means repeatable read
objConn.open "ViewRidgeDSN"
```

13.34 To create an object that represents the results of a SQL statement.

13.35

```
Dim objRecordSet, varSql
Const adoCursorType = 3 ' static cursor
```

```
Const adoLockType = 3 ' optimistic locking

varSql = "SELECT * FROM [ARTIST]"
Set objRecordSet = Server.CreateObject("ADODB.Recordset")
objRecordSet.CursorType = adoCursorType
objRecordSet.LockType = adoLockType
objRecordSet.Open varSql, objConn
```

13.36 The fields collection contains the names of the columns in a recordset. Used when the program needs to process fields by name and does not already know the fields in the recordset.

13.37
```
Dim varI, varNumCols, objField
varNumCols = objRecordSet.Fields.Count

For varI = 0 to varNumCols - 1
   Set objField = objRecordSet.Fields(varI)
   '  objField.Name now has the name of the field
   '  objField.Value now has the value of the field
   '  can do something with them here
Next
```

13.38 From zero to many errors that resulted during the processing of some ADO command.

13.39
```
Dim varErrorCount, varI, objError

On Error Resume Next
varErrorCount = objConn.Errors.Count
If varErrorCount > 0 Then
   For varI = 0 to varErrorCount - 1
     Set objError = objConn.Errors(varI)
     ' objError.Description contains
     ' a description of the error
   Next
End If
```

13,40 To execute queries and stored procedures that are stored with the database.

13.41

```
Dim objCommand

Set objCommand = Server.CreateObject("AdoCommand")
' assume objConn has the current connection as above
Set objCommand.ActiveConnection = objConn
objCommand.CommandText = "ArtistModify"
objCommand.CommandType = adCmdStoredProcedure
                              ' from ADOVBS.inc
cmd.Parameters(0)= "A"
cmd.Parameters(1)= "B"  ' note these are values
```

cmd.Execute

13.42 They mark script that is to be executed on the ASP server rather than on the browser.

13.43 They save the connection and session variables so that they do not have to be recreated for a particular browser session.

13.44 To set the capitalization correctly for the surrogate key columns.

13.45 Indicates whether data values are to be passed as parameters or in a Form object.

13.46 The variable varTableName is set to the value of the control text1 that was passed to it via the Form object.

13.47

```
objMyRecordSet.AddNew
objMyRecordSet("A")= AValue
objMyRecordSet("B")= BValue
objMyRecordSet.Update
```

13.48 Write something back to the browser.

Answers to Group II Questions

13.49 I believe that almost everything Microsoft does has the goal of promoting the sale of Windows. Whereas Windows is the predominant operating system on the desktop, Windows NT has not had the same success on servers. Unix and Linex are serious competitors. I believe all of these efforts are made to increase the marketshare of Windows NT (and 2000) on servers.

13.50 Here is a summary of cursor types for the three pages:

Page	Isolation Level	Cursor Type	Lock Type
AddArtist.asp	Cursor Stability	Dynamic	Optimistic
Artist.asp	Cursor Stability	Static	Optimistic
Customer.asp	Cursor Stability	Static	Optimistic

Concurrent users of AddArtist will be able to view each other's work when that work is committed to the database. Artist and Customer users will see data that is current when their recordset is opened, but they will not see changes that occur while they process that recordset. Since that is likely to be a short period of time, this is not too much of a problem. I think these are set correctly.

13.51 The View Ridge database is available on www.prenhall.com/kroenke/. The asp pages that are generated will be very similar to those shown in this chapter. The point of this exercise is for the students to see Access's use of asp.

Answers to Projects

13.52 The changes are straightforward. Suppose we want to add a new customer and set the values for Name, AreaCode, and LocalNumber. Change the asp in Figure 13-23a to accept values for AreaCode and LocalNumber instead of for Nation. This involves adding one more text box with the appropriate name. Then, change the code in Figure 13-23(b) so that varSQL is set to "SELECT * FROM CUSTOMER". After objectRecordSet.AddNew, replace the statement to set Nationality with two statements to set AreaCode and LocalNumber. The source for these asp pages can be found on www.prenhall.com/kroenke/.

A. Use same strategy as in Figure 13-21. In the page in Figure 13-21(a) input form will need to obtain and pass the name of the table, and the names of columns to be changed along with their new values. Then, to do the update, modify the page in Figure 13-23(b) to pass the name of the table as a variable into the SELECT statement and then process the Fields collection to find the field and set its value.

B. The trick here is to get the correct CustomerID value. The easy way to do this is to use two pages as in Figure 13-21. In the first page, present the CUSTOMER data along with the CustomerID value. Show a textbox and ask the user to enter the CustomerID value of the row they want to delete. Pass that value to the second asp page. Replace the SELECT statement in, say, Figure 13-23(b) with a DELETE statement.

The problem with this approach is that if the user enters the wrong CustomerID value, the wrong row will be deleted. Another safer but more difficult approach is to present the non-CustomerID values to the user in the first page, and have them click on the row they want deleted. Trap the click event and then pass the Name and other data to the second page. On that page, look up that data to find the correct surrogate key value. Use that value to delete the row. This is similar to the approach shown in Chapter 10 for finding a surrogate key value after an insert.

Chapter 14

Sharing Enterprise Data

Objectives

- Learn the different system architectures that can be used to support multi-user database processing and the advantages and disadvantages of each
- Understand the benefits and problems of downloading data
- Learn the purpose, characteristics, and basic terminology of OnLine Analytical Processing (OLAP)
- Learn the purpose, nature, and concepts of data warehousing and data marts
- Understand that organizational data is an asset that needs not only to be protected, but also to be effectively used
- Learn the scope, role, and basic functions of data administration

Teaching Suggestions

1. The chief difference between data and database administration is scope. Data administration is organization-wide; database administration is database wide.

2. Ask the students to think about ways in which data can be made more useful to decision makers. How can data be made more relevant? Think about a continuum of ways that data can be brought closer — downloading, data warehouses, etc.

3. If every department wants to download data, the management problems become immense. Data warehousing is an attempt to centralize and specialize the skills and facilities for bringing data closer to end users.

4. Data warehousing is a new idea. It may turn out to be one of those concepts that sound great in theory, but never quite deliver on their promise. The Internet may turn out to be a different and more effective way for people to bring data closer to the users.

Answers to Group I Questions

14.1 Teleprocessing, client-server, file-processing, distributed, and Internet-technology (three-tier).

14.2 See Figure 14-1. All programs reside on the centralized computer: the application programs, the communications control programs (OS communications), the DBMS and the operating system.

14.3 Limited processing power in dumb terminals.

14.4 See Figure 14-2. Several client computers; one server computer, usually all are microcomputers. Application programs and OS_{net} client computers, OS_{net}, OS_{dm}, DBMS on server computer.

14.5 Usually, all microcomputers. Can use mainframe as server, however.

14.6 There can be many servers in a client-server system. Some of them may be non-database servers. If there is more than one database server, then the servers must process different databases.

14.7 See Figure 14-3. Multiple computers, usually micros. One file server computer and multiple user computers. OS_{net}, DBMS, applications, all on user computers. OS_{net} and OS_{dm} on file server computer.

14.8 In a file-sharing system, all of the data would need to be downloaded onto the user's computer and the DBMS on that computer would process the SQL. In a client-server system, the raw data would remain on the server, the DBMS on the server would process the SQL, and only the results would be returned.

14.9 Because too much data must be sent from the server to the user computer.

14.10 Partitioned data refers to sections or pieces of the database that are distributed on different computers. Replicated refers to whether or not data is duplicated on more than one computer.

14.11 A vertical fragment refers to a table that is split into two more or tables by columns; a horizontal fragment refers to a table that is split into two or more tables by rows.

14.12 See the discussion of Figures 14-5 and 14-6.

14.13 Move the data closer to the user; allow users to perform their own query and reporting without creating a performance problem on the operational database.

14.14 The data cannot be updated nor can it be returned to the operational database.

14.15 They run a data extraction program that was written by the MIS Department.

14.16 – 14.19 See Figure 14-9.

14.20 See Figure 14-10.

14.21 An OLAP cube is a presentation having axes on which dimensions are placed. Measures of data to be displayed are organized within the dimensions on the axes. Slices are cuts through the data made by holding certain data values constant. A cube of class data having years and quarters on the vertical axis, departments and professors on the horizontal axis, and average number of students per class as a measure. Slices could be undergraduate and graduate classes.

14.22 An axis is a physical construct; a dimension is a semantic construct taken from the data.

14.23 The measure is the item to be displayed; measures are often aggregates of data.

14.24 One or more data values that are held constant in an OLAP presentation.

14.25 A member is a value of a dimension that is displayed on an axis. Members of Time are 1999, 2000, 2001, 2002; members of Location are USA, Canada, Mexico, Brazil, Chile, and Argentina.

14.26 Levels are shown for the time and the geographic dimensions. Time levels are year, quarter, month; geographic levels are state, city.

14.27 The term is used to refer to the construct having certain dimensions, levels, and measures and is also used to refer to a particular materialization of a cube construct.

14.28

Mary		Lynda	
Sailing	Skiing	Sailing	Skiing

and

Sailing		Skiing	
Mary	Lynda	Mary	Lynda

14.29

```
SELECT      CROSSJOIN ({California.Children, Nevada}, {Existing
            Structure, New Structure}) ON ROWS,
            {1998.Q1.Children, 1998.Q2, 1998.Q3, 1998.Q4,
            1999.Q1.Children, 1999.Q2, 1999.Q3, 1999.Q4} ON
            COLUMNS
FROM        HousingSalesCube
WHERE       (SalesPrice, HousingType = 'SingleFamily')
```

14.30 Relational OLAP, Multi-dimensional OLAP, Hybrid OLAP. Using a relational DBMS to support OLAP; using a purpose-built engine to support OLAP, using both.

14.31 To provide OLAP processing on Web servers and personal computers.

14.32 An abstraction of a cube called a *datset* has been created on top of the rowset abstraction. Methods and properties have been defined for datasets.

14.33 ADO MD is ADO for multi-dimensional (or OLAP) processing. Dataset methods and properties have been defined and exposed through ADO MD.

14.34 A store of enterprise data that is designed to facilitate management decision making.

14.35 Processing downloaded data must be done on a department by department basis. A data warehouse is a centralized resource for solving the problem using specialized programs, resources, and personnel.

14.36 See Figure 14-19

14.37 When the reporting requirements change, the contents, sorting, or grouping of the report changes. This differs from printing the same report over different data.

14.38 In a law firm, aggregate client billings into a client total or aggregate subject matter billings into a subject matter total.

14.39 In a construction company, drill down project data into building construction data, into floor construction data, into room construction data.

14.40 Timing inconsistencies and domain inconsistencies. Timing: In a software development project, equipment costs are by week; personnel costs are by payment period. The two may differ in ways that become important when they are combined. Domain: Two sets of data may have different department name domains — one set is before a company reorganization and another is after a company re-organization.

14.41 Tools that have different paradigms will have different user interfaces that may be very difficult to reconcile. Those that are licensed by different vendors may have interfaces that do not work well together or in which it is difficult to get customer support.

14.42 Those that cannot be purchased outside — particularly those for managing the warehouse meta-data and data from different DBMS products and from different data sources.

14.43 Information systems are structured and respond best to requests that follow a pattern.

14.44 A data mart is a data warehouse for a restricted domain.

14.45 Restricted to: particular data inputs, particular business functions, particular business units.

14.46 Data is not only used for operational purposes, but it can be used for management decision making as well. Data characteristics the organization; information is knowledge produced from data about those characteristics. Such information becomes more valuable all of the time.

14.47 Sales trend analysis, employee effectiveness assessment, simulation of changes in organization and products.

14.48 Not only protect the data resource, but also invest it for maximum return to the company.

14.49 Without it, data anarchy rules. What data exists, what format does it have, how is it to be protected, how should it be used, etc., are questions that go unanswered without data administration.

14.50 See Figure 14-25.

14.51 See Figure 14-26.

14.52 See Figure 14-26.

14.53 The department or individual that manages the official definition and format for a data item.

14.54 None. Data owner just sounds too possessive.

14.55 See Figure 14-26.

14.56 See text discussion on pages 405-406.

14.57 See text discussion on page 406.

Chapter 15

Relational Implementation with DB2

Objectives

- Explain the database constructs employed by Database 2 (DB2)
- Illustrate the use of DB2 data definition language to create tables, views, and indexes
- Illustrate the use of DB2 to modify and delete various database constructs
- Illustrate the use of SQL as implemented in DB2 to manipulate database data
- Explain how application programs can access DB2
- Overview the ways DB2 handles the issues of concurrent processing, backup and recovery, and security

Teaching Suggestions

1. This chapter is a long one. Consider treating it in two sessions, rather than one. The first session could address everything through DB2 Data Definition Language. The second session could address DB2 Data Manipulation Language: SQL through the end of the chapter.

2. Much of this chapter is devoted to a case study. If time is short, have students skim this material. But if time permits, think the case study helps to bring many concepts together.

3. Even if your students don't (or won't) use DB2, this is a good foundation chapter on relational implementation. It shows many of the issues regarding workgoup and organizational system implementation that are missed if the students are only exposed to microcomputer DBMS products.

4. The major purpose of the COBOL coding example is to show how the "impedance-mismatch" between the relation-oriented nature of SQL and the row-oriented nature of COBOL (or other procedural languages) is resolved. This strategy is used for the interface between SQL and all other programming languages.

Answers to Group I Questions

15.1 Because that was the data that the product marketing personnel needed and KDK did not want to tie up their transaction-processing mainframe with the processing of queries and reports from product managers.

15.2 The INVOICE as needed in the Information Center is really just a view of the actual invoice: it contains only those fields germane to the PMs' processing requirements.

15.3 The PRODUCT-AD relation is an intersection relation that stores the many-to-many relationship between products and ads.

15.4 DB2 can be accessed interactively (via SQL statements interpreted by DB2I) and in batch mode (via SQL statements embedded in application programs written in COBOL, PL/I, FORTRAN, or assembler language).

15.5 A table is a physical database construct containing stored data. A view is a virtual database construct whose definition is stored in the database. When referenced, a view is constructed by the DBMS from stored data. The table from which a view is constructed is called the base table.

15.6 A user authorized to access a view can get at only the data defined as part of the view, and not at other data in the base table. Thus a view provides security at the field value level.

15.7 Users and application programmers reference only tables and views.

15.8 Tables, views, and indexes refer to collections of database data, but not their actual physical storage properties. Storage groups, table spaces, and index spaces refer to physical storage devices or locations. A data base is the collection of all the above, and more.

15.9
```
CREATE    TABLE CUST
          (NAME      CHAR(20)    NOT NULL,
          ADDR       CHAR(50),
          ACCT-NO    DECIMAL(5) NOT NULL)

CREATE    UNIQUE INDEX CSTNUMS
          ON CUST (ACCT-NO)

CREATE    VIEW CNAMES
    AS    SELECT UNIQUE NAME
          FROM CUST
```

15.10
```
ALTER TABLE CUST
ADD AGE DECIMAL(2)
```

15.11
```
INSERT    INTO CUST
          VALUES    ('Mike Thompson', 'Madison', 456, 45),
                    ('Paul Hand', 'New Haven', 722, 20),
                    ('Karen Munroe', 'Gales Ferry', 076, 27)
```

15.12	DROP	TABLE CUST
	DROP	INDEX CSTNUMS
	DROP	VIEW CNAMES

15.13 The DB2 precompiler translates embedded SQL statements into host language definitions (in DATA DIVISION) or subroutine calls (in PROCEDURE DIVISION).

15.14 SQL instructions are flagged with the keywords EXEC SQL.

15.15 A cursor is used when an application program retrieves multiple rows from the database. A cursor is a placemarker that "points" to the next row to be processed.

15.16 When a shared lock is applied, multiple programs can read the same data, but not update it. When an exclusive lock is applied only one application can access the locked data.

15.17 If data were modified without an exclusive lock in effect, then two or more programs could copy data into their workareas, update it simultaneously, then rewrite it onto the database. Only the last update would be saved (all others would be overlaid) and the database data would be incorrect.

15.18 If tablespace-level locks are applied, then the entire tablespace containing the data being processed is locked, including all other data stored there. This approach requires less administrative overhead, but can cause delays with other applications needing access to data in the tablespace. Page-level locks lock only the page on which the data being processed resides. This approach requires more administrative overhead, but it does not cause the problems of delay mentioned above because less data is being locked.

15.19 The COMMIT statement makes database changes permanent; the ROLLBACK statement removes database changes not yet committed.

15.20 DB2 solves deadlock by terminating the application with the fewest log records since the most recent commitment.

15.21 DB2 recovers from a system crash by applying all before images created since the most recent checkpoint, then applying all after images of committed transactions. Uncommitted transactions need to be restarted.

To recover a DB2 database after database damage the organization uses DB2 utilities that combine data from logs and backup copies of pages.

15.22 The GRANT statement is used to bestow explicit permissions to users. The GRANT statement includes the option to bestow the same grant authority to another user.

15.23 The REVOKE statement takes away authority that had been previously granted. The cascade effect refers to the fact that if the user whose authority is revoked had granted the same authority to another user, that user's (and any other generation's) authority is also revoked.

Chapter 16

Transaction Processing and Data Language/I

Objectives

- Understand the historical importance of the hierachrical and network data models
- Learn the basic data structures of DL/I and basic DL/I data manipulation constructs
- Learn the basic data structures of the CODASYL DBTG model DL/I and basic DBTG data manipulation constructs

Teaching Suggestions

1. The hierarchical and network data models have become rare and students are unlikely to work with them except in maintenance or conversion projects. If your students do not accept jobs with companies that are still using DBMS from either of these categories, I would skip this chapter.

2. The goal here is to explain the basic constructs of each model so that the students know the fundamental terminology — to the level that they could talk with collegues and co-workers about these models.

Answers to Group I Questions

16.1 Relational — relationships carried in data; hierarchical, all data structures must be converted to hierarchies before they can be represented; network, all data structures must be converted to simple networks before they can be represented.

16.2 A field is the smallest logical unit of data; a segment is a collection of related fields — it is a node on the tree; a data base record is a collection of related segments; a data base is a collection of data base records.

16.3 A segment is a node on a tree.

16.4 DL/I data base records are defined via assembler language macros because DL/I does not include a DDL.

16.5 DL/I can process only hierarchies, not simple or complex networks.

16.6 DL/I eliminates data duplication by storing data only once, then pointing to it within subsequent references.

16.7 A physical data base record refers to the physical storage of data base data; a logical data base record is an application's view of data base data. An LDBR is constructed from one or several PDBRs by DL/I.

16.8 See discussion pages 455-458.

16.9 See discussion page 458.

16.10 See discussion page 458, 459.

16.11 A user executes a program. The execution of a program on behalf of a user is called a run-unit. The application program views the database via a subschema. This subschema contains a logical view of the database for that application. The schema may have records, fields, and relationships not available to the subschema. The data structure description describes the physical aspects of the database. The database is stored according to the DSD description. The DBMS uses the schema, subschema, and DSD to determine what can be obtained by the run-unit and how to obtain the data from the database.

16.12 A data-item is a field. Data-items arise from domains, but domains are not recognized in the CODASYL model.

16.13 A record is a collection of data-items; it can contain vectors, or repeating groups.

16.14 A set is a 1:N relationship between records. The owner of the set is the parent of the relationship. Set members are the children. A set occurrence is one instance of a particular owner record and its members.

16.15 Set with INVOICE as owner and LINE-ITEM as member.

INVOICE 123   Owner Record

Line-item 1	Shovel	$22.99	Member Records
Line-item 2	Fertilizer	$13.45	
Line-item 3	Roses	$75.18	

	INVOICE 456		Owner Record
Line-item 1	Bulbs	$11.55	Member Records
Line-item 2	Rake	$22.9	
Line-item 3	Shovel	$22.99	

16.16

DISTRICT record owns SET1 of SCHOOL member records.
SCHOOL record owns SET2 of PUPIL member records.
SCHOOL record owns SET3 of TEACHER member records.
TEACHER record owns SET4 of PAST-ASSIGN member records.

16.17

FATHER record owns SET1 of CHILDREN member records.
TEACHER record owns SET2 of CHILDREN member records.

16.18

CHILDREN record owns SET1 of CHILD-HOBBY member records.
HOBBY record owns SET2 of CHILD-HOBBY member records.

16.19

a. MOVE 'ABC CONSTRUCTION' TO NAME IN CUSTOMER
   FIND ANY CUSTOMER USING NAME
   GET CUSTOMER

b. MOVE 12345 TO NUMBER IN ORDER
   FIND ANY ORDER USING NUMBER
   GET ORDER

c. MOVE 'ABC CONSTRUCTION' TO CUST-NAME IN ORDER
   FIND ANY ORDER USING CUST-NAME
   DOWHILE DB-STATUS = 0
   GET ORDER

```
                    FIND DUPLICATE ORDER USING CUST-NAME
            END-DO


16.20   MOVE 'PARKS' TO SALESPERSON-NAME IN ORDER
        FIND FOR UPDATE ANY ORDER USING SALESPERSON-NAME
        DOWHILE DB-STATUS = 0
                ERASE ORDER
                FIND FOR UPDATE DUPLICATE ORDER USING
                SALESPERSON-NAME
        END-DO


16.21   MOVE 'ABC CONSTRUCTION' TO NAME IN CUSTOMER
        FIND FOR UPDATE ANY CUSTOMER USING NAME
        IF DB-STATUS = 0
                THEN MOVE 'J' TO INDUSTRY-TYPE
                    MODIFY INDUSTRY-TYPE
                ELSE DO ERROR-PROCESSING
        END-IF


16.22   MOVE 'CURTIS' TO NAME IN SALESPERSON
        MOVE 39 TO AGE IN SALESPERSON
        MOVE 65000 TO SALARY IN SALESPERSON
        STORE SALESPERSON
        IF DB-STATUS NOT = 0
                THEN DO ERROR-PROCESSING
        END-IF
```

Chapter 17

Object-Oriented Database Processing

Objectives

- Describe the characteristics of object oriented programming and the necessity for object databases and ODBMS
- Understand the advantages and disadvantages of object persistence via traditional file processing, relational database processing, and ODBMS processing
- Learn the prominent characteristics of SQL3 and understand how objects are bound to relations
- Learn the prominent characteristics of the ODMB proposed standard

Teaching Suggestions

1. The approach that you take with this chapter depends how much object oriented programming your students know. If they have done OOP, then you can start immediately with the problems of object persistence. If not, you'll have to teach object programming ideas for the students to be able to understand the need for object persistence.

2. The SQL committee had a problem in that they needed to make the SQL3 standard upward compatible with SQL-92. This forced the committee to make objects (or ADTs) an extension of relations. SQL3 seems to me to effectively meet that requirement. Whether or not SQL3 becomes important depends, of course, on whether any vendors pay attention to it. See suggestion 4, below.

3. The ODMG Committee was able to start with a clean slate. They did not need to consider migration from the relational model, so their proposal is pure object thinking. Since today's ODBMS products are much closer to the ODMG model than to SQL3, it is likely that it will be a more important standard.

4. I wonder how important standards are today. Microsoft is so powerful and influential that it seems that they force standards by the products and architectures they develop or endorse. There may be niches in which ODMG or SQL3 are important, but until Microsoft decides to develop a product based on one of them, it's all just talk. You might discuss this situation with your students.

Answers to Group I Questions

17.1 Objects are data structures that have both data attributes and procedures (methods). Object programming differs in design in that, rather than start with programming logic, designers start first with objects, determine their interface, and then their implementation. Cohesion should be much better in OOP.

17.2 They are more common, far more data is in relational format, practitioners are more familiar and comfortable with relational databases.

17.3 An OOP object is an encapsulated structure having both attributes and methods.

17.4 Encapsulated means that an object is complete in itself; programs external to the object need know nothing about the object's internal structure to interface with it. An attribute is a data element of an object; a method is a program associated with an object.

17.5 The external appearance of an object is its interface — it consists of public attributes and public methods. An implementation is the encapsulated internals of the object. An object would have just one interface but could, conceivably, have many implementations.

17.6 Objects can be arranged in a supertype, subtype hierarchy. An object inherits the attributes and methods of its supertypes.

17.7 Polymorphism occurs when the same name is used to refer to different methods in an object hierarchy. The compiler invokes the correct method depending on the type of object that is being called.

17.8 An object class is the logical structure of an object; a class library is a group of object classes; an object instance is a particular object — including particular data elements and the methods of the class.

17.9 Object constructors obtain memory and create the structures necessary to instantiate a new object. Object destructors unbind object and free memory.

17.10 A transient object exists only in transient memory and lasts only as long as a program is in execution. A persistent object is stored on disk and survives the termination of a program.

17.11 The first expression invokes the Find member of CUSTOMER and the second refers to the ZipCode data attribute of CUSTOMER.

17.12 It can be used to determine if a pointer to an object is null.

17.13 It can be used to qualify references to methods or attributes or to refer to the current object instance that is running.

17.14 A callback is a means by which an object registers itself with another object; callbacks are used for many purposes — one of which is to allow an object to free its reference to another object before the second object destroys itself.

17.15 It refers to the process of converting an in-memory address to a permanent identifier (and sometimes to the reverse process as well).

17.16 See Figure 17-8, column three.

17.17 See Figure 17-8, column two.

17.18 Designed for OOP so easy to use, easy to invoke, swizzling is automatic, performance is tuned for OOP. However, not much data is in this format, few know how to use ODBMS products, lack of query and reporting facilities, performance is unknown for large-scale database transaction processing.

17.19 See discussion, page 434, 435.

17.20 See discussion, page 435, 436.

17.21 An extension to the SQL-92 standard that incorporates object persistence; it is upwardly compatible with the SQL-92 standard.

17.22 A user-defined structure that has methods, data items, and persistent identifiers; equivalent to an object.

17.23 An Object ADT is an identifiable, independent data structure that can be referred to by its identifier. A value ADT has no identifier and can only be referred to via a table or a function — depending on how it was created.

17.24 An OID is a pointer to an object ADT. An OID can be used to provide a reference to an object instance.

17.25 Returns DeptName by accessing the row of DEPT, returns Manager.Phone by following the OID that is stored to refer to Manager. The instance of Admin that has been stored as part of the Dept row will be used to return Admin.Phone.

17.26 The name of the employee who is the manager of each department will be set to John Jacob Astor. The manager of every department will have this name, although the instances of the managers of the department will be unchanged.

17.27 See second UPDATE example on page 440.

17.28 A row identifier is what we have called a surrogate key in this text. It is a unqiue identifier for a row of a table.

17.29 A set is a table with no duplicate rows; a multiset is a table with duplicate rows; a list is a table that has an order defined by one or more columns.

17.30 A subtable is a subset of another table. A supertable is a table that has at least one subtable. A table is a relation that is one of the three types SET, MULTISET, LIST.

17.31 The ODMG-93 is a definition of interfaces for object data management products.

17.32 See Figure 17-15.

17.33 A class is a logical group of objects; it is an interface. A type is an implementation of a class in a particular language.

17.34 A property can be either a data attribute or a relationship; an attribute is a data value.

17.35 The set of all instances of an object (class or type).

17.36 Properties are either a data attribute or a relationship.

17.37 Data values or relationships to other objects.

17.38 Data values, only.

17.39 Connections between objects.

17.40 If method persistence is not supported, two objects that were created or changed by different versions of a method would appear the same, but would not necessarily be logically the same.

17.41 Like ODMG, the properties of a semantic object are either data value or relationships. They can be either singular or plural. In SOM, relationships are always binary; in ODMG, they need not necessarily be binary. SOM has little provision for methods.

Appendix A

Data Structures for Database Processing

Answers to Selected Group I Questions

A.1　A flat file is a file in which the records have no repeating groups. Examples will vary with students, but one might be an Employee file containing no repeating groups; a non-flat file might be an Employee file containing repeating fields for employee deductions.

Flat file:

Emp#	Name	Title
107	Ahalt	Instructor
109	Wampler	Instructor
215	Meyers	Professor
350	Ko	Professor

Non-flat file:

Emp#	Name	Deductions
107	Ahalt	Insurance 35 Retirement 30 Savings 45
109	Wampler	Insurance 40 Savings 50
215	Meyers	
350	Ko	Savings 50

A.2　Two files are required, one sorted on Emp#, the other on Name:

Emp#	Name	Title
107	Ahalt	Instructor
109	Wampler	Instructor
215	Meyers	Professor
350	Ko	Professor

Emp#	Name	Title
107	Ahalt	Instructor
350	Ko	Professor
215	Meyers	Professor
109	Wampler	Instructor

A.3   Store the file in Emp# order, and use linked list to keep the file in order by name:

Emp#	Name	Title	Link
107	Ahalt	Instructor	4
109	Wampler	Instructor	Null
215	Meyers	Professor	2
350	Ko	Professor	3

Start of alphabetic list = 1

A.4   The data would be stored as in Question A.3, but there would be no link field. This would be the inverted list:

Ahalt	1
Ko	4
Meyers	3
Wampler	2

A.5   A tree is a set of records and one-to-many relationships in which a child can have at most one parent. An example is a checking account (parent) that has many deposits (children) and checks (children).

```
              ACCOUNT
    1:N                   1:N
  DEPOSIT               CHECK
```

A.6

ACCOUNT 123

DEP 188   DEP 243   CHK 455   CHK456   CHK457

140

A.9 A simple network is a set of records and relationships in which all relationships are one-to-many, but a child can have more than one parent if they are different record types. An example is the relationships among salesperson (parent), customer (parent), and invoice (child).

| SALESPERSON | | CUSTOMER |

| INVOICE |

A.16 A primary key is normally used to determine where a record is stored. The primary key is the key by which the record is normally accessed. Primary keys are unique. Secondary keys are other fields whose values may be used to access the record. Secondary keys can be unique or non-unique. If the secondary key is non-unique it can be used to access groups of records that contain the same value for the key.

A.17 With a unique key only one record can have a specific key value; each key value must be unique within the file. Non-unique keys do not have to have different values. Multiple records can have the same value for a non-unique key.

A.18

Note: this Student file will be used for Questions A.18, A.19, and A.20.

RRN	Number	Name	Major
1	1234	Joanie Wampler	Acct
2	2311	Jon Miley	Comp
3	3451	Jersey Eng	Acct
4	3561	Sandy Merrow	Comp
5	4566	Bob Adams	Acct

The primary key is Number. The unique secondary key is Name. The non-unique secondary key is Major. Unique secondary key represented via inverted list:

Name	RRN
Bob Adams	5
Jersey Eng	3
Sandy Merrow	4
Jon Miley	2
Joanie Wampler	1

A.19

RRN	Number	Name	Major	Major Link
1	1234	Joanie Wampler	Acct	3
2	2311	Jon Miley	Comp	4
3	3451	Jersey Eng	Acct	5
4	3561	Sandy Merrow	Comp	Null
5	4566	Bob Adams	Acct	Null

Head Acct = 1
Head Comp = 2

A.20

Major	Addr	Addr	Addr	Addr
Acct	1	3	5	Null
Comp	2	4	Null	Null

142

Appendix B

Using SQL Server

SQL Server is an enterprise class DBMS. We have just touched the surface of it in this Appendix. If you have time in your course, you might want to add additional material. However, this course is already so packed with material that it is difficult to imagine adding much more. Still, if you have advanced students, or if you want to continue with special projects after this course, here are some possible topic areas:

- SQL Server security facilities

- Backup and recovery and use of the log file

- Creating stored procedures for enforcing business rules

- Creating stored procedures for common activity (adding an artist interest to a customer in the View Ridge case, for example)

- Accessing SQL Server using ADO from ASP pages

- Importing / Exporting data using SQL Server

Answers to Exercises

B.1 These exercises are straightforward. If the students have trouble getting started, make sure that SQL Server is running. Use the Service Manager program to start it as described in the Appendix. The rest should be obvious. Here's the second query involving the join of authors and titles with the predicate on State of California:

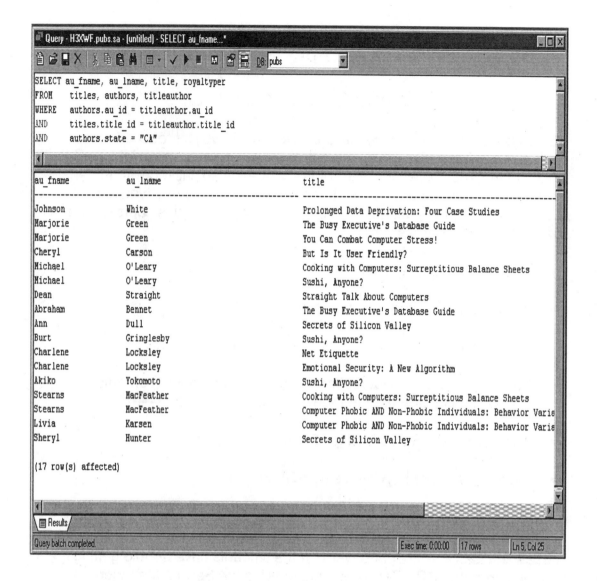

B.2 This is easier to do with Access 2000 because you can create a project based on SQL Server and both the tables will be automatically available. Otherwise, with Access 97, attach the two tables as described in this appendix.

B.3 Here are the three tables. For illustration purposes, I set the seed of ID_ in CUSTOMER to be 100 so that surrogate key values would be different between CUSTOMER and ARTIST in the intersection tables. The tables were created by DBApp so it appended the model name to the (here Model 3):

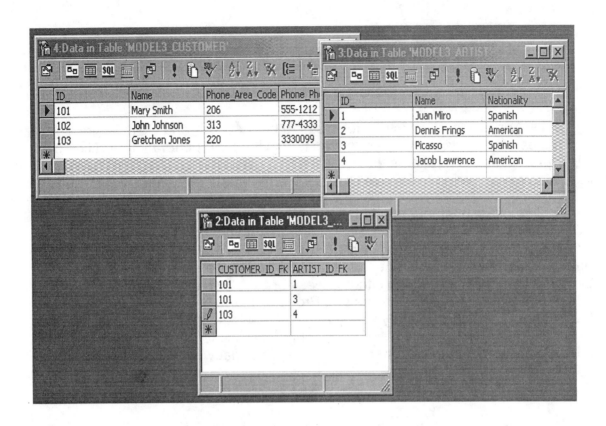

Appendix C

Working with DBApp

DBApp is very easy to use for creating both Access and SQL Server databases. Even if you do not have time to use the ASP generation facilities of DBApp, be sure to have the students use it to create tables. They will find it much faster than using the native DBMS table generation facilities.

One of the best features of DBApp is its database migration capability. You can create a database, fill it with data, and then change the model. Both the schema and the underlying data will be changed. For example, you can reverse engineer Northwind (or even better, just take the Suppliers and Products tables). Create a copy database using either Access or SQL Server. DBApp will create a 1:N relationship between Suppliers and Products in the new database because that's what it will find in the key structure. You can then change the relationship to N:M and DBApp will modify the underlying database to create the intersection table and fill it with data — correctly using the data that was already in the tables.

Answers to Exercises

C.1 This model is located on www.prenhall.com/kroenke/ under the name Fig413.apm. Copy it down and save as under a new name. Say No to use existing databases if you are asked so that you can create new databases.

C.2 Make up your own tables or use the example in the answers to questions 4.15 to 4.19.

C.3 It is interesting to generate this model and see how many tables are created. This will illustrate the power of working with a tool from a higher-level model than working at the table level.

C.4 Even if you do not have time to assign the exercise to the students, it's well worth demo-ing it in the lab. The hardest part is setting IIS on NT. As of spring, 1999, make sure you have NT Server with Service Pack 4 installed. Using the IIS Manager to mark the root directory (or a new one you create) as Execute and enable ASP processing. If you try to run the application and the JScript shows up in the browser, that means that IIS does not think the directory is marked for executing script. Make sure when you use the DBApp publishing wizard that you place your pages in a directory subordinate to the InetPub or whatever other directory you have created.

A good demonstration is to reverse the Supplier and Products tables of Northwind as described above and then do query by form. Query on products having more than UnitsInStock with a supplier name of New*. DBApp will create the underlying in SQL. Then, change the max cardinality of Supplier (in Products) and regenerate the pages (if you didn't use the Exit button when you exited the browser, IIS will have a lock on the pages for 20 min (the default). So, when you regenerate, put the pages in a different directory.

C.5   Here is the model during the reverse engineering process:

Here is the revision to the model:

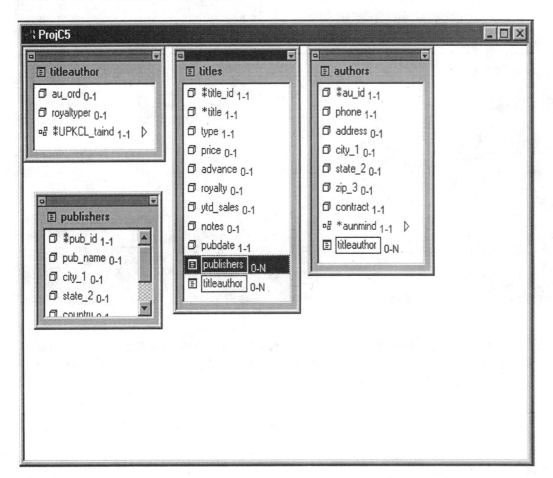

Here is the SQL Server database after DBApp has created the new intersection table between titles and publishers:

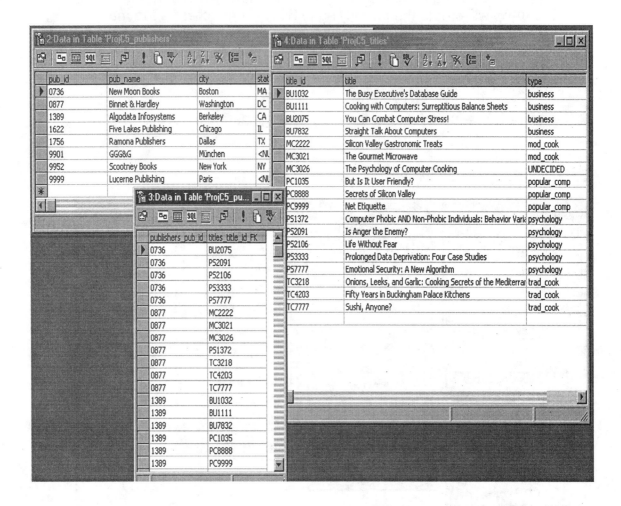

C.6   This is straightforward. You might have to show the students how to use the generated pages to create relationships. (The browser help is pretty good — have them look there as well.)

DATABASE PROCESSING

Seventh Edition

David M. Kroenke

Prentice Hall
Upper Saddle River, New Jersey 07458

CHAPTER 1 TEST QUESTIONS

TRUE-FALSE QUESTIONS

T   1.   The purpose of a database is to help people keep track of things.
Reference: Section   1.1

T   2.   End users often have a consultant develop a database and database application for them.
Reference: Section   1.1

F   3.   A DBMS extracts data from reports.
Reference: Section   1.1

T   4.   A DBMS stores data in tables.
Reference: Section   1.1

F   5.   A database can only store text.
Reference: Section   1.1

T   6.   A *personal* database typically has only one user at a time.
Reference: Section   1.1

F   7.   A *workgroup* database typically has hundreds of concurrent users.
Reference: Section   1.1

F   8.   A user can directly access the database.
Reference: Section   1.2

T   9.   Most DBMS products contain form generators and report writers.
Reference: Section   1.2

T 10.   The first business information systems were called *file-processing systems*.
Reference: Section   1.3

F 11.   Data is never duplicated in a file-processing system.
Reference: Section   1.3

T 12.   With file processing, application programs depend on the file format.
Reference: Section   1.3

F 13.   Database-processing programs access the stored data directly.
Reference: Section   1.4

F 14.   Data is never duplicated in a database-processing system.
Reference: Section   1.4

T 15.   In a database-processing environment, application programmers do not have to be concerned with the ways in which data are physically stored.
Reference: Section   1.4

T 16. In a database system, all the application data is stored in a single facility called the *database*.
Reference: Section   1.4

T 17. A database is self-describing.
Reference: Section   1.5

T 18. A character is composed of bits.
Reference: Section   1.5

F 19. A field is composed of records.
Reference: Section   1.5

T 20. Transactions are representations of events.
Reference: Section   1.5

F 21. Early database systems let end users easily access the data themselves.
Reference: Section   1.6

T 22. In the *relational database model* data are stored as tables, with rows and columns.
Reference: Section   1.6

F 23. Relational DBMSs require less computer resources than earlier systems.
Reference: Section   1.6

T 24. Microcomputer DBMSs generally have friendlier user interfaces than mainframe systems.
Reference: Section   1.6

T 25. Processing is shared among more than one CPUs in a *client-server architecture*.
Reference: Section   1.6

F 26. Database applications cannot be delivered across networks such as the Internet.
Reference: Section   1.6

T 27. In a *distributed database* the organization's data are stored in more than one computer.
Reference: Section   1.6

F 28. Performance in a distributed database environment is generally better than in a centralized one.
Reference: Section   1.6

T 29. Most *object-oriented* DBMS products are designed to store complex, non-business data.
Reference: Section   1.6

T 30. An important characteristic of Internet technology is the use of standard browsers to display forms and reports.
Reference: Section   1.6

MULTIPLE CHOICE QUESTIONS

1.   The purpose of a database is to:
      a.   eliminate paperwork
      b.   use computer resources
      c.   help people keep track of things
      d.   reduce the need for people to communicate
      e.   all of the above
      Answer: c   Reference: Section   1.1

2.   To obtain an effective database, the user:
      a.   must specify the outputs desired
      b.   must know how to design the tables, forms, and reports
      c.   often has a technical person design the tables, forms, and reports
      d.   a and b
      e.   a and c
      Answer: e   Reference: Section   1.1

3.   Multi-user databases:
      a.   allow more than one concurrent user
      b.   must keep one user's work from interfering with another's
      c.   allow each user to make changes independently
      d.   a and b
      e.   a and c
      Answer: d   Reference: Section   1.1

4.   Multimedia databases can store:
      a.   text
      b.   sound
      c.   pictures
      d.   movies
      e.   all of the above
      Answer: e   Reference: Section   1.1

5.   Organizations having less than 25 concurrent users generally utilize a _____ type of database.
      a.   personal
      b.   workgroup
      c.   organizational
      d.   multimedia
      e.   none of the above
      Answer: b   Reference: Section   1.1

6.   In a database processing system:
      a.   the database application(s) interact with the DBMS
      b.   the database application(s) access the database data
      c.   the DBMS accesses the database data
      d.   a and b
      e.   a and c
      Answer: e   Reference: Section   1.2

7.   In a file-processing system:
        a.   the user interacts with the application
        b.   the user accesses the file data
        c.   the application accesses the file data
        d.   a and b
        e.   a and c
        Answer: e   Reference: Section   1.3

8.   When data are duplicated, the most serious problem is:
        a.   storage space is wasted
        b.   data may be in different formats
        c.   the same fields may contain different values in different files
        d.   the files may be of different sizes
        Answer: c   Reference: Section   1.3

9.   In file-processing systems, the physical file formats are:
        a.   in the metadata
        b.   part of the application code
        c.   in the application metadata
        d.   in the DBMS
        e.   in the data file
        Answer: b   Reference: Section   1.3

10.   In file-processing systems, the physical file formats are dependent on:
        a.   the language or product used to generate them
        b.   the type of data being stored
        c.   the DBMS
        d.   the size of the file
        e.   the user's preference
        Answer: a   Reference: Section   1.3

11.   In a database processing system, application programmers must know how:
        a.   data are physically stored
        b.   to ask the DBMS to access data
        c.   to eliminate duplicate data
        d.   all of the above
        e.   a and b
        Answer: b   Reference: Section   1.4

12.   In a database processing system, program/data independence means that:
        a.   application programs need contain only the length and type of the fields they need from
                the database
        b.   in general, application programs need not be aware of changes to the structure of the
                database
        c.   whenever data items are added, changed, or deleted from the database, only those
                programs that use these particular data items have to be modified
        d.   all of the above
        e.   none of the above
        Answer: d   Reference: Section   1.4

13.   A database is self-describing because:
    a.   all the data is in one place
    b.   it is well documented
    c.   it contains a description of its own structure
    d.   it contains a listing of all the programs that use it
    e.   all of the above
    Answer: c   Reference: Section   1.5

14.   The standard hierarchy of data is as follows:
    a.   bytes are aggregated into characters, characters are aggregated into fields, fields are aggregated into records, and records are aggregated into files
    b.   bits are aggregated into characters, characters are aggregated into fields, fields are aggregated into records, and records are aggregated into files
    c.   bits are aggregated into characters, characters are aggregated into fields, fields are aggregated into files, and files are aggregated into records
    d.   bits are aggregated into characters, characters are aggregated into records, records are aggregated into files, and files are aggregated into databases
    e.   bits are aggregated into characters, characters are aggregated into fields, fields are aggregated into files, and files are aggregated into databases
    Answer: b   Reference: Section   1.5

15.   A database contains:
    a.   user data
    b.   metadata
    c.   indexes
    d.   application metadata
    e.   all of the above
    Answer: e   Reference: Section   1.5

16.   The description of the structure of a database is called:
    a.   user data
    b.   metadata
    c.   indexes
    d.   application metadata
    e.   none of the above
    Answer: b   Reference: Section   1.5

17.   An index is used to:
    a.   represent relationships among the data
    b.   eliminate duplicate data
    c.   improve the performance of database applications
    d.   a and b
    e.   a and c
    Answer: e   Reference: Section   1.5

18.   When the description of the forms and reports are part of a database, it is called:
a.   user data
b.   metadata
c.   indexes
d.   application metadata
e.   none of the above

Answer: d   Reference: Section   1.5

19.   A database is a model of:
a.   the actual business
b.   the users' model of the business
c.   the programmers' view of the business
d.   the managers' model of the business
e.   all of the above
Answer: b   Reference: Section   1.5

20.   Transactions:
a.   are representations of events
b.   are initiated by a human entering data
c.   alter the database
d.   usually produce displays or printouts
e.   all of the above
Answer: e   Reference: Section   1.5

21.   Disadvantages of early database technologies included:
a.   they were slow and unreliable
b.   applications had to be developed in procedural languages
c.   they could not store as much data as was needed
d.   a and b
e.   b and c
Answer: d   Reference: Section   1.6

22.   Advantages of the relational model include:
a.   data duplication is minimized
b.   most processing errors can be eliminated
c.   most users can obtain information from the database themselves
d.   all of the above
e.   a and b
Answer: e   Reference: Section   1.6

23.   Reasons for the initial resistance to the relational model included:
a.   slow response time caused by greater need for computer resources
b.   programmers had to learn a new way to think about data processing
c.   users objected to the new view of the data
d.   all of the above
e.   a and b
Answer: e   Reference: Section   1.6

24. Modern microcomputer DBMS products:
     a.   are truly relational
     b.   provide easier to use interfaces than mainframe systems
     c.   still have poor response time
     d.   a and b
     e.   b and c
     Answer: d   Reference: Section   1.6

25. In a client-server database architecture:
     a.   only the mainframe does the processing
     b.   processing is shared by independent computers
     c.   all of the computers are connected by a network
     d.   a and c
     e.   b and c
     Answer: e   Reference: Section   1.6

26. In a distributed database, coordinating and synchronizing the data can be difficult because:
     a.   data is stored in more than one computer system
     b.   there are multiple users
     c.   the users are in remote locations and must communicate over networks
     d.   a and b
     e.   b and c
     Answer: a   Reference: Section   1.6

27. Reasons for the resistance to object-oriented database systems for business information systems
     include:
     a.   object-oriented programming has not been widely accepted
     b.   most organizations are unwilling to convert their relational databases
     c.   most OODBMSs do not have appropriate features and functions
     d.   all of the above
     e.   b and c
     Answer: d   Reference: Section   1.6

28. The process of converting a table from a form that is not desirable into two or more tables in a
     more desirable form is called:
     a.   indexing
     b.   normalization
     c.   relating
     d.   file-sharing
     e.   none of the above
     Answer: b   Reference: Section   1.6

29. A database that utilizes the Internet is designed to be used by:
     a.   a few users within the organization
     b.   many users within the organization
     c.   a few users outside the organization
     d.   many users outside the organization
     e.   none of the above
     Answer: d   Reference: Section   1.6

30.   Multimedia applications are currently delivered via:
    a.   large public networks, like the Internet
    b.   large private networks (intranets)
    c.   e-mail
    d.   a and b
    e.   a and c
    Answer: d   Reference: Section   1.6

FILL IN THE BLANKS

1.   A database application uses forms   for entering data.

    Reference: Section   1.1

2.   A database application uses reports   for displaying data.

    Reference: Section   1.1

3.   A single-user database that is used by only one person at a time is called a personal database.

    Reference: Section   1.1

4.   A database that is used by more than one person at a time is called a   multi-user   database.

    Reference: Section   1.1

5.   A   workgroup database is typically used by fewer than 25 concurrent users.

    Reference: Section   1.1

6.   An   organizational   database is typically used by hundreds of concurrent users.

    Reference: Section   1.1

7.   The first business information systems stored groups of records in separate files and were called   file-processing systems   .

    Reference: Section   1.3

8.   Loss of   data integrity   is a common result of duplication of data.

    Reference: Section   1.3

9.   In a database system, the   DBMS   acts as an intermediary between the database application and the database.

    Reference: Section   1.3

10.   The self-contained structure of a database, known as the data dictionary or data directory, is also called   metadata   .

Reference: Section   1.5

11.   An   index   is used to represent relationships among the data and to improve the performance of database applications.

Reference: Section   1.5

12.   When the structure of a form or report is part of the database it is called application metadata .

Reference: Section   1.5

13.   A byte/character is composed of   bits   .

Reference: Section   1.5

14.   A field is composed of   bytes/characters   .

Reference: Section   1.5

15.   A record is composed of   fields   .

Reference: Section   1.5

16.   A file is composed of   records   .

Reference: Section   1.5

17.   A   transaction   is a representation of an event.

Reference: Section   1.5

18.   Data are separate and isolated in a file processing system, while in a database system data are   integrated   .

Reference: Section   1.5

19.   A database is a model of the   users'   model or view of the business.

Reference: Section   1.5

20.   The   relational   database model stores data as tables, with rows and columns.

Reference: Section   1.6

21.   Normalization   is a process which can change tables that are in an undesirable form into two or more tables which are in a desirable form.
Reference: Section   1.6

22.   In 1979, a company called Ashton-Tate introduced a microcomputer DBMS called dBASE II .

        Reference: Section   1.6

23.   Microcomputers are often connected together using a   local area network .

        Reference: Section   1.6

24.   Small organizations can share data among multiple users by utilizing a mode of processing
        known as file-sharing architecture .

        Reference: Section   1.6

25.   Larger organizations can share data *and processing* among multiple CPUs by utilizing a mode of
        processing known as   client-server architecture   .

        Reference: Section   1.6

26.   A   multimedia   database can store complex data including text, sound, and pictures.

        Reference: Section   1.6

27.   Data and applications can be delivered from one organization to another on the public network
        called the Internet .

        Reference: Section   1.6

28.   Internet-based applications use a browser to display the data.

        Reference: Section   1.1

29.   A   distributed   database is logically integrated but physically located in more than one place.

        Reference: Section   1.6

30.   A new category of non-relational DBMSs called   object-oriented   database systems is
        evolving, primarily to support engineering applications.

        Reference: Section   1.6

ESSAY

1.   Describe the characteristics of the organization that is likely to use a personal, workgroup,
        organizational, or Internet technology type of database for its fundamental record keeping.

2.   Contrast file-processing systems and database processing systems.

3.   Give the history of database processing.

4.   Describe the hierarchy of data.

5.   Describe the characteristics that differentiate Internet-based database processing systems.

CHAPTER 2 TEST QUESTIONS

TRUE-FALSE QUESTIONS

T   1.   A relation is a table of data.
Reference: Section   2.1

F   2.   The columns of a table contain records.
Reference: Section   2.1

T   3.   Unnormalized relations generally contain duplicate data.
Reference: Section   2.1

T   4.   A poorly structured relation has data concerning two or more topics.
Reference: Section   2.1

T   5.   In an unnormalized relation, if a value for a field changes, it may have to be changed in several rows.
Reference: Section   2.1

F   6.   Most DBMSs store the metadata in a separate database.
Reference: Section   2.1

T   7.   Knowledgeable users can query the system tables for information about the structure of the DBMS.
Reference: Section   2.1

F   8.   When a new record is added to a table, only the index for the primary key field is updated.
Reference: Section   2.1

F   9.   Creating and using an index does not require additional processing.
Reference: Section   2.1

T   10.   Rows in a table can be sorted into a desired sequence.
Reference: Section   2.1

F   11.   Only one index can be created for each table.
Reference: Section   2.1

F   12.   Most DBMSs let developers access the application metadata directly.
Reference: Section   2.1

T   13.   Most DBMSs have a design tools subsystem to facilitate the design and creation of the database and its applications.
Reference: Section   2.2

F   14.   Most DBMSs do not include a programming language.
Reference: Section   2.2

T 15. The run-time subsystem processes the application components that are developed using the design tools.
Reference: Section   2.2

F 16. Data in a database cannot be accessed by standard file-processing languages.
Reference: Section   2.2

F 17. The DBMS engine is the intermediary between the user and the design tools.
Reference: Section   2.2

T 18. A database schema contains the design of the database.
Reference: Section   2.3

T 19. The term *1:N* means that one row of the first table is related to many rows of the second table.
Reference: Section   2.3

F 20. Business rules cannot be included in a database schema.
Reference: Section   2.3

T 21. A field in one table is called a foreign key when it is the primary key of another table.
Reference: Section   2.3

F 22. A data entry form is independent of any tables.
Reference: Section   2.4

T 23. A query can be used to specify which rows in a table are to be retrieved.
Reference: Section   2.4

F 24. A query cannot contain data from more than one table.
Reference: Section   2.4

T 25. A DBMS's programming language is often a variant of a standard language, such as BASIC.
Reference: Section   2.4

F 26. If the development team is thoroughly knowledgeable about the DBMS, they do not need to become familiar with the users' model.
Reference: Section   2.5

T 27. The *top-down* development strategy proceeds from the general to the specific.
Reference: Section   2.5

F 28. *Bottom-up* development generally does not produce useful systems quickly.
Reference: Section   2.5

T 29. Database developers generally examine the outputs that the users require, and then work backward to determine the data that must be stored in the database.
Reference: Section   2.5

T   30.   A problem with a multiuser system is that different users may have inconsistent models of the system to be developed.
Reference: Section   2.5

MULTIPLE CHOICE QUESTIONS

1.   The columns of a table contain:
    a.   records
    b.   attributes
    c.   files
    d.   rows
    e.   relations
    Answer: b   Reference: Section 2.1

2.   A normalized, well-structured relation:
    a.   has data concerning only one topic
    b.   has little, if any, duplicate data
    c.   only has to be updated once when a field's value changes
    d.   all of the above
    e.   a and b
    Answer: d   Reference: Section 2.1

3.   Metadata contains:
    a.   the large data records
    b.   the structure of the database
    c.   the application programs
    d.   the indexes
    e.   all of the above
    Answer: b   Reference: Section 2.1

4.   An index:
    a.   is used for processing the table in a specified order
    b.   is used to rapidly access an individual record
    c.   requires additional processing and storage overhead
    d.   all of the above
    e.   a and b
    Answer: d   Reference: Section 2.1

5.   Application metadata:
    a.   contains the structure of the database
    b.   contains the structure and format of user forms, reports, and queries
    c.   can be directly accessed by developers
    d.   all of the above
    e.   a and b
    Answer: e   Reference: Section 2.1

6.   The design tools subsystem of the DBMS includes tools for creating:
        a.   tables
        b.   forms
        c.   queries
        d.   reports
        e.   all of the above
        Answer: e   Reference: Section 2.2

7.   The run-time subsystem of the DBMS:
        a.   processes the application components developed with the design tools subsystem
        b.   processes requests from application programs to read and write database data
        c.   is also known as a run-time product
        d.   all of the above
        e.   a and b
        Answer: e   Reference: Section 2.2

8.   The DBMS engine:
        a.   contains the design tools and run-time subsystems
        b.   processes requests from the design tools and run-time subsystems
        c.   is responsible for transaction management, locking, and backup and recovery
        d.   a and c
        e.   b and c
        Answer: e   Reference: Section 2.2

9.   A schema is:
        a.   a diagram of the database
        b.   the users' view of the data
        c.   the design of the database
        d.   all of the above
        e.   a and b
        Answer: c   Reference: Section 2.3

10.   The set of values that a column may have is known as its:
        a.   domain
        b.   schema
        c.   relationships
        d.   foreign keys
        e.   business rules
        Answer: a   Reference: Section 2.3

11.   Business rules are:
        a.   constraints on allowed data values
        b.   completely enforced by the DBMS
        c.   generally enforced by application programs
        d.   a and b
        e.   a and c
        Answer: e   Reference: Section 2.3

12.   Indexing is a property of a:
    a.   table
    b.   field
    c.   record
    d.   relation
    e.   domain
    Answer: b   Reference: Section 2.3

13.   A relationship is created between two tables by specifying a field in the first table as a:
    a.   domain
    b.   index
    c.   foreign key
    d.   constraint
    e.   business rule
    Answer: c   Reference: Section 2.3

14.   A data entry form can contain:
    a.   text boxes containing identifying labels
    b.   text boxes which hold values for attributes
    c.   data from more than one table
    d.   all of the above
    e.   a and b
    Answer: d   Reference: Section 2.4

15.   A query can be expressed using:
    a.   the data access language SQL
    b.   query by example (QBE)
    c.   query by form
    d.   all of the above
    e.   b and c
    Answer: d   Reference: Section 2.4

16.   A *parameterized* query is one in which criteria values:
    a.   are accepted at run time
    b.   are specified using the query by example design tool
    c.   are entered into a form
    d.   a and b
    e.   a and c
    Answer: a   Reference: Section 2.4

17.   A report differs from the printout of the table in that:
    a.   it can contain formatting to enhance readability
    b.   data can be grouped
    c.   fields to be printed can be selected, rather than all fields being shown
    d.   all of the above
    e.   a and c
    Answer: d   Reference: Section 2.4

18.   Menus make an application more user-friendly by:
   a.   showing what options are available
   b.   helping the users select those actions they want performed
   c.   providing shortcut (hot) keys
   d.   all of the above
   e.   a and b
   Answer: d   Reference: Section 2.4

19.   Application programs:
   a.   are written when functionality beyond the capability of the design tools is required
   b.   must be written in a language specific to the DBMS
   c.   must be written in a standard language that interfaces with the DBMS
   d.   a and b
   e.   a and c
   Answer: a   Reference: Section 2.4

20.   A prototype is a:
   a.   completed database and applications
   b.   simplified working model of the system to be created
   c.   part of the statement of requirements for the system to be created
   d.   a and c
   e.   b and c
   Answer: e   Reference: Section 2.5

21.   The strategy for developing a database, which begins with studying strategic goals, is called:
   a.   bottom-up development
   b.   top-down development
   c.   prototyping
   d.   modeling
   e.   none of the above
   Answer: b   Reference: Section 2.5

22.   The strategy for developing a database, which begins with the need to create a specific system, is called:
   a.   bottom-up development
   b.   top-down development
   c.   prototyping
   d.   modeling
   e.   none of the above
   Answer: a   Reference: Section 2.5

23.   Database developers generally:
   a.   examine the available data and determine what reports can be generated
   b.   examine the reports desired and determine what data needs to be stored in the database
   c.   examine the schema and determine what reports can be generated
   d.   all of the above
   e.   a and b
   Answer: b   Reference: Section 2.5

24.   Modeling a multiuser system is complicated because:
   a.   different users may envision different data models for the system
   b.   the developers have to reconcile different and inconsistent data models
   c.   the developers have to consolidate separate and consistent data models
   d.   all of the above
   e.   a and b
   Answer: d   Reference: Section   2.5

25.   The development team builds a data model from the users' statements about:
   a.   forms
   b.   reports
   c.   structure of the data
   d.   all of the above
   e.   a and b
   Answer: e   Reference: Section   2.5

FILL IN THE BLANKS

1.   The columns of a table contain ___fields/attributes___ .

   Reference: Section   2.1

2.   The process of creating well-structured relations is called ___normalization___ .

   Reference: Section   2.1

3.   Most DBMSs store their metadata in ___system tables___ .

   Reference: Section   2.1

4.   ___Indexes___ improve the performance and accessibility of the database.

   Reference: Section   2.1

5.   The structure and format of user forms and other application components is known as
   ___application metadata___ .

   Reference: Section   2.1

6.   The ___design tools___ subsystem of the DBMS facilitates the design and creation of the database
   and its applications.

   Reference: Section   2.2

7.   The ___run-time___ subsystem processes the application components.

   Reference: Section   2.2

8. DBMS products must provide an __application program interface__ for standard programming languages.

    Reference: Section   2.2

9. The DBMS __engine__ is the intermediary between the design tools and run-time subsystems and the data.

    Reference: Section   2.2

10. End users need to buy only the __run-time product__ , rather than the entire DBMS.

    Reference: Section   2.2

11. A database __schema__ defines a database's structure, its tables, relationships, domains, and business rules.

    Reference: Section   2.3

12. A __domain__ is a set of values that a column may have.

    Reference: Section   2.3

13. __Business rules__ specify the constraints on allowed data values.

    Reference: Section   2.3

14. A __foreign key__ is used to declare a relationship between two tables.

    Reference: Section   2.3

15. Users generally enter data into __forms__ rather than directly into tables.

    Reference: Section   2.4

16. Specifying the desired outcomes in a query window is called __query by example (QBE)__ .

    Reference: Section   2.4

17. Entering the desired criteria for a query on a data entry form is called __query by form__ .

    Reference: Section   2.4

18. A __parameterized__ criterion in a query lets the user enter the criterion *value* at the time the query is run.

    Reference: Section   2.4

19. A __report__ is a formatted display of data.

    Reference: Section   2.4

20. __Menus__ show users what options are available and help the users select a desired action.

    Reference: Section   2.4

21. A __prototype__ is a sample database and application used during development to clarify requirements.

    Reference: Section   2.5

22. __Top-down__ development begins with a study of the strategic goals of the organization.

    Reference: Section   2.5

23. __Bottom-up__ development begins with the need to develop a specific system.

    Reference: Section   2.5

24. Developers generally need to use the art of __inferencing__ when implementing the design for the database from information supplied by users.

    Reference: Section   2.5

25. Modeling a __multiuser__ database is complicated because many users may have different views of the data.

    Reference: Section   2.5

ESSAY

1. Describe the purpose of overhead data such as indexes and linked lists.

2. What is application metadata?

3. Describe the function of the DBMS engine.

4. Describe the function of forms, queries, and reports.

5. Discuss why data modeling is more complicated for multiuser systems.

CHAPTER 3 TEST QUESTIONS

TRUE-FALSE QUESTIONS

F   1.   There is one generally accepted standard E-R model.
Reference: Section   3.1

T   2.   An entity is something that the users want to track.
Reference: Section   3.1

F   3.   An *entity group* is the collection of all entities of a given type.
Reference: Section   3.1

T   4.   An *entity class* contains the structure of the entities in the class.
Reference: Section   3.1

T   5.   A particular occurrence of an entity is known as an instance.
Reference: Section   3.1

T   6.   An entity's characteristics are described by its attributes.
Reference: Section   3.1

F   7.   All instances of a given entity class do not have to have the same attributes.
Reference: Section   3.1

T   8.   Each instance of an entity has at least one attribute used as an identifier.
Reference: Section   3.1

F   9.   Every identifier of an entity must be unique.
Reference: Section   3.1

F 10.   An identifier can consist of only one attribute.
Reference: Section   3.1

T 11.   Entities are associated with one another in relationships.
Reference: Section   3.1

F 12.   Relationships cannot have attributes.
Reference: Section   3.1

F 13.   The maximum number of entities in a relationship is two.
Reference: Section   3.1

F 14.   The minimum number of entities in a relationship is two.
Reference: Section   3.1

F 15.   In a relationship, an instance of one entity is always related to more than one instance of the other entity.
Reference: Section   3.1

T 16.   A relationship may exist among instances of the same class.
Reference: Section   3.1

T 17.   Some entities cannot exist in the database unless another type of entity also exists in the database.
Reference: Section   3.1

F 18.   The identifier of one entity cannot include the identifier of another entity.
Reference: Section   3.1

T 19.   Subtype entities are defined when an entity can have optional attributes.
Reference: Section   3.1

T 20.   Subtype entities have the same identifier as their supertype.
Reference: Section   3.1

F 21.   A subtype is a generalization of the supertype.
Reference: Section   3.1

T 22.   The entities in subtypes inherit the attributes of the supertype entity class.
Reference: Section   3.1

F 23.   Subtypes are shown on an E-R diagram by rounding the corners of the relationship symbol.
Reference: Section   3.1

F 24.   The minimum cardinality in a relationship is one.
Reference: Section   3.1

T 25.   Business rules are not included in the E-R model.
Reference: Section   3.1

MULTIPLE CHOICE QUESTIONS

1.   An entity class:
    a.   contains the structure or format of the entities
    b.   represents something that the users want to track
    c.   contains one instance of a particular entity
    d.   a and b
    e.   b and c
    Answer: d   Reference: Section   3.1

2.   All instances of a given entity:
    a.   have the same attributes
    b.   have the same values for the attributes
    c.   belong to the same entity class
    d.   a and b
    e.   a and c
    Answer: e   Reference: Section   3.1

3.   An identifier of an entity instance:
       a.   may be unique
       b.   must be unique
       c.   may consist of more than one attribute
       d.   a and c
       e.   b and c
       Answer: d   Reference: Section   3.1

4.   Depending on the system being modeled, a relationship can have _____ entities:
       a.   one
       b.   two
       c.   three
       d.   all of the above
       e.   zero
       Answer: d   Reference: Section   3.1

5.   The maximum cardinality in a binary relationship can be:
       a.   0
       b.   1
       c.   N
       d.   a or c
       e.   b or c
       Answer: e   Reference: Section   3.1

6.   The minimum cardinality in a binary relationship can be:

       a.   0
       b.   1
       c.   N
       d.   all of the above
       e.   a or b
       Answer: d   Reference: Section   3.1

7.   The *degree* of a relationship refers to the:
       a.   number of entities
       b.   maximum cardinality
       c.   minimum cardinality
       d.   number of attributes in the identifiers
       e.   number of attributes in the entities
       Answer: a   Reference: Section   3.1

8.   A relationship which exists among entities of the same class is:
       a.   ID-dependent
       b.   recursive
       c.   weak
       d.   strong
       e.   binary
       Answer: b   Reference: Section   3.1

9.   A *weak* entity is one which:
      a.   is not in a relationship with any other entities
      b.   does not have a unique identifier
      c.   cannot exist in the database by itself
      d.   is a subtype
      e.   has a minimum cardinality of zero
      Answer: c   Reference: Section   3.1

10.   An *ID-dependent* entity is one which:
      a.   has an identifier that includes the identifier of another entity
      b.   does not have a unique identifier
      c.   has an identifier that consists of only one attribute
      d.   has an identifier inherited from its supertype
      e.   has not been assigned an identifier
      Answer: a   Reference: Section   3.1

11.   A *strong* entity is one which:
      a.   must be in a relationship with another entity
      b.   can exist in the database by itself
      c.   is not in a relationship with any other entities
      d.   is a supertype
      e.   has a minimum cardinality of one
      Answer: b   Reference: Section   3.1

12.   A subtype entity:
      a.   inherits the attributes of its supertype
      b.   contains optional attributes not contained in its supertype
      c.   is always mutually exclusive
      d.   all of the above
      e.   a and b
      Answer: e   Reference: Section   3.1

13.   A supertype entity:
      a.   is a generalization of its subtypes
      b.   contains attributes common to its subtypes
      c.   may not have any subtype instances
      d.   all of the above
      e.   a and b
      Answer: d   Reference: Section   3.1

14.   E-R diagrams created with a CASE tool are:
      a.   generally more visually pleasing
      b.   easier to modify
      c.   more compact
      d.   all of the above
      e.   a and b
      Answer: e   Reference: Section   3.1

15.   Business rules:
    a.   are not part of an E-R diagram
    b.   may be enforced by the DBMS
    c.   may be enforced by application programs
    d.   all of the above
    e.   b and c
    Answer: d   Reference: Section   3.1

FILL IN THE BLANKS

1.   A(n) __entity__ is something that can be identified in the users' work environment.

    Reference: Section   3.1

2.   Entities of a given type are grouped into __entity classes__ .

    Reference: Section   3.1

3.   A(n) __instance__ of an entity class is the representation of a particular entity.

    Reference: Section   3.1

4.   Properties that describe an entity's characteristics are called __attributes__ .

    Reference: Section   3.1

5.   __Identifiers__ are attributes that name, or identify, entity instances.

    Reference: Section   3.1

6.   Identifiers that consist of two or more attributes are called __composite__ identifiers.

    Reference: Section   3.1

7.   Entities can be associated with one another in __relationships__ .

    Reference: Section   3.1

8.   The number of entities in a relationship is the __degree__ of the relationship.

    Reference: Section   3.1

9.   Relationships which associate two entities are called __binary__ relationships.

    Reference: Section   3.1

10. In a(n) one-to-one (1:1) relationship, a single-entity instance of one type is related to a single entity instance of another type.

    Reference: Section   3.1

11. In a(n) one-to-many (1:N) relationship, a single-entity instance of one type is related to more than one entity instance of another type.

    Reference: Section   3.1

12. In a(n) many-to-many (N:M) relationship, more than one entity instance of one type is related to more than one entity instance of another type.

    Reference: Section   3.1

13. The maximum number of entities that can occur on one side of a relationship is called the maximum cardinality .

    Reference: Section   3.1

14. The minimum cardinality that can occur on one side of a relationship is either one or zero.

    Reference: Section   3.1

15. Relationships among entities of a single class are called recursive relationships.

    Reference: Section   3.1

16. A(n) weak entity is one that cannot exist in the database unless another type of entity also exists in the database.

    Reference: Section   3.1

17. An entity that can exist by itself in the database is called a(n) strong entity.

    Reference: Section   3.1

18. A weak entity in which the identifier of one entity includes the identifier of another entity is called a(n) ID-dependent entity.

    Reference: Section   3.1

19. A(n) subtype entity contains optional attributes.

    Reference: Section   3.1

20. A subtype entity belongs to, or is owned by, a(n) supertype entity.

    Reference: Section   3.1

21.   The entities in subtypes __inherit__ the attributes of the supertype.

Reference: Section   3.1

22.   The relationship between a subtype and its supertype is called a(n) __IS-A__ relationship.

Reference: Section   3.1

23.   Structures of subtypes and supertypes are sometimes called __generalization hierarchies__ .

Reference: Section   3.1

ESSAY

1.   What is a composite identifier? Give an example.

2.   Describe the different possible cardinalities. Give an example of each type.

2.   How is a multi-valued attribute represented in a database? Give an example.

3.   Describe what is meant by a generalization hierarchy? Give an example.

5.   How can business rules be added to the E-R model?

CHAPTER 4 TEST QUESTIONS

TRUE-FALSE QUESTIONS

F   1.   A *semantic object* is the same as an object created with an object-oriented programming language.
Reference: Section 4.1

T   2.   A semantic object has a collection of attributes.
Reference: Section 4.1

F   3.   All objects represent a physical entity.
Reference: Section 4.1

T   4.   *Group* attributes are composites of other attributes.
Reference: Section 4.1

F   5.   The attributes of a semantic object are known as *semantic object attributes.*
Reference: Section 4.1

F   6.   The cardinality of a group attribute is inherited by all of the attributes in the group.
Reference: Section 4.1

T   7.   A semantic object can contain a link to another object.
Reference: Section 4.1

T   8.   Object attributes always occur as a pair.
Reference: Section 4.1

F   9.   Object identifiers are always unique.
Reference: Section 4.1

T 10.   An attribute's domain can be an *enumerated list*.
Reference: Section 4.1

T 11.   In an existing system, developers often work backward to derive the semantic objects from the existing reports, forms, and queries.
Reference: Section 4.2

T 12.   For a totally new application, developers begin by determining what objects the users need to track.
Reference: Section 4.2

F 13.   A *semantic object specification* contains the same information as a semantic object diagram.
Reference: Section 4.2

T 14.   A single-valued attribute is an attribute whose maximum cardinality is 1.
Reference: Section 4.3

F 15. A simple object is a semantic object that contains only a single attribute.
Reference: Section 4.3

F 16. A composite object is a semantic object that contains nonobject and object attributes.
Reference: Section 4.3

T 17. A compound object is a semantic object that contains at least one object attribute.
Reference: Section 4.3

T 18. A hybrid object is a semantic object with at least one multivalued group attribute that includes a semantic object attribute.
Reference: Section 4.3

T 19. The identifier of an association object is usually the combination of the identifiers of the objects being associated.
Reference: Section 4.3

F 20. The minimum cardinality of a subtype attribute is 1.
Reference: Section 4.3

F 21. A supertype object inherits all of the attributes of its subtype.
Reference: Section 4.3

T 22. The first attribute of a subtype is the parent attribute.
Reference: Section 4.3

F 23. A semantic object can contain only one subtype attribute.
Reference: Section 4.3

T 24. Subtypes may exclude one another.
Reference: Section 4.3

F 25. Subtypes cannot be nested.
Reference: Section 4.3

F 26. An *archetype* object is also called a *version* object.
Reference: Section 4.3

T 27. The identifier of a version object includes the archetype object.
Reference: Section 4.3

T 28. Semantic objects are more closely related to actual data than are entities and relationships.
Reference: Section 4.3

F 29. Semantic objects contain less metadata than entities.
Reference: Section 4.3

T 30. Object attributes in the semantic object model perform the same function as relationships in the E-R model.
Reference: Section 4.3

MULTIPLE CHOICE QUESTIONS

1.   Comparing the E-R model and the Semantic Object Model, we can say that:
    a.   in the E-R methodology, the development team analyzes the users' reports, forms, and queries to construct the data model
    b.   in the Semantic Object Model methodology, the development team analyzes the users' reports, forms, and queries to construct the data model
    c.   in the E-R methodology, the data model consists of entities and relationships
    d.   in the Semantic Object Model methodology, the data model consists of semantic objects
    e.   all of the above
    Answer: e   **Reference:**   Section 4.0

2.   Stating that the collection of attributes of a semantic object is a *sufficient description* means that:
    a.   the attributes do not represent all of the characteristics that the users need in order to do their work
    b.   the attributes represent all of the characteristics that the users need in order to do their work
    c.   the attributes represent all of the characteristics that the users need in order to do their work, and there are additional attributes also
    d.   the attributes represent all of the characteristics of the actual physical object
    e.   b and d
    Answer: b   **Reference:**   Section 4.1

3.   A *single-value* attribute must have:
    a.   a minimum cardinality of 0
    b.   a minimum cardinality of 1
    c.   a maximum cardinality of 1
    d.   no minimum cardinality (N)
    e.   no maximum cardinality (N)
    Answer: c   **Reference:**   Section 4.1

4.   An attribute that must have exactly one value has:
    a.   a minimum cardinality of 0
    b.   a minimum cardinality of 1
    c.   a maximum cardinality of 1
    d.   a and c
    e.   b and c
    Answer: e   **Reference:**   Section 4.1

5.   If a group attribute is optional:
        a.   all of the attributes in the group must be optional
        b.   the first attribute in the group must be optional
        c.   the first attribute in the group cannot be optional
        d.   all of the attributes in the group may be optional
        e.   all of the attributes in the group cannot be optional
        Answer: d   **Reference:**   Section 4.1

6.   A paired attribute is:
        a.   one that has a minimum cardinality of 2
        b.   one that has a maximum cardinality of 2
        c.   one that appears in two objects
        d.   one that has a matching object attribute in the object corresponding to the attribute
        e.   one that has the same value in two instances of the objects
        Answer: d   **Reference:**   Section 4.1

7.   An object identifier:
        a.   is employed by users to identify object instances
        b.   must be unique
        c.   may be unique
        d.   a and b
        e.   a and c
        Answer: e   **Reference:**   Section 4.1

8.   A group identifier:
        a.   has more than one attribute
        b.   identifies a group of instances
        c.   identifies a group of attributes in an object
        d.   is the identifier for a group of semantic objects
        e.   links two objects
        Answer: a   **Reference:**   Section 4.1

9.   The physical description portion of an attribute domain indicates:
        a.   the type of data
        b.   the length of the data
        c.   other restrictions or constraints
        d.   all of the above
        e.   a and b
        Answer: d   **Reference:**   Section 4.1

10.   The semantic description portion of an attribute domain:
        a.   indicates the type of wording in the description
        b.   distinguishes this attribute from other attributes that have the same physical description
        c.   distinguishes this attribute from other attributes that have a similar identifier
        d.   is a description of the attribute's specific values
        e.   describes the restrictions on the attribute's values
        Answer: b   **Reference:**   Section 4.1

11.   Views are used:
    a.   when the database is being designed from existing forms, reports, and queries
    b.   after the database structure has been created to support new forms, reports, and queries
    c.   to restrict access to some of an object's attributes
    d.   all of the above
    e.   a and b
Answer: d   **Reference:**   Section 4.1

12.   Developing semantic objects from existing form, reports, and queries is known as:
    a.   query by example
    b.   reverse engineering
    c.   top-down development
    d.   forward engineering
    e.   structured development
Answer: b   **Reference:**   Section 4.2

13.   Repeating groups in a report may represent:
    a.   data concerning another object
    b.   several values of a group attribute
    c.   different attributes of the object
    d.   all of the above
    e.   a and b
Answer: e   **Reference:**   Section 4.2

14.   A database model can be specified by:
    a.   a set of semantic object diagrams
    b.   a semantic object specifications table
    c.   a domain specifications table
    d.   a and c, or b and c
    e.   a and b, or b and c
Answer: d   **Reference:**   Section 4.2

15.   The type of attribute domain whose values are computed from other values is known as a(n):
    a.   enumerated domain
    b.   object domain
    c.   formula domain
    d.   group domain
    e.   set domain
Answer: c   **Reference:**   Section 4.2

16.   An attribute whose maximum cardinality is greater than one is called a(n) _____ attribute.
    a.   single-valued
    b.   multivalued
    c.   object
    d.   non-object
    e.   paired
Answer: b   **Reference:**   Section 4.3

17.   A *simple object* is a semantic object that contains only _____ attributes.
    a.   single-valued, nonobject
    b.   single-valued, object
    c.   multivalued, nonobject
    d.   multivalued, object
    e.   group
    Answer: a   **Reference:**   Section 4.3

18.   A *composite object* is a semantic object that contains only _____ attributes.
    a.   single-valued, nonobject
    b.   single-valued, object
    c.   multivalued, nonobject
    d.   multivalued, object
    e.   group
    Answer: c   **Reference:**   Section 4.3

19.   A *compound object* is a semantic object that contains at least one _____ attribute.
    a.   single-valued
    b.   object
    c.   group
    d.   multivalued
    e.   nested
    Answer: b   **Reference:**   Section 4.3

20.   Paired attributes can represent relationships with cardinalities shown as:
    a.   1:1
    b.   1:N
    c.   M:1
    d.   M:N
    e.   all of the above
    Answer: e   **Reference:**   Section 4.3

21.   A *hybrid object* is a semantic object that contains at least one _____ attribute.
    a.   single-valued group attribute that does not include a semantic object
    b.   single-valued group attribute that includes a semantic object
    c.   multivalued group attribute that does not include a semantic object
    d.   multivalued group attribute that includes a semantic object
    e.   paired
    Answer: d   **Reference:**   Section 4.3

22.   An *association object* is a semantic object that:
    a.   relates two (or more) objects
    b.   stores data that is peculiar to that relationship
    c.   has two (or more) object attributes
    d.   all of the above
    e.   a and b
    Answer: d   **Reference:**   Section 4.3

23.   The identifier of an association object can be:
    a.   a composite identifier consisting of the identifiers of the objects that are associated
    b.   a unique single-attribute identifier of its own
    c.   a unique composite identifier of its own
    d.   any of the above
    e.   a or c
    Answer: d   **Reference:**   Section 4.3

24.   Regarding a subtype object:
    a.   the first attribute must be the parent attribute
    b.   it inherits all of the attributes of its parent
    c.   it has a paired attribute in its parent
    d.   all of the above
    e.   a and b
    Answer: d   **Reference:**   Section 4.3

25.   A *version object*:
    a.   can exist on its own
    b.   must contain the archetype object in its identifier
    c.   is a subtype of an archetype object
    d.   a and b
    e.   b and c
    Answer: b   **Reference:**   Section 4.3

FILL IN THE BLANKS

1.   The collection of attributes in an object is a(n) sufficient description , meaning that the
    attributes represent all of the characteristics that the users need in order to do their work.

    Reference: Section 4.1

2.   Simple attributes have a single value.

    Reference: Section 4.1

3.   Group attributes are composites of other attributes.

    Reference: Section 4.1

4.   Object attributes are attributes that establish a relationship between one semantic object and
    another.

    Reference: Section 4.1

5.   The minimum cardinality indicates the number of instances of the attribute that must exist in
    order for the object to be valid.

    Reference: Section 4.1

6.   Object attributes are also known as paired attributes.

    Reference: Section 4.1

7.   An object __identifier__ is one or more attributes that the users employ to identify object instances.

   Reference: Section 4.1

8.   A(n) __group identifier__ is an identifier that has more than one attribute.

   Reference: Section 4.1

9.   The __physical__ description of a domain indicates the type of data.

   Reference: Section 4.1

10.   The __semantic__ description of a domain specifies the application area of the attribute.

   Reference: Section 4.1

11.   A(n) __enumerated list__ specifies the physical description of a domain when it consists of a set of specific values.

   Reference: Section 4.1

12.   The portion of an object that is visible to a particular application is called the semantic object __view__ .

   Reference: Section 4.1

13.   Data modeling is a(n) __iterative__ process.

   Reference: Section 4.2

14.   A database can be represented by a complete set of __semantic object diagrams__ .

   Reference: Section 4.2

15.   When the values for an attribute are computed from other values, it has a __formula__ domain.

   Reference: Section 4.2

16.   A(n) __single-valued__ attribute is an attribute whose maximum cardinality is 1.

   Reference: Section 4.3

17.   A(n) __multivalued__ attribute is an attribute whose maximum cardinality is greater than 1.

   Reference: Section 4.3

18.   A(n) __nonobject__ attribute is a simple or a group attribute.

   Reference: Section 4.3

19.   A(n)   simple   object is a semantic object that contains only single-valued, nonobject attributes.

Reference: Section 4.3

20.   A(n)   composite   object is a semantic object that contains one or more multivalued, nonobject attributes.

Reference: Section 4.3

21.   A(n)   compound   object contains at least one object attribute.

Reference: Section 4.3

22.   A(n)   hybrid   object is a semantic object with at least one multivalued group attribute that includes a semantic object attribute.

Reference: Section 4.3

23.   A(n)   association   object relates two (or more) objects and stores data that are peculiar to that relationship.

Reference: Section **4.3**

24.   A(n)   subtype   object has specific, restricted attributes not suitable for all instances of its parent type.

Reference: Section 4.3

25.   A subtype   inherits   all of the attributes of its parent.

Reference: Section 4.3

26.   A(n)   archetype   object is a semantic object that produces other semantic objects that represent versions.

Reference: Section 4.3

27.   Nested   subtypes are ones which contain subtypes within subtypes.

Reference: Section 4.3

28.   The first part of the ID in a version object must be the   archetype   object.

Reference: Section 4.3

29.   The E-R model sees the concept of   entity   as basic.

Reference: Section 4.4

30.   The semantic object model sees the concept of   semantic object   as basic.

Reference: Section 4.4

ESSAY

1.   Describe the difference between a *simple attribute* and a *single-value attribute*.

2.   How is a relationship between two objects represented in the Semantic Object Model?

3.   Explain what is meant by attribute cardinality in the Semantic Object Model.

4.   Describe the difference between the physical description and the semantic description portions of the domain of an attribute.

5.   Describe the differences between the Semantic Object Model and the E-R Model.

CHAPTER 5 TEST QUESTIONS

TRUE-FALSE QUESTIONS

T   1.   A relation is a two-dimensional table.
Reference: Section 5.1

F   2.   Rows are called attributes.
Reference: Section 5.1

F   3.   Columns are called tuples.
Reference: Section 5.1

T   4.   A *functional dependency* is a relationship between or among attributes.
Reference: Section 5.1

T   5.   The known or given attribute is called the *determinant* in a functional dependency.
Reference: Section 5.1

F   6.   The relationship in a functional dependency is one-to-one (1:1).
Reference: Section 5.1

F   7.   If a composite attribute is a determinant, then the individual attributes also functional determine the same attribute as the composite attribute.
Reference: Section 5.1

T   8.   A *key* is a group of one or more attributes that uniquely identifies a row.
Reference: Section 5.1

F   9.   The selection of the attributes to use for the key is determined by the database programmers.
Reference: Section 5.1

T 10. Rows in a relation must be unique.
Reference: Section 5.1

T 11. A *deletion anomaly* occurs when deleting one entity results in deleting facts about another entity.
Reference: Section 5.2

T 12. An *insertion anomaly* occurs when we cannot insert some data into the database without inserting another entity first.
Reference: Section 5.2

F 13. Modification anomalies do not occur in tables that meet the definition of a relation.
Reference: Section 5.2

T 14. *Normalization* is the process of splitting a relation into two or more relations.
Reference: Section 5.2

T 15. Relations are classified into *normal forms*, based on the type of modification anomalies to which they are vulnerable.
Reference: Section 5.2

T 16. A table of data that meets the minimum definition of a relation is automatically in *first normal form*.
Reference: Section 5.3

F 17. The order of the rows in a relation is determined by the key chosen.
Reference: Section 5.3

F 18. A relation is in *first normal form* if all of its non-key attributes are dependent on part of the key.
Reference: Section 5.3

T 19. A relation is in *second normal form* if all of its non-key attributes are dependent on all of the key.
Reference: Section 5.3

T 20. A *transitive dependency* occurs when one non-key attribute determines another non-key attribute.
Reference: Section 5.3

F 21. A relation can be in third normal form without being in second normal form.
Reference: Section 5.3

T 22. A relation often has two or more attributes or attribute collections that can be a key.
Reference: Section 5.3

T 23. A relation is in *Boyce-Codd normal form* if every determinant is a candidate key.
Reference: Section 5.3

F 24. A multivalued dependency occurs when an attribute that has multiple values depends on another attribute.
Reference: Section 5.3

F 25. *Fifth normal form* is the highest normal form.
Reference: Section 5.4

F 26. A relation can be converted into *domain/key normal form* using an algorithm specified by R. Fagin.
Reference: Section 5.4

T 27. A relation in *domain/key normal form* is guaranteed to have no modification anomalies.
Reference: Section 5.4

T 28. Two attributes in a relation can determine each other.
Reference: Section 5.5

F 29. If attribute A determines B, but B does not determine A, the relationship among their data values is one-to-one.
Reference: Section 5.5

T 30. Normalized relations are sometimes de-normalized to improve performance.
Reference: Section 5.7

MULTIPLE CHOICE QUESTIONS

1.   A *relation* is analogous to a:
      a.   file
      b.   field
      c.   record
      d.   row
      e.   column
      Answer: a   **Reference:**   Section 5.1

2.   A *tuple* is analogous to a:
      a.   file
      b.   row
      c.   column
      d.   field
      e.   table
      Answer: b   **Reference:**   Section 5.1

3.   An *attribute* is analogous to a:
      a.   field
      b.   file
      c.   row
      d.   table
      e.   record
      Answer: b   **Reference:**   Section 5.1

4.   In a relation:
      a.   the order of the rows and the columns is significant
      b.   the order of the rows is significant, but the order of the columns is not
      c.   the order of the columns is significant, but the order of the rows is not
      d.   neither the order of the rows nor the columns is significant
      e.   the order of the rows and the columns is specified when the relation is defined
      Answer: b   **Reference:**   Section 5.1

5.   In a functional dependency, the determinant:
      a.   will be paired with one value of the dependent attribute
      b.   may be paired with one or more values of the dependent attribute
      c.   may consist of more than one attribute
      d.   a and c
      e.   b and c
      Answer: d   **Reference:**   Section 5.1

6.   When the determinant contains two attributes:
      a.   the first attribute determines the dependent attribute
      b.   the second attribute determines the dependent attribute
      c.   both attributes determine the dependent attribute
      d.   either the first or second attribute determines the dependent attribute
      e.   the first attribute determines the second
      Answer: c   **Reference:**   Section 5.1

7.   A key in a relation:
      a.   may not functionally determine any attribute in the row
      b.   functionally determines only one attribute in the row
      c.   functionally determines at least one attribute in the row
      d.   functionally determines all the attributes in the row
      e.   functionally determines all duplicate rows
      Answer: d   **Reference:**   Section 5.1

8.   An *anomaly* in a relation is:
      a.   an unusual data value
      b.   a duplicate data value caused by changing the data
      c.   an undesirable consequence of changing the data
      d.   an error in the design
      e.   a conflict between the users' and developers' views
      Answer: c   **Reference:**   Section 5.2

9.   Restrictions on operations on a relation are called:
      a.   deletion anomalies
      b.   insertion anomalies
      c.   modification anomalies
      d.   domains
      e.   referential integrity constraints
      Answer: e   **Reference:**   Section 5.2

10.   The normalization process generally:
      a.   reduces the number of relations
      b.   increases the number of relations
      c.   reduces the number of functional dependencies
      d.   increases the number of functional dependencies
      e.   reduces the number of duplicate rows
      Answer: b   **Reference:**   Section 5.2

11.   A relation is automatically in:
      a.   First Normal Form
      b.   Second Normal Form
      c.   Third Normal Form
      d.   Boyce-Codd Normal Form
      e.   Fourth Normal Form
      Answer: a   **Reference:**   Section 5.3

12. A relation is in second normal form if all its non-key attributes are: .
    a.   dependent on part of the key
    b.   dependent on all of the key
    c.   independent of the key
    d.   independent of each other
    e.   independent of any other relation
    Answer: b   **Reference:**   Section 5.3

13. A relation is in third normal form if all its non-key attributes are:
    a.   dependent on part of the key
    b.   dependent on all of the key
    c.   independent of the key
    d.   independent of each other
    e.   independent of any other relation
    Answer: d   **Reference:**   Section 5.3

14. A relation is in Boyce-Codd normal form if:
    a.   every determinant is a candidate key
    b.   every determinant is a primary key
    c.   every attribute is a candidate key
    d.   there is more than one candidate key
    e.   there is more than one primary key
    Answer: a   **Reference:**   Section 5.3

15. The primary key is:
    a.   selected by the developers
    b.   selected by the users
    c.   automatically determined by the design
    d.   determined by the DBMS
    e.   determined by the sequence selected for the rows
    Answer: b   **Reference:**   Section 5.3

16. A *multivalued dependency* exists when a relation has:
    a.   at least two attributes, both of them are multivalued, and their values depend on each
         other
    b.   at least two attributes, one of them is multivalued, and its value depends on the other
    c.   at least three attributes, two of them are multivalued, and their values depend on only the
         third attribute
    d.   at least three attributes, one of them is multivalued, and its value depends on the other
         two attributes
    e.   at least three attributes, all of them are multivalued, and their values depend on each
         other
    Answer: c   **Reference:**   Section 5.3

17.   A relation is in fourth normal form if it is in BCNF and it has no:
   a.   transitive dependencies
   b.   multivalued dependencies
   c.   deletion anomalies
   d.   insertion anomalies
   e.   referential integrity conflicts
   Answer: b   **Reference:**   Section 5.3

18.   A relation is in domain/key normal form if:
   a.   every key of the relation is a logical consequence of the definition of constraints and determinants
   b.   every key of the relation is a logical consequence of the definition of constraints and domains
   c.   every constraint on the relation is a logical consequence of the definition of keys and determinants
   d.   every constraint on the relation is a logical consequence of the definition of keys and domains
   e.   every domain of the relation is a logical consequence of the definition of keys and constraints
   Answer: d   **Reference:**   Section 5.4

19.   The advantage of having a relation in domain/key normal form is that:
   a.   it takes less storage space than other normal forms
   b.   it is easily obtained from Boyce-Codd normal form
   c.   there is an algorithm for obtaining DK/NF
   d.   it is obtained by enforcing referential integrity constraints
   e.   it is guaranteed to have no modification anomalies
   Answer: e   **Reference:**   Section 5.4

20.   Synthesizing relations means that the developers start with a:
   a.   relation and normalize it
   b.   relation and determine its functional dependencies
   c.   set of attributes and determine what relations should be formed
   d.   set of attributes and normalize them
   e.   set of attributes and remove any modification anomalies
   Answer: c   **Reference:**   Section 5.5

21.   If two attributes A and B have a one-to-one attribute relationship, it would be shown as:
   a.   A - > B and B - > A
   b.   A - > B, but B not - > A
   c.   B - > A, but A not - > B
   d.   A not - > B and B not - > A
   e.   A < - > B
   Answer: a   **Reference:**   Section 5.5

22.   If two attributes *A* and *B* have a many-to-one attribute relationship, it would be shown as:
  a.   A - > B and B - > A
  b.   A - > B, but B not - > A
  c.   B - > A, but A not - > B
  d.   A not - > B and B not - > A
  e.   A < - > B
  Answer: b   **Reference:**   Section 5.5

23.   If two attributes *A* and *B* have a many-to-many attribute relationship, it would be shown as:
  a.   A - > B and B - > A
  b.   A - > B, but B not - > A
  c.   B - > A, but A not - > B
  d.   A not - > B and B not - > A
  e.   A < - > B
  Answer: d   **Reference:**   Section 5.5

24.   When a relation has a key consisting of multiple attributes, you can add a new attribute to the relation:
  a.   without any restriction
  b.   so long as it is functionally dependent on part of the key
  c.   so long as it is functionally dependent on all of the key
  d.   so long as it is functionally dependent on a non-key attribute
  e.   so long as it is a candidate key
  Answer: c   **Reference:**   Section 5.5

25.   Relations should be normalized to the greatest extent possible except when:
  a.   it would take too long
  b.   performance would be adversely affected
  c.   the database is too large
  d.   the DBMS can't support the restrictions
  e.   data duplication is desired
  Answer: b   **Reference:**   Section 5.7

FILL IN THE BLANKS

1.   A   relation   is a two-dimensional table.

  Reference: Section 5.1

2.   Rows are called   tuples   .

  Reference: Section 5.1

3.   Columns are called   attributes   .

  Reference: Section 5.1

4.   A __functional dependency__ is a relationship between or among attributes.

     Reference: Section 5.1

5.   The known or given attribute in a functional dependency is called the __determinant__ .

     Reference: Section 5.1

6.   A __key__ is a group of one or more attributes that uniquely identifies a row.

     Reference: Section 5.1

7.   __Normalization__ is the process of redefining or splitting a relation into two or more relations that have more desirable properties.

     Reference: Section 5.1

8.   For some relations, changing the data can have undesirable consequences, called __modification anomalies__ .

     Reference: Section 5.2

9.   A __deletion anomaly__ occurs when deleting facts about one entity causes facts about another entity to be deleted.

     Reference: Section 5.2

10. An __insertion anomaly__ occurs when we can't insert facts about one entity until we insert facts about another entity.

     Reference: Section 5.2

11. __Referential integrity constraints__ require that before an attribute of a relation can be stored as an attribute in another relation, the value of the attribute must be stored in the first relation.

     Reference: Section 5.2

12. Relations can be classified into classes called __normal forms__ , based on the types of modification anomalies to which they are vulnerable.

     Reference: Section 5.2

13. Any table of data that meets the definition of a relation is said to be in __first normal form__ .

     Reference: Section 5.3

14. A relation is in __second normal form__ if all its non-key attributes are dependent on the entire key.
     Reference: Section 5.3

15. A relation is in third normal form if it is in second normal form and has no <u>transitive dependencies</u> .

Reference: Section 5.3

16. Two or more attributes or attribute collections that can be a key are called <u>candidate keys</u> .

Reference: Section 5.3

17. The attribute or attribute collection which is used to uniquely identify each row is called the <u>primary key</u> .

Reference: Section 5.3

18. A relation is in Boyce-Codd normal form if every <u>determinant</u> is a candidate key.

Reference: Section 5.3

19. A <u>multivalued dependency</u> exists when a relation has at least three attributes, two of them are multivalued, and their values depend on only the third attribute.

Reference: Section 5.3

20. A relation is in <u>domain/key normal form</u> if every constraint on the relation is a logical consequence of the definition of keys and domains.

Reference: Section 5.4

21. If two attributes have a <u>one-to-one</u> relationship, they functionally determine each other.

Reference: Section 5.5

22. If attribute A determines B, but B does not determine A, the relationship among their data values is <u>many-to-one</u> .

Reference: Section 5.5

23. If attribute A does not determine B and B does not determine A, the relationship among their data values is <u>many-to-many</u> .

Reference: Section 5.5

24. Relations are sometimes purposely left unnormalized or are normalized and then de-normalized in order to <u>improve performance</u> .

Reference: Section 5.7

25.   In some cases, creating __repeating columns__ is preferred to the standard normalization techniques.

   Reference: Section 5.7

ESSAY

1.   Describe the relationship between functional dependencies, keys, and uniqueness.

2.   Describe the different types of modification anomalies.

3.   What is meant by a *referential integrity constraint*?

4.   Give the requirements for a table to be in First, Second, and Third Normal forms.

5.   Give the requirements for a table to be in Domain/Key Normal Form, and give the advantage and the disadvantage of the technique.

CHAPTER 6 TEST QUESTIONS

TRUE-FALSE QUESTIONS

T   1. The first step in representing entities using the relational model is to define a relation for each entity.
     Reference: Section 6.1

T   2. The attributes of the relation are the attributes of the entity.
     Reference: Section 6.1

F   3. When it is not obvious from the data model which attribute identifies an entity, the developers make the selection.
     Reference: Section 6.1

F   4. DK/NF relations are always preferred over lower normal forms.
     Reference: Section 6.1

T   5. A processing constraint needs to be implemented so that when the parent is deleted, any weak entities are also deleted.
     Reference: Section 6.1

T   6. When creating a relation for an ID-dependent entity, we must ensure that the key of both the parent and the key of the entity itself appear in the relation.
     Reference: Section 6.1

F   7. When the key of one relation is stored in a second relation, it is called a candidate key.
     Reference: Section 6.1

F   8. Representing a 1:1 relationship with the relational model requires placing the key of each relation into the other.
     Reference: Section 6.1

F   9. In a 1:1 relationship, we can navigate from either relation to the other.
     Reference: Section 6.1

T 10. When a 1:1 relationship is mandatory in both directions, and both relations have the same key, the relations should be combined into one relation.
     Reference: Section 6.1

F 11. In a one-to-many relationship, the parent relation is on the many side of the relationship.
     Reference: Section 6.1

T 12. In a 1:N relationship, we can navigate from either relation to the other.
     Reference: Section 6.1

T 13. Representing a 1:N relationship with the relational model requires placing the key of the parent entity into the relation representing the child entity.
     Reference: Section 6.1

F 14. Relations in a data structure diagram are represented by diamonds.
     Reference: Section 6.1

T 15. Many-to-many relationships cannot be directly represented by relations, without creating modification anomalies.
Reference: Section 6.1

T 16. An M:N relationship between two entities is represented by creating three relations.
Reference: Section 6.1

T 17. An intersection relation contains the keys of the relations in the M:N relationship.
Reference: Section 6.1

F 18. A recursive relationship cannot be of the many-to-many type.
Reference: Section 6.1

T 19. In a 1:1 or 1:N recursive relation, both the child and parent rows reside in the same relation.
Reference: Section 6.1

F 20. Relationships are limited to a maximum of two entities.
Reference: Section 6.1

F 21. All business rules that are constraints can be represented in the relational model.
Reference: Section 6.1

T 22. A *MUST NOT* constraint indicates combinations of attribute values that are not allowed to occur.
Reference: Section 6.1

T 23. A subtype is called an *IS-A* relationship.
Reference: Section 6.1

F 24. Subtype relations generally have their own key, independent of the key of the supertype.
Reference: Section 6.1

T 25. Each row of the supertype relation can correspond to only one row in the same subtype.
Reference: Section 6.1

F 26. A tree is a data structure in which the elements of the structure have only one-to-one relationships.
Reference: Section 6.3

T 27. Each element of a tree has at most one parent.
Reference: Section 6.3

F 28. Every node of a tree has one parent.
Reference: Section 6.3

T 29. In a simple network, the elements may have more than one parent, as long as the parents are of different types.
Reference: Section 6.3

T 30. A complex network is a data structure of elements in which at least one of the relationships is many-to-many.
Reference: Section 6.3

MULTIPLE CHOICE QUESTIONS

1.   The first step in database design using an E-R model is to:
       a.   define a relation for each entity
       b.   name each relation
       c.   determine the attributes of each relation
       d.   normalize each relation
       e.   determine the key for each relation
       Answer: a   **Reference:**   Section 6.1

2.   When creating a relation for an ID-dependent entity, we must ensure that:
       a.   the key of the parent appears in the relation
       b.   the key of the entity itself appears in the relation
       c.   the key of the parent and the key of the entity itself appear in the relation
       d.   the key of the supertype appears in the relation
       e.   the key of the supertype and the key of the entity itself appear in the relation
       Answer: c   **Reference:**   Section 6.1

3.   When the key of one relation is stored in a second relation, it is called a _____ key.
       a.   candidate
       b.   foreign
       c.   primary
       d.   secondary
       e.   subtype
       Answer: b   **Reference:**   Section 6.1

4.   When a relationship between two entities is 1:1 they should be:
       a.   converted to an IS-A relationship
       b.   eliminated if they have different keys
       c.   combined if they have different keys
       d.   eliminated if they have the same key
       e.   combined if they have the same key
       Answer: e   **Reference:**   Section 6.1

5.   The separation of an entity into two relations can be justified for:
       a.   performance reasons
       b.   security reasons
       c.   normalization reasons
       d.   a and b
       e.   a and c
       Answer: d   **Reference:**   Section 6.1

6.   In a one-to-many relationship:
    a.   the key of the parent entity is placed in the relation representing the child entity
    b.   the key of the child entity is placed in the relation representing the parent entity
    c.   the key of the parent entity is placed in the relation representing the child entity, and the key of the child entity is placed in the relation representing the parent entity
    d.   neither key is placed in the other relation
    e.   both keys are modified to include the key of the other relation
    Answer: a   **Reference:**   Section 6.1

7.   A one-to-one relationship can be processed:
    a.   from the parent to the child only
    b.   from the child to the parent only
    c.   in both directions
    d.   depends on whether the parent key is placed in the child relation
    e.   depends on whether the child key is placed in the parent relation
    Answer: c   **Reference:**   Section 6.1

8.   Many-to-many relationships are represented by:
    a.   two relations with an M:N relationship
    b.   two relations with a 1:N relationship
    c.   by an intersection relation which has M:N relationships with the two relations
    d.   by an intersection relation which has 1:N relationships with the two relations
    e.   by two intersection relations which each have 1:N relationships with the two relations
    Answer: d   **Reference:**   Section 6.1

9.   Recursive relationships can be:
    a.   1:1 only
    b.   1:N only
    c.   M:N only
    d.   any of the above depending on the application
    e.   none of the above
    Answer: d   **Reference:**   Section 6.1

10.   In a recursive relationship:
    a.   the parent rows reside in the parent relation
    b.   the child rows reside in the child relation
    c.   both of the above
    d.   the parent rows and the child rows reside in the same relation
    e.   the parent rows and the child rows reside in the intersection relation

    Answer: d   **Reference:**   Section 6.1

11.   A relationship between two instances of the same type is called a _____ relationship.
    a.   binary
    b.   reclusive
    c.   recursive
    d.   ternary
    e.   weak
    Answer: c   **Reference:**   Section 6.1

12.   A relationship between two entities of different logical types is called a_____ relationship.
        a.   binary
        b.   reclusive
        c.   recursive
        d.   ternary
        e.   weak
        Answer: a   **Reference:**   Section 6.1

13.   A relationship among three entities of different logical types is called a_____ relationship.
        a.   binary
        b.   reclusive
        c.   recursive
        d.   ternary
        e.   weak
        Answer: d   **Reference:**   Section 6.1

14.   A supertype-subtype relationship is known as a(n) _____ relationship.
        a.   binary
        b.   HAS-A
        c.   IS-A
        d.   recursive
        e.   weak
        Answer: c   **Reference:**   Section 6.1

15.   In a supertype-subtype structure, the relationship between a row in the supertype and a row in one of the subtypes is:
        a.   1:1
        b.   1:N
        c.   N:1
        d.   M:N
        e.   N:N
        Answer: a   **Reference:**   Section 6.1

16.   A tree is a data structure in which the elements of the structure have _____ relationship(s).
        a.   only 1:1
        b.   only 1:N
        c.   only N:1
        d.   at least one M:N
        e.   only M:N
        Answer: b   **Reference:**   Section 6.3

17.   The element at the top of the tree is called the:
        a.   branch
        b.   child
        c.   node
        d.   parent
        e.   root
        Answer: e   **Reference:**   Section 6.3

18.   Nodes having the same parent are called:
    a.   children
    b.   twins
    c.   elements
    d.   branches
    e.   leaves
    Answer: b   **Reference:**   Section 6.3

19.   In a simple network the child elements may:
    a.   have more than one parent
    b.   have more than one parent so long as the parents are of the same type
    c.   have more than one parent so long as the parents are of different types
    d.   not have a parent at all
    e.   be directly connected by a branch
    Answer: c   **Reference:**   Section 6.3

20.   In a complex network, at least one of the relationships is:
    a.   1:1
    b.   1:N
    c.   N:1
    d.   N:N
    e.   M:N
    Answer: e   **Reference:**   Section 6.3

21.   The unique feature of a *bill of materials* data structure is that it generally contains _____ relationships.
    a.   binary
    b.   reclusive
    c.   recursive
    d.   ternary
    e.   weak
    Answer: c   **Reference:**   Section 6.3

FILL IN THE BLANKS

1.   In the E-R model, things that users want to keep track of are called __entities__ .

    Reference: Section 6.1

2.   In the E-R model, entities are related by explicitly defined __relationships__ .

    Reference: Section 6.1

3.   The attribute that identifies an entity becomes the __key__ of the relation.

    Reference: Section 6.1

4.   In many cases the database design can be improved by normalizing the relations into
      __Domain-Key__ normal form.

      Reference: Section 6.1

5.   A(n) __weak__ entity depends for its existence on another entity.

      Reference: Section 6.1

6.   When creating a relation for a(n) __ID-dependent__ entity, we must ensure that the key of both the
      parent and the key of the entity itself appear in the relation.

      Reference: Section 6.1

7.   A relationship among entities of different logical types is called a(n) __HAS-A__ relationship.

      Reference: Section 6.1

8.   When the key of one relation is stored in a second relation, it is called a(n) __foreign__ key.

      Reference: Section 6.1

9.   A relationship between two entities of different logical types is called a __binary__ relationship.

      Reference: Section 6.1

10.   When two relations have the same __key__ they should generally be combined into a single
      relation.

      Reference: Section 6.1

11.   In 1:N relationships, the __parent__ relation is on the *one* side of the relationship.

      Reference: Section 6.1

12.   In 1:N relationships, the __child__ relation is on the *many* side of the relationship.

      Reference: Section 6.1

13.   A __data structure__ diagram is another technique for showing relations and relationships.

      Reference: Section 6.1

14.   In a 1:N relationship, the __key__ of the parent relation must be placed in the child relation.

      Reference: Section 6.1

15.   When representing a many-to-many relationship, an __intersection__ relation must be created.

Reference: Section 6.1

16.   A recursive relationship is a relationship among entities of the same __class/type__ .

Reference: Section 6.1

17.   In a recursive relationship, both the parent and child rows reside in the same __relation.__

Reference: Section 6.1

18.   A relationship among three entities of different logical types is called a __ternary__ relationship.

Reference: Section 6.1

19.   The key of subtypes is generally the key of the __supertype__ .

Reference: Section 6.1

20.   A(n) __tree/hierarchy__ is a data structure in which the elements of the structure have only one-to many relationships with one another.

Reference: Section 6.3

21.   Each element in a tree is called a(n) __node__ .

Reference: Section 6.3

22.   Relationships among elements in a tree are called __branches__ .

Reference: Section 6.3

23.   The element at the top of the tree is called the __root__ .

Reference: Section 6.3

24.   Every node of a tree, except the root, has a(n) __parent__ .

Reference: Section 6.3

25.   The descendants of a node are called __children__ .

Reference: Section 6.3

26.   Nodes having the same parent are called __twins/siblings__ .

Reference: Section 6.3

27.   A(n) __simple network__ is a data structure having only 1:N relationships, but permitting elements to have more than one parent, as long as the parents are of different types.

   Reference: Section 6.3

28.   A(n) __complex network__ is a data structure having at least one many-to-many relationship.

   Reference: Section 6.3

29.   A complex network can only be implemented using a(n) __intersection__ relation.

   Reference: Section 6.3

30.   A(n) __bill of materials__ is a data structure frequently occurring in manufacturing applications, and is commonly described as a network with recursive M:N relationships.

   Reference: Section 6.3

ESSAY

1.   Describe how weak entities are represented in a relational database design.

2.   Give the definition of a *foreign key* and describe how it is used.

3.   Describe how *recursive relationships* are represented in a relational database design.

4.   Describe how *ternary relationships* are represented in a relational database design.

5.   Describe the role of normalization in representing entities with the relational model.

CHAPTER 7 TEST QUESTIONS

TRUE-FALSE QUESTIONS

F   1. A simple object has no multivalued attributes but may have object attributes.
   Reference: Section 7.1

T   2. A simple object can be represented by a single relation.
   Reference: Section 7.1

T   3. The attributes of the relation are the attributes of the object.
   Reference: Section 7.1

T   4. A composite object has one or more multivalued attributes but no object attributes.
   Reference: Section 7.1

F   5. A composite object can be represented by a single relation.
   Reference: Section 7.1

T   6. Composite objects are transformed by defining one relation for the object itself and another relation for each multivalued attribute.
   Reference: Section 7.1

F   7. The key of each relation created for a multivalued group is the identifier of the object.
   Reference: Section 7.1

T   8. The key of a relation created for a nested group is the composite of the key of the containing group and the identifier of the nested group.
   Reference: Section 7.1

T   9. A compound object contains one or more object attributes.
   Reference: Section 7.1

T 10. One-to-one compound objects are represented by two relations.
   Reference: Section 7.1

F 11. 1:N and N:1 compound objects are represented by N relations.
   Reference: Section 7.1

F 12. M:N compound objects are represented by a number of relations equal to the greater of M or N.
   Reference: Section 7.1

T 13. An intersection relation formed to represent compound objects never contains non-key data.
   Reference: Section 7.1

F 14. Hybrid objects are transformed into relational designs using the same techniques as for compound objects.
   Reference: Section 7.1

F 15. The relation created to represent an association object always has a composite key consisting of the keys of the parents.
   Reference: Section 7.1

F 16. An association relation is also called an intersection relation.
    Reference: Section 7.1

T 17. For parent/subtype objects, one relation is created for the parent and one for each of the subtypes.
    Reference: Section 7.1

T 18. The performance of relations created for parent/subtype objects can be improved by the use of one or more type indicator attributes in the parent relation.
    Reference: Section 7.1

T 19. Archetype/version objects are represented by two relations.
    Reference: Section 7.1

T 20. In the child relation formed for a version, the key of the archetype object is both a local and a foreign key.
    Reference: Section 7.1

MULTIPLE CHOICE QUESTIONS

1. A simple object can be represented by a(n):
    a.   single relation
    b.   intersection relation
    c.   relation for the base object and another for the repeating group attribute
    d.   association relation
    e.   multivalued relation
    Answer: a   **Reference:**   Section 7.1

2. A composite object can be represented by a(n):
    a.   single relation
    b.   intersection relation
    c.   relation for the base object and another for the repeating group attribute
    d.   association relation
    e.   multivalued relation
    Answer: c   **Reference:**   Section 7.1

3. The key of a relation created to represent a repeating group must contain:
    a.   the identifier of the object
    b.   the identifier of the group
    c.   the identifier of the object and the identifier of the group
    d.   the identifier of the intersection relation
    e.   the identifier of the association relation
    Answer: c   **Reference:**   Section 7.1

4.   When an object contains nested groups:
   a.   the relation representing the containing group is the supertype of the relation that represents the nested group
   b.   the relation representing the nested group is the supertype of the relation that represents the containing group
   c.   the relation representing the containing group is made subordinate to the relation that represents the nested group
   d.   the relation representing the nested group is made subordinate to the relation that represents its containing group
   e.   the relation representing the containing group is on the same level as the relation that represents the nested group

   Answer: d   **Reference:**   Section 7.1

5.   For a 1:1 relationship between two objects, we place:
   a.   the key of the first relation into the second as a foreign key
   b.   the key of the second relation into the first as a foreign key
   c.   the key of either relation into the other as a foreign key
   d.   the key of either relation into the other as a part of the primary key
   e.   the key of both relations into the other as a part of both primary keys

   Answer: c   **Reference:**   Section 7.1

6.   For a 1:N relationship between two objects, we place:
   a.   the key of the first relation into the second as a foreign key
   b.   the key of the second relation into the first as a foreign key
   c.   the key of either relation into the other as a foreign key
   d.   the key of either relation into the other as a part of the primary key
   e.   the key of both relations into the other as a part of both primary keys

   Answer: a   **Reference:**   Section 7.1

7.   For an M:N relationship between two objects, we place:
   a.   the key of the first relation into the second as a foreign key
   b.   the key of the second relation into the first as a foreign key
   c.   the key of either relation into the other as a foreign key
   d.   the key of either relation into the intersection relation as a part of the primary key
   e.   the key of both relations into the intersection relation as a part of the primary key

   Answer: e   **Reference:**   Section 7.1

8.   For an association relationship between two objects, we place:
   a.   the key of the first relation into the second as a foreign key
   b.   the key of the second relation into the first as a foreign key
   c.   the key of either relation into the other as a foreign key
   d.   the key of either relation into the association relation as a part of the primary key
   e.   the key of both relations into the association relation as a foreign key

   Answer: e   **Reference:**   Section 7.1

9. The difference between an association relation and an intersection relation is that:
    a. the association relation does not have any non-key attributes and the intersection relation does
    b. the intersection relation does not have any non-key attributes and the association relation does
    c. the association relation cannot have a unique key and the intersection relation can
    d. the intersection relation cannot have a unique key and the association relation can
    e. the association relation can relate more than two objects and the intersection relation cannot

    Answer: b   **Reference:**   Section 7.1

10. The performance of parent/subtype relationships can be improved by:
    a. combining the relations
    b. creating an intersection relation
    c. creating an association relation
    d. adding a type indicator attribute to the parent relation
    e. adding a type indicator attribute to the subtype relation

    Answer: d   **Reference:**   Section 7.1

FILL IN THE BLANKS

1. A(n) _simple_ object is transformed into a single relation.

    Reference: Section 7.1

2. A composite object contains one or more _multivalued_ attributes.

    Reference: Section 7.1

3. The key of a relation representing a group of multivalued attributes is a composite of the
    identifier of the object/parent plus the identifier of the group.

    Reference: Section 7.1

4. 1:1 compound objects are represented by how many relations? (_two_)

    Reference: Section 7.1

5. 1:N compound objects are represented by how many relations? (_two_)

    Reference: Section 7.1

6. M:N compound objects are represented by how many relations? (_three_)

    Reference: Section 7.1

7. A(n) _intersection_ relation represents the relationship of two objects.

    Reference: Section 7.1

8.   A(n) __hybrid__ object is a combination of the basic types of objects.

      Reference: Section 7.1

9.   A(n) __association__ relation differs from an intersection relation in that it contains non-key attributes.

      Reference: Section 7.1

10.   The performance of relations resulting from the representation of parent/subtype objects may be improved by including an additional attribute called a __type indicator__ in the parent relation.

      Reference: Section 7.1

11.   Archetype/version objects are represented by how many relations? (__two__)

      Reference: Section 7.1

12.   A __surrogate__ key is created by the DBMS or the developers, has no semantic meaning, and is hidden from the users.

      Reference: Section 7.1

ESSAY

1.   Describe how a simple object is transformed into a relational design.

2.   Discuss how an attribute of a relation can be both a local and a foreign key.

3.   Describe how a hybrid object is transformed into a relational design.

4.   Describe how parent and subtype objects are transformed into a relational design.

5.   Describe how performance can be improved when parent and subtype objects are transformed into a relational design and the subtypes are mutually exclusive.

CHAPTER 8 TEST QUESTIONS

TRUE-FALSE QUESTIONS

F 1. Multiple values are allowed in some relations.
      Reference: 8.1

T 2. All the entries in any column are of the same kind.
      Reference: 8.1

T 3. Each attribute has a *domain*, which is a physical and logical description of allowed values.
      Reference: 8.1

F 4. Duplicate rows are permitted in some relations.
      Reference: 8.1

T 5. A *logical key* is a unique identifier.
      Reference: 8.1

F 6. A *physical key* is the implementation of a logical key.
      Reference: 8.1

T 7. Sorting rows is facilitated by defining an index for the ordering attribute.
      Reference: 8.1

F 8. Accessing a row quickly is facilitated by sorting the rows.
      Reference: 8.1

T 9. An index can be used to prohibit duplicate values for an attribute in more than one row.
      Reference: 8.1

F 10. A database designed using the relational model can be directly implemented on any DBMS product.
      Reference: 8.1

T 11. The structure of a database is generally defined graphically on personal computer DBMS products.
      Reference: 8.1

F 12. All DBMS products allocate physical media storage space automatically.
      Reference: 8.1

T 13. The best case for creating the database data is for all of the data to already be in a format that the DBMS can import from.
      Reference: 8.1

T 14. *Relational algebra* requires the user to know what is wanted but also how to get it.
      Reference: 8.2

T 15. *Relational calculus* does not require the user to know how to get the desired results.
      Reference: 8.2

F 16. *Transform-oriented languages* require the user to know how to get the desired results.
Reference: 8.2

F 17. *Query-By-Example* and *Query-By-Form* are examples of transform-oriented languages.
Reference: 8.2

T 18. A form is a common type of interface to a database.
Reference: 8.2

T 19. A *query language* generally selects rows from a relation based on criteria supplied by the user.
Reference: 8.2

F 20. A database cannot be accessed from traditional file-processing programming languages.
Reference: 8.2

T 21. In relational algebra, the variables are relations.
Reference: 8.3

F 22. Any two relations can be combined using the *union* operator.
Reference: 8.3

F 23. The *difference* of two relations is a third relation containing tuples that occur in the second relation but not in the first.
Reference: 8.3

T 24. The *intersection* of two relations is a third relation containing the tuples that appear in both the first and second relations.
Reference: 8.3

T 25. The *product* of two relations is the concatenation of every tuple of one relation with every tuple of the second relation.
Reference: 8.3

F 26. *Projection* is an operation that selects specified rows from a relation.
Reference: 8.3

F 27. *Selection* is an operation that selects specified rows from a relation.
Reference: 8.3

T 28. The *join* operation is a combination of the product, selection, and optionally the projection operations.
Reference: 8.3

T 29. The number of columns resulting from an *equijoin* is greater than the number of columns resulting from a *natural join*.
Reference: 8.3

T 30. The attributes in the condition of a join must have the same domain.
Reference: 8.3

MULTIPLE CHOICE QUESTIONS

1.   The intersection of a row and a column in a relation can contain:
        a.   only one value
        b.   multiple values depending on the attribute type
        c.   multiple values regardless of the attribute type
        d.   multiple values depending on the cardinality
        e.   multiple values regardless of the cardinality
        Answer: a   **Reference:**   8.1

2.   The domain of an attribute includes:
        a.   only the description of physical values allowed
        b.   only the description of logical values allowed
        c.   the description of physical and logical values allowed
        d.   the description of its functional dependencies
        e.   the description of its index
        Answer: c   **Reference:**   8.1

3.   The relation structure plus the allowable constraints on data values is called the:
        a.   data definition language
        b.   data manipulation language
        c.   transform-oriented language
        d.   relational schema
        e.   domain
        Answer: d   **Reference:**   8.1

4.   A group of one or more attributes that uniquely identifies a tuple in a relation is called a(n):
        a.   logical key
        b.   physical key
        c.   functional dependency
        d.   relational schema
        e.   domain
        Answer: a   **Reference:**   8.1

5.   A group of one or more attributes that is supported by a data structure that facilitates fast retrieval
        or rapid sequential access is called a(n):
        a.   logical key
        b.   physical key
        c.   functional dependency
        d.   relational schema
        e.   domain
        Answer: b   **Reference:**   8.1

6.   Which of the following reflects the relationships between a logical key and a physical key?
        a.   A logical key cannot be a physical key.
        b.   A physical key cannot be a logical key.
        c.   A logical key cannot be a physical key but a physical key can be a logical key.
        d.   A logical key can be a physical key, but a physical key cannot be a logical key.
        e.   A logical key can be a physical key, and a physical key can be a logical key.
        Answer: e   **Reference:**   8.1

7.   An index is another name for a(n):
    a.   logical key
    b.   physical key
    c.   functional dependency
    d.   relational schema
    e.   domain
    Answer: b   **Reference:**   8.1

8.   An index:
    a.   must be unique
    b.   cannot be unique
    c.   may be unique, as specified by the developers
    d.   may be unique, as determined by the DBMS
    e.   may be unique, depending on the domain
    Answer: c   **Reference:**   8.1

9.   When a relational design is to be implemented using a relational DBMS:
    a.   the design must first be converted into a semantic object model design
    b.   the design must first be converted into a CODASYL DBTG model design
    c.   the design must first be converted into relational algebra
    d.   the design must first be converted into a transform-oriented language
    e.   the design can be directly defined to the DBMS without being converted
    Answer: e   **Reference:**   8.1

10.   Graphical design tools are commonly used to describe the structure of the database to DBMS products on:
    a.   mainframes
    b.   servers
    c.   personal computers
    d.   all computers
    e.   none of the above
    Answer: c   **Reference:**   8.1

11.   A text file used to describe the structure of the database to the DBMS is written using:
    a.   data definition language
    b.   data manipulation language
    c.   transform-oriented language
    d.   relational algebra
    e.   relational calculus
    Answer: a   **Reference:**   8.1

12.   When allocating media space for a database on a server or mainframe:
    a.   all tables should be stored on the same disk
    b.   each table should be stored on a different disk
    c.   the developer must determine the best place to locate the data
    d.   the DBMS determines the best place to locate the data
    e.   the user determines the best place to locate the data
    Answer: c   **Reference:**   8.1

13.   The easiest way to create the database data is to:
     a.   manually key in the data from original source documents
     b.   manually key in the data from printouts of the data in traditional computer files
     c.   scan the data from original source documents
     d.   scan the data from printouts of the data in traditional files
     e.   import the data from traditional computer files
Answer: e   **Reference:**   8.1

14.   A *procedural* language:
     a.   requires you to know what you want but not how to do it
     b.   requires you to know what you want and how to do it
     c.   requires you to be able to express what you want graphically using a form
     d.   requires you to be able to express what you want graphically using a spreadsheet
     e.   requires you to be able to express what you want using a query
Answer: b   **Reference:**   8.2

15.   _____ is a procedural data manipulation language that uses operators that work on relations.
     a.   A transform-oriented language
     b.   Query-By-Example
     c.   Query-By-Form
     d.   Relational algebra
     e.   Relational calculus
Answer: d   **Reference:**   8.2

16.   _____ is a nonprocedural data manipulation language that uses relations as input and produces a single relation as the result.
     a.   A transform-oriented language
     b.   Query-By-Example
     c.   Query-By-Form
     d.   Relational algebra
     e.   Relational calculus
Answer: a   **Reference:**   8.2

17.   _____ is a nonprocedural data manipulation language that is used largely for theoretical rather than practical purposes.
     a.   A transform-oriented language
     b.   Query-By-Example
     c.   Query-By-Form
     d.   Relational algebra
     e.   Relational calculus
Answer: e   **Reference:**   8.2

18.   The single most important query language is:
     a.   Query-By-Example
     b.   Query-By-Form
     c.   Relational algebra
     d.   Relational calculus
     e.   SQL
Answer: e   **Reference:**   8.2

19.   A common data manipulation language interface that lets the user see multiple rows at a time or shows each row as an independent entity is a(n):
   a.   application program interface
   b.   form
   c.   precompiler
   d.   query language
   e.   stored program interface
   Answer: b   **Reference:**   8.2

20.   A common data manipulation language interface that lets the user enter commands that specify the desired actions is a(n):
   a.   application program interface
   b.   form
   c.   precompiler
   d.   query language
   e.   stored program interface
   Answer: d   **Reference:**   8.2

21.   A common data manipulation language interface that lets the user execute stored procedures written by a specialist is a(n):
   a.   application program interface
   b.   form
   c.   precompiler
   d.   query language
   e.   stored program interface
   Answer: e   **Reference:**   8.2

22.   A common data manipulation language interface that lets traditional file-processing programs access the database is a(n):
   a.   application program interface
   b.   form
   c.   precompiler
   d.   query language
   e.   stored program interface
   Answer: a   **Reference:**   8.2

23.   Relational algebra is said to be _____ , meaning that the results of one or more relational operations are always a relation.
   a.   procedural
   b.   nonprocedural
   c.   closed
   d.   open
   e.   transform-oriented
   Answer: c   **Reference:**   8.3

24.   The _____ of two relations is formed by adding the tuples from one relation to those of the
        second relation to produce a third relation.
        a.   difference
        b.   intersection
        c.   join
        d.   product
        e.   union
        Answer: e   **Reference:**   8.3

25.   The _____ of two relations is a third relation containing tuples that occur in the first
        relation but not in the second.
        a.   difference
        b.   intersection
        c.   join
        d.   product
        e.   union
        Answer: a   **Reference:**   8.3

26.   The _____ of two relations is a third relation containing the tuples that appear in both
        the first and second relations.
        a.   difference
        b.   intersection
        c.   join
        d.   product
        e.   union

        Answer: b   **Reference:**   8.3

27.   The _____ is the concatenation of every tuple of one relation with every tuple of a
        second relation.
        a.   difference
        b.   intersection
        c.   join
        d.   product
        e.   union
        Answer: d   **Reference:**   8.3

28.   The _____ operation is a combination of the product, selection, and (possibly) projection
        operations.
        a.   difference
        b.   intersection
        c.   join
        d.   product
        e.   union
        Answer: c   **Reference:**   8.3

29.   _____ is an operation that selects specified attributes from a relation and places them into the result relation.
    a.   Difference
    b.   Intersection
    c.   Join
    d.   Product
    e.   Union
Answer: d   **Reference:**   8.3

30.   The _____ operator takes tuples meeting specified criteria and places them into the result relation.
    a.   difference
    b.   intersection
    c.   product
    d.   projection
    e.   selection
Answer: e   **Reference:**   8.3

FILL IN THE BLANKS

1.   A two-dimensional table is known as a(n) __relation__ .

    Reference: 8.1

2.   The physical and logical description of allowed values is called the __domain__ .

    Reference: 8.1

3.   The columns of a relation are called __attributes__ .

    Reference: 8.1

4.   The relation structure plus constraints is called the __relational schema__ .

    Reference: 8.1

5.   A(n) __(logical) key__ is a group of one or more attributes that uniquely identifies a tuple in a relation.

    Reference: 8.1

6.   A physical key is also called a(n) __index__ .

    Reference: 8.1

7.   A row in a relation is called a(n) __tuple__ .

    Reference: 8.1

8.   The language used to describe the structure of a database is called data definition language
      (DDL) .

      Reference: 8.1

9.   DBMS products on personal computers generally use graphical means to define the structure
      of the database.

      Reference: 8.1

10.   Relational algebra defines operators that work on relations.

      Reference: 8.2

11.   Relational calculus is a second type of relational data manipulation, used largely for
       theoretical rather than practical purposes.

      Reference: 8.2

12.   Transform-oriented languages are a class of languages that transform input data expressed as
       relations into results expressed as a single relation.

      Reference: 8.2

13.   Procedural data manipulation techniques require you to know not only what you want
       but also how to get it.

      Reference: 8.2

14.   Instructions for processing relations are expressed in terms of a(n) data manipulation language .

      Reference: 8.2

15.   Query-By-Example and Query-By-Form provide a graphical interface for the user to
       provide processing instructions to the DBMS.

      Reference: 8.2

16.   A form is a common type of data manipulation interface for the user.

      Reference: 8.2

17.   SQL is the single most important query language.

      Reference: 8.2

18.   End users often ask database specialists to write queries and save them as stored procedures
      that the users can execute.

      Reference: 8.2

19.   Most DBMSs provide some form of __application program interface__ which enables traditional file-processing programs to access the database.

Reference: 8.2

20.   Relational algebra is said to be __closed__, meaning that the results of one or more relational operations are always a relation.

Reference: 8.3

21.   The __union__ of two relations is formed by adding the tuples from one relation to those of the second relation to produce a third relation.

Reference: 8.3

22.   Two relations that do not have the same attributes are said to be __union incompatible__ .

Reference: 8.3

23.   The __difference__ of two relations is a third relation containing tuples that occur in the first relation but not in the second.

Reference: 8.3

24.   The __intersection__ of two relations is a third relation containing the tuples that appear in both the first and second relations.

Reference: 8.3

25.   The __(Cartesian) product__ is the concatenation of every tuple of one relation with every tuple of a second relation.

Reference: 8.3

26.   __Projection__ is an operation that selects specified attributes from a relation and places them into the result relation.

Reference: 8.3

27.   The __selection__ operator takes tuples meeting specified criteria and places them into the result relation.

Reference: 8.3

28.   The __join__ operation is a combination of the product, selection, and (possibly) projection operations.

Reference: 8.3

29.   With the __equijoin__ operation, the result contains all of the attributes in the condition.

Reference: 8.3

30.   With the   natural join   operation, the result contains no duplicate attributes from the condition.

Reference: 8.3

ESSAY

1.   Discuss the differences between a *logical* key and a *physical* key.

2.   Describe the four categories of relational data manipulation language.

3.   Discuss potential strategies for allocating media space so as to improve performance.

4.   Describe the two types of *outer join* operations.

5.   Explain why the intersection operation is commutative while the difference operation is not.

CHAPTER 9 TEST QUESTIONS

TRUE-FALSE QUESTIONS

F   1. SQL stands for *Standard Query Language*.
    Reference: Section 9.0

T   2. SQL has become the standard language for information exchange among computers.
    Reference: Section 9.0

T   3. The American National Standards Institute (ANSI) maintains the standards for SQL.
    Reference: Section 9.0

F   4. SQL commands can only be used interactively.
    Reference: Section 9.0

T   5. SQL is a transform-oriented language.
    Reference: Section 9.0

F   6. SQL is not considered a *closed* language.
    Reference: Section 9.0

F   7. SQL can only query a single table.
    Reference: Section 9.1

F   8. The SQL language is case sensitive.
    Reference: Section 9.1

T   9. The keyword *SELECT* is used to specify the columns to be obtained.
    Reference: Section 9.1

F   10. The SQL verb *SELECT* performs the same operation as the relational algebra operator *selection*.
    Reference: Section 9.1

T   11. The keyword *FROM* is used to specify the table to be used.
    Reference: Section 9.1

T   12. The result of an SQL *SELECT* operation can contain duplicate rows.
    Reference: Section 9.1

T   13. An asterisk (*) following the *SELECT* verb means that all columns are to be obtained.
    Reference: Section 9.1

T   14. The SQL phrase *WHERE* performs the same operation as the relational algebra operator *selection*.
    Reference: Section 9.1

F   15. The *WHERE* clause contains the condition that specifies which columns are to be selected.
    Reference: Section 9.1

F   16. A *WHERE* clause can contain only one condition.
    Reference: Section 9.1

T 17. The rows of the result relation can be sorted by the values in one or more columns.
Reference: Section 9.1

F 18. Sorting is specified by the use of the *SORT BY* phrase.
Reference: Section 9.1

T 19. The clause *SELECT COUNT(*)* results in a table with a single row and a single column.
Reference: Section 9.1

F 20. The built-in function *SUM* can be used with any column.
Reference: Section 9.1

T 21. The SQL keyword *GROUP BY* instructs the DBMS to group together those rows that have the same value of a column.
Reference: Section 9.1

F 22. The *GROUP BY* phrase always returns all of the groups in the table.
Reference: Section 9.1

F 23. If two tables use the same name for a column, the DBMS will be confused and not know which table's column is being referred to.
Reference: Section 9.2

T 24. A *WHERE* clause can contain a subquery.
Reference: Section 9.2

T 25. Two or more tables can be joined by giving the table names in the *FROM* clause and specifying the equality of the respective column names as the condition in the *WHERE* clause.
Reference: Section 9.2

F 26. Every subquery can be alternatively expressed by a join.
Reference: Section 9.2

T 27. *EXISTS* and *NOT EXISTS* are logical operators whose value is either true or false depending on the presence or absence of rows that fit the qualifying conditions.
Reference: Section 9.3

F 28. The *INSERT* clause can only be used to insert a single row into a table.
Reference: Section 9.4

T 29. Using the *DELETE* clause to delete a row from one table can cause an integrity problem in another table.
Reference: Section 9.4

F 30. The keyword *MODIFY* is used to change a column value.
Reference: Section 9.4

MULTIPLE CHOICE QUESTIONS

1.   The *SELECT* verb accomplishes the _____ operation.
        a.   join
        b.   product
        c.   projection
        d.   selection
        e.   union
        Answer: c   **Reference:**   Section 9.1

2.   Which keyword must be used to remove duplicate rows?
        a.   DELETE
        b.   DISTINCT
        c.   NOT EXISTS
        d.   SET
        e.   UPDATE
        Answer: b   **Reference:**   Section 9.1

3.   Which keyword is used to state the condition that specifies which rows are to be selected?
        a.   EXISTS
        b.   FROM
        c.   SELECT
        d.   SET
        e.   WHERE
        Answer: e   **Reference:**   Section 9.1

4.   Which keyword is used to specify the table(s) to be used?
        a.   EXISTS
        b.   FROM
        c.   SELECT
        d.   SET
        e.   WHERE
        Answer: b   **Reference:**   Section 9.1

5.   Which keyword is used to separate two conditions when both must be true for the rows to be selected?
        a.   AND
        b.   EXISTS
        c.   HAVING
        d.   IN
        e.   OR
        Answer: a   **Reference:**   Section 9.1

6.   Which keyword is used to determine if a column value is equal to any one of several values?
        a.   AND
        b.   EXISTS
        c.   HAVING
        d.   IN
        e.   OR
        Answer: d   **Reference:**   Section 9.1

7.   Which keyword is used to sort the result relation by the values in one or more columns?
    a.   GROUP BY
    b.   ORDER BY
    c.   SELECT
    d.   SORT BY
    e.   WHERE
Answer: b   **Reference:**   Section 9.1

8.   Which built-in function is used to compute the number of rows in a table?
    a.   AVG
    b.   COUNT
    c.   MAX
    d.   MIN
    e.   SUM
Answer: b   **Reference:**   Section 9.1

9.   Which built-in function is used to total numeric columns?
    a.   AVG
    b.   COUNT
    c.   MAX
    d.   MIN
    e.   SUM
Answer: e   **Reference:**   Section 9.1

10.   Which built-in function is used to compute the average value of numeric columns?
    a.   AVG
    b.   COUNT
    c.   MAX
    d.   MIN
    e.   SUM
Answer: a   **Reference:**   Section 9.1

11.   Which built-in function is used to obtain the largest value of numeric columns?
    a.   AVG
    b.   COUNT
    c.   MAX
    d.   MIN
    e.   SUM
Answer: c   **Reference:**   Section 9.1

12.   Which built-in function is used to obtain the smallest value of numeric columns?
    a.   AVG
    b.   COUNT
    c.   MAX
    d.   MIN
    e.   SUM
Answer: d   **Reference:**   Section 9.1

13.   Which keyword is used to collect those rows that have the same value of a specified column?
   a.   GROUP BY
   b.   ORDER BY
   c.   SELECT
   d.   SORT BY
   e.   WHERE
   Answer: a   **Reference:**   Section 9.1

14.   Which keyword is used to select those groups meeting specified criteria?
   a.   AND
   b.   EXISTS
   c.   HAVING
   d.   IN
   e.   OR
   Answer: c   **Reference:**   Section 9.1

15.   Which keyword is used to implement a subquery?
   a.   GROUP BY
   b.   HAVING
   c.   ORDER BY
   d.   SELECT
   e.   SORT BY
   Answer: d   **Reference:**   Section 9.2

16.   Which keyword is used to specify the names of tables to be joined?
   a.   FROM
   b.   HAVING
   c.   JOIN
   d.   SELECT
   e.   WHERE
   Answer: a   **Reference:**   Section 9.2

17.   Which keyword is used to specify the condition(s) for a join operation?
   a.   FROM
   b.   HAVING
   c.   JOIN
   d.   SELECT
   e.   WHERE
   Answer: e   **Reference:**   Section 9.2

18.   Regarding the interchangeability of subqueries and joins:
   a.   A join can always be used as an alternative to a subquery, and a subquery can always be used as an alternative to a join.
   b.   A join can sometimes be used as an alternative to a subquery, and a subquery can sometimes be used as an alternative to a join.
   c.   A join can always be used as an alternative to a subquery, and a subquery can sometimes be used as an alternative to a join.
   d.   A join can sometimes be used as an alternative to a subquery, and a subquery can always be used as an alternative to a join.
   e.   A join can never be used as an alternative to a subquery, and a subquery can never be used as an alternative to a join.
   Answer: b   **Reference:**   Section 9.2

19.   Which keyword is a logical operator whose value is either true or false depending on the presence or absence of rows that meet the qualifying conditions.
a.   AND
b.   EXISTS
c.   HAVING
d.   IN
e.   OR
Answer: b   **Reference:**   Section 9.3

20.   Rows in the same table can be compared to each other by:
a.   joining the table to itself
b.   sorting the table on the column to be compared
c.   grouping the table on the column to be compared
d.   assigning two different names to the table
e.   removing duplicate rows
Answer: d   **Reference:**   Section 9.3

21.   Which keyword is used to add one or more rows to a table?
a.   DELETE
b.   INSERT
c.   SELECT
d.   SET
e.   UPDATE
Answer: b   **Reference:**   Section 9.4

22.   Which keyword is used to remove one or more rows from a table?
a.   DELETE
b.   INSERT
c.   SELECT
d.   SET
e.   UPDATE
Answer: a   **Reference:**   Section 9.4

23.   Which keyword is used to change one or more rows in a table?
a.   DELETE
b.   INSERT
c.   SELECT
d.   SET
e.   UPDATE
Answer: e   **Reference:**   Section 9.4

24.   Which keyword is used to change a column value?
a.   DELETE
b.   INSERT
c.   SELECT
d.   SET
e.   UPDATE
Answer: d   **Reference:**   Section 9.4

25.   When a row is added to a table but the value for a column is not known, the DBMS places a(n)
_____ value for the column in the new row.
   a.   blank
   b.   null
   c.   previous
   d.   unknown
   e.   zero
   Answer: b   **Reference:**   Section 9.4

FILL IN THE BLANKS

1.   SQL stands for ___Structured Query Language___ .

   Reference: Section 9.0

2.   The ___American National Standards Institute (ANSI)___ maintains the standards for SQL.

   Reference: Section 9.0

3.   The keyword ___SELECT___ is used to specify the columns to be obtained.

   Reference: Section 9.1

4.   The keyword ___FROM___ is used to specify the table(s) to be used.

   Reference: Section 9.1

5.   To obtain all columns, use a(n) ___asterisk (*)___ instead of listing all the column names.

   Reference: Section 9.1

6.   To remove duplicate rows from the result of a query, specify the qualifier ___DISTINCT___ .

   Reference: Section 9.1

7.   The ___WHERE___ clause contains the condition that specifies which rows are to be selected.

   Reference: Section 9.1

8.   When two conditions must both be true for the rows to be selected, the conditions are separated
by the keyword ___AND___ .

   Reference: Section 9.1

9.   To refer to a set of values in a condition, the values are placed inside ___square brackets [ ]___ and
separated by commas.

   Reference: Section 9.1

10. Multiple values in a set have the same effect as using the __OR__ logical operator.

   Reference: Section 9.1

11. To exclude one or more values in a condition, the keyword __NOT__ must be used.

   Reference: Section 9.1

12. To sort the rows of the result relation, the __ORDER BY__ clause is specified.

   Reference: Section 9.1

13. Columns to be sorted can be declared to be in the opposite of ascending sequence by using the keyword __DESC__ .

   Reference: Section 9.1

14. The built-in function __COUNT__ computes the number of rows in a table.

   Reference: Section 9.1

15. The built-in function __SUM__ totals numeric columns.

   Reference: Section 9.1

16. The built-in function __AVG__ computes the average value of numeric columns.

   Reference: Section 9.1

17. The built-in function __MAX__ obtains the largest value of numeric columns.

   Reference: Section 9.1

18. The built-in function __MIN__ obtains the smallest value of numeric columns.

   Reference: Section 9.1

19. To exclude duplicate values when computing the number of rows in a table the keyword __DISTINCT__ must be included.

   Reference: Section 9.1

20. The SQL keyword __GROUP BY__ is used to collect those rows that have the same value of a specified column.

   Reference: Section 9.1

21. A nested SELECT statement (one within another SELECT statement) is called a __subquery__ , and must be enclosed in parentheses.

   Reference: Section 9.2

22.   The names of tables to be joined are listed in the __FROM__ clause.

Reference: Section 9.2

23.   A join operation is achieved by specifying the equality of the respective column names as the condition in the __WHERE__ clause.

Reference: Section 9.2

24.   The keyword __EXISTS__ is a logical operator whose value is either true or false depending on the presence or absence of rows that fit the qualifying conditions.

Reference: Section 9.3

25.   One or more rows can be added to a table by using the __INSERT__ statement.

Reference: Section 9.4

26.   When a row is added to a table but the value for a column is not known, the DBMS places a __null__ value for the column in the new row.

Reference: Section 9.4

27.   Rows can be copied from one table to another by the use of a __SELECT__ statement to specify the rows to be copied.

Reference: Section 9.4

28.   Rows can be removed from a table by using the __DELETE__ statement.

Reference: Section 9.4

29.   Rows in a table can be changed by using the __UPDATE__ statement.

Reference: Section 9.4

30.   The keyword __SET__ is used to change a column value.

Reference: Section 9.4

ESSAY

1.   Describe how to use the *LIKE* operator in comparisons.

2.   Describe the five built-in functions available in SQL.

3.   Describe the use of the *EXISTS* and *NOT EXISTS* keywords.

4.   When a relationship exists between tables, discuss how the sequence in which *DELETE* operations are performed affects referential integrity.

5.   Describe how specified rows from one table can be copied into another table using the *INSERT* keyword.

CHAPTER 10 TEST QUESTIONS

TRUE-FALSE QUESTIONS

T 1. A fundamental purpose of a database application is to create, read, update, and delete views.
   Reference: Section 10.1

F 2. Materializing an object means adding a row to a relation.
   Reference: Section 10.1

F 3. An application view is constructed from rows in a table.
   Reference: Section 10.1

T 4. An application should provide an easy-to-use interface.
   Reference: Section 10.2

F 5. Table data can be removed using the *UPDATE* SQL statement.
   Reference: Section 10.3

T 6. When a DBMS supports cascading deletions, they are performed automatically..
   Reference: Section 10.3

T 7. Table data can be added using the *INSERT* SQL statement.
   Reference: Section 10.3

F 8. A *form* is a screen display used only to present data to the user.
   Reference: Section 10.4

T 9. The structure of a form should reflect the structure of the object that it materializes.
   Reference: Section 10.4

T 10. Data which are semantically related should be placed graphically close to one another on a form.
   Reference: Section 10.4

T 11. A drop-down list box on a form can be designed so that users cannot add data to it.
   Reference: Section 10.4

T 12. The alternatives in a group of option buttons are mutually exclusive.
   Reference: Section 10.4

F 13. The alternatives in a group of check boxes are mutually exclusive.
   Reference: Section 10.4

F 14. Special-purpose keys such as *ESC* should be allowed to have different actions on different forms.
   Reference: Section 10.4

T 15. A report may be based on a *set of objects*, rather than a single object.
   Reference: Section 10.5

T 16. The structure of a report should reflect the structure of the underlying object.
   Reference: Section 10.5

F 17. In an application with a 1:N relationship, the form for the many-side relation can be used to change data in either relation.
Reference: Section 10.6

T 18. Uniqueness constraints are best enforced by the DBMS.
Reference: Section 10.6

F 19. A row that exists inappropriately without a required parent or child is called an orphan.
Reference: Section 10.6

F 20. A parent of a Mandatory-Optional relationship can always be deleted without violating relationship constraints.
Reference: Section 10.6

T 21. A child of a Mandatory-Mandatory relationship can only be deleted if a sibling exists.
Reference: Section 10.6

F 22. A blank is an example of a *null* value.
Reference: Section 10.6

F 23. Modern DBMS products automatically enforce all constraints.
Reference: Section 10.6

T 24. A properly designed application can reduce the consequences of user errors.
Reference: Section 10.6

F 25. The semantic component of an attribute's domain can be enforced automatically by the DBMS.
Reference: Section 10.6

F 26. Most users want to see all of the data available in an object.
Reference: Section 10.7

T 27. By creating multiple views of an object, sensitive data can be hidden from unauthorized users.
Reference: Section 10.7

T 28. Vertical security can be used to limit access to specified rows..
Reference: Section 10.7

MULTIPLE CHOICE QUESTIONS

1.   A named subset of an object is called a(n):
    a.   child
    b.   materialization
    c.   subtype
    d.   table
    e.   view
    Answer: e   **Reference:**   Section 10.3

2.   A named subset of an object plus user-specified formatting is called a:
    a.   child
    b.   materialization
    c.   subtype
    d.   table
    e.   view
    Answer: b   **Reference:**   Section 10.3

3.   Which SQL statement is used to add rows to a table?
    a.   CREATE
    b.   DELETE
    c.   INSERT
    d.   SELECT
    e.   UPDATE
    Answer: c   **Reference:**   Section 10.3

4.   Which SQL statement is used to remove rows from a table?
    a.   CREATE
    b.   DELETE
    c.   INSERT
    d.   SELECT
    e.   UPDATE
    Answer: b   **Reference:**   Section 10.3

5.   Which SQL statement is used to modify rows in a table?
    a.   CREATE
    b.   DELETE
    c.   INSERT
    d.   SELECT
    e.   UPDATE
    Answer: e   **Reference:**   Section 10.3

6.   Which SQL statement is used to retrieve rows from a table?
    a.   CREATE
    b.   DELETE
    c.   INSERT
    d.   SELECT
    e.   UPDATE
    Answer: d   **Reference:**   Section 10.3

7.   The result of a SQL statement is called a:
    a.   form
    b.   query
    c.   recordset
    d.   table
    e.   view
    Answer: c   **Reference:**   Section 10.3

8.   A _____ is used for data entry and edit.
      a.   form
      b.   query
      c.   relation
      d.   report
      e.   table
      Answer: a   **Reference:**   Section 10.4

9.   The structure of a form should reflect the underlying:
      a.   objects
      b.   queries
      c.   relations
      d.   reports
      e.   tables
      Answer: a   **Reference:**   Section 10.4

10.   A GUI form feature that presents a list of items from which the user can choose is called a(n):
      a.   check box
      b.   drop-down list box
      c.   menu
      d.   option or radio button
      e.   text box
      Answer: b   **Reference:**   Section 10.4

11.   A GUI form feature that enables the user to select one alternative condition from a sequence of possibilities is called a(n):
      a.   check box
      b.   drop-down list box
      c.   menu
      d.   option or radio button
      e.   text box
      Answer: d   **Reference:**   Section 10.4

12.   A GUI form feature that enables the user to select one or more alternative conditions from a sequence of possibilities is called a(n):
      a.   check box
      b.   drop-down list box
      c.   menu
      d.   option or radio button
      e.   text box
      Answer: a   **Reference:**   Section 10.4

13.   The actions of special-purpose keys such as *ESC*:
      a.   can't be utilized
      b.   can be different on different forms in the application
      c.   can be selected by the user of the form
      d.   should be the same on all forms in the application
      e.   are determined by the DBMS
      Answer: d   **Reference:**   Section 10.4

14. The cursor should move through the form:
   a. following the pattern of the telephone conversation if data is supplied that way
   b. following the pattern of the source document if data is supplied that way
   c. following the preference of the user entering the data
   d. all of the above
   e. a and b

   Answer: b   **Reference:**   Section 10.4

15. The structure of a report should reflect the underlying:
   a. forms
   b. objects
   c. queries
   d. relations
   e. tables

   Answer: b   **Reference:**   Section 10.5

16. An *implied object* is based on:
   a. an instance of an object type
   b. an instance of more than one object type
   c. a request by a developer
   d. a request by a user
   e. the most frequently used objects

   Answer: d   **Reference:**   Section 10.5

17. The part of an attribute's domain that often can be automatically enforced by the DBMS is called the _____ component:
   a. business rule
   b. format
   c. implied
   d. physical
   e. semantic

   Answer: d   **Reference:**   Section 10.6

18. A row that exists inappropriately without a required parent or child is called a(n):
   a. fragment
   b. implied object
   c. orphan
   d. subtype
   e. supertype

   Answer: a   **Reference:**   Section 10.6

19. A child row that exists without a mandatory parent is called a(n):
   a. fragment
   b. implied object
   c. orphan
   d. subtype
   e. supertype

   Answer: c   **Reference:**   Section 10.6

20.   A(n) _____ constraint means that neither the parent or child can exist without the other.
    a.   Mandatory-Mandatory
    b.   Mandatory-Optional
    c.   Optional -Mandatory
    d.   Optional - Optional
    e.   relationship
    Answer: a   **Reference:**   Section 10.6

21.   A(n) _____ constraint means that a parent can exist without a child.
    a.   Mandatory-Mandatory
    b.   Mandatory-Optional
    c.   Optional -Mandatory
    d.   Optional - Optional
    e.   relationship
    Answer: b   **Reference:**   Section 10.6

22.   A(n) _____ constraint means that either the parent or child can exist without the other.
    a.   Mandatory-Mandatory
    b.   Mandatory-Optional
    c.   Optional -Mandatory
    d.   Optional - Optional
    e.   relationship
    Answer: d   **Reference:**   Section 10.6

23.   A(n) _____ constraint means that a child can exist without a parent.
    a.   Mandatory-Mandatory
    b.   Mandatory-Optional
    c.   Optional -Mandatory
    d.   Optional - Optional
    e.   relationship
    Answer: c   **Reference:**   Section 10.6

24.   A parent of a(n) _____ relationship can be inserted only if at least one child is created.
    a.   Mandatory-Mandatory
    b.   Mandatory-Optional
    c.   Optional -Mandatory
    d.   Optional - Optional
    e.   relationship
    Answer: a   **Reference:**   Section 10.6

25.   The key of a child of a(n) _____ relationship can be modified only if a sibling exists.
    a.   Mandatory-Mandatory
    b.   Mandatory-Optional
    c.   Optional -Mandatory
    d.   Optional - Optional
    e.   relationship
    Answer: c   **Reference:**   Section 10.6

26.   A parent of a(n) _____ relationship can be inserted only if at least one child is created or an appropriate child already exists.
   a.   Mandatory-Mandatory
   b.   Mandatory-Optional
   c.   Optional -Mandatory
   d.   Optional - Optional
   e.   relationship
   Answer: c   **Reference:**   Section 10.6

27.   The key of a parent or of a child of a(n) _____ relationship can be modified without restriction.
   a.   Mandatory-Mandatory
   b.   Mandatory-Optional
   c.   Optional -Mandatory
   d.   Optional - Optional
   e.   relationship
   Answer: d   **Reference:**   Section 10.6

28.   An attribute which does not contain a value is known as a(n):
   a.   fragment
   b.   implied object
   c.   modification anomaly
   d.   null
   e.   orphan
   Answer: d   **Reference:**   Section 10.6

29.   _____ security is used to limit access to specified rows of a table.
   a.   horizontal
   b.   password
   c.   user name
   d.   transaction boundary
   e.   vertical
   Answer: e   **Reference:**   Section 10.7

FILL IN THE BLANKS

1.   A database application must construct or __materialize__ objects from the underlying relations.

   Reference: Section 10.2

2.   Objects such as a sales analysis report must be __materialized__ from the underlying relations.

   Reference: Section 10.2

3.   A(n) ____view____ is a structured list of data items.

   Reference: Section 10.3

4.   The result of a SQL statement is called a(n) __recordset__ .

   Reference: Section 10.3

5.   Data can be modified using the _____UPDATE_____ SQL statement.

Reference: Section   10.3

6.   Data can be removed using the _____DELETE_____ SQL statement.

Reference: Section   10.3

7.   Some DBMSs support _____cascading deletions__ which remove <u>dependent</u> rows when the primary row is removed.

Reference: Section   10.3

8.   Data can be added using the _____INSERT_____ SQL statement

Reference: Section   10.3

9.   A(n) __form__ is a screen display used for data entry and edit.

Reference: Section   10.4

10.   A(n) __drop-down list box__ is a GUI control that presents a list of items from which the user can choose.

Reference: Section   10.4

11.   A(n) __option button/radio button__ is a display technique that enables users to select one alternative condition or state from a list of possibilities.

Reference: Section   10.4

12.   A(n) __check box__ is a display technique that enables users to select one <u>or more</u> alternative conditions or states from a list of possibilities.

Reference: Section   10.4

13.   The actions of special-purpose keys such as *ESC* should be __consistent/pervasive__ throughout an application.

Reference: Section   10.4

14.   A(n) __implied__ object is generally created by sorting a set of objects.

Reference: Section   10.5

15.   A row that exists inappropriately without a required parent or child is called a(n) __fragment__ .

Reference: Section   10.6

16.   A child row that exists without a mandatory parent is called a(n) __orphan__ .

Reference: Section   10.6

17.   A(n) __Mandatory-Mandatory/M-M__ constraint means that neither the parent or child can exist without the other.

Reference: Section 10.6

18.   A(n) __Mandatory-Optional/M-O__ constraint means that a parent can exist without a child.

Reference: Section 10.6

19.   A(n) __Optional - Optional /O-O__ constraint means that either the parent or child can exist without the other.

Reference: Section 10.6

20.   A(n) __Optional - Mandatory /O-M__ constraint means that a child can exist without a parent.

Reference: Section 10.6

21.   A parent of a(n) __Mandatory-Mandatory/M-M__ relationship can be inserted only if at least one child is created.

Reference: Section 10.6

22.   The key of a child of a(n) __Optional-Mandatory/O-M__ relationship can be modified only if a sibling exists.

Reference: Section 10.6

23.   A parent of a(n) __Optional-Mandatory/O-M__ relationship can be inserted only if at least one child is created or an appropriate child already exists.

Reference: Section 10.6

24.   The key of a parent or of a child of a(n) __Optional- Optional /O-O__ relationship can be modified without restriction.

Reference: Section 10.6

25.   A(n) __null (value)__ for an attribute arises when either no value has ever been entered into the database, or no value is appropriate.

Reference: Section 10.6

26.   A(n) __trigger__ is a program segment that is invoked when a specified event occurs in the database.

Reference: Section 10.6

27.   One technique for protecting an application's security is to ask the user to enter a(n) __password__ before he or she can access the application.

Reference: Section 10.7

28.   ___Horizontal___ security limits access to specified columns.

   Reference: Section 10.7

29.   ___Vertical___ security limits access to specified rows.

   Reference: Section 10.7

30.   ___Transaction___ boundaries identify work that must be completed as a unit.

   Reference: Section 10.7

ESSAY

1.   Describe the difference between the data content of a view and the appearance of that content (the format or materialization).

2.   Discuss the factors that should be considered when designing a form.

3.   Discuss the difference between those constraints that can be enforced by the DBMS and those that must be enforced by the application. Give examples.

4.   Describe the various relationship cardinality constraints and how they can be enforced.

5.   Describe the uses of menus for providing control in database applications.

CHAPTER 11 TEST QUESTIONS

TRUE-FALSE QUESTIONS

T   1. A *network* is a collection of computers that communicate with each other using a standardized protocol.
Reference: Section 11.1

F   2. A *private* network is one that anyone can use by paying a fee, directly or indirectly.
Reference: Section 11.1

F   3. The *Internet* was created for military use in the early 1990s.
Reference: Section 11.1

T   4. *TelNet* allows an Internet user to sign on to a remote computer.
Reference: Section 11.1

F   5. *Internet mail services* allow users to send or retrieve files from remote computers.
Reference: Section 11.1

T   6. The essential characteristic of an *HTML* document is that it can include links to other documents.
Reference: Section 11.1

T   7. The *World Wide Web* is a network of distributed hypertext documents.
Reference: Section 11.1

F   8. All internet files are HTML documents.
Reference: Section 11.1

F   9. WWW servers send requests for activity to users.
Reference: Section 11.1

F   10. An *intranet* is a private network that cannot be connected to a public network.
Reference: Section 11.1

T   11. The transmission speed of an intranet is generally much faster than the speed of the Internet.
Reference: Section 11.1

T   12. Every document on the Internet can be accessed by its *universal resource locator*, or address.
Reference: Section 11.1

F   13. A server on the Internet uses a browser to send HTML documents to client computers.
Reference: Section 11.1

T   14. In *static report publishing*, all of the data flow from the server to the user.
Reference: Section 11.1

T   15. A crucial difference between a traditional network and the Internet is that an HTML file can be processed by any computer having a browser and access to the Internet.
Reference: Section 11.1

F 16. In an Internet database application, all of the application processing is always performed by the *client* computer.
Reference: Section 11.1

F 17. The *database server* is the middle tier in the three-tier architecture.
Reference: Section 11.2

T 18. In the three-tier architecture, view CRUD is best performed by the Web server.
Reference: Section 11.2

F 19. In network database applications, the client browser sends SQL requests to the Web server.
Reference: Section 11.2

T 20. *Perl* is used to create application programs that run on network servers.
Reference: Section 11.3

F 21. *Java Script* refers to an HTML standard for defining forms and sending and receiving form data.
Reference: Section 11.3

T 22. An HTML page can contain embedded programs to handle complex logic.
Reference: Section 11.3

T 23. The bytecode resulting from compiling a Java program is machine-independent.
Reference: Section 11.3

F 24. An advantage of scripting languages is that they are supported by all browsers.
Reference: Section 11.3

T 25. An ActiveX control contains properties and methods.
Reference: Section 11.3

T 26. HTML permits the user to modify a page element <u>locally</u>.
Reference: Section 11.4

F 27. Storing data locally on the client is called *binding*.
Reference: Section 11.4

T 28. The most important advantage of XML over HTML is that heterogeneous systems can exchange data.
Reference: Section 11.4

T 29. A Web server must keep track of those clients that are performing database transactions.
Reference: Section 11.5

F 30. Java programs are only executed on the client machines.
Reference: Section 11.5

MULTIPLE CHOICE QUESTIONS

1.   The communications protocol used by the Internet is called:
        a.   FTP
        b.   HTML
        c.   MIME
        d.   TCP/IP
        e.   URL
        Answer: d   **Reference:**   Section 11.1

2.   _____ are places on the Internet where users with common interests can conduct
        public discussions with one another.
        a.   FTP
        b.   Internet mail services
        c.   MIME
        d.   Newsgroups
        e.   TelNet
        Answer: d   **Reference:**   Section 11.1

3.   _____ is an Internet service that allows a user to sign on to a remote computer.
        a.   FTP
        b.   Internet mail services
        c.   MIME
        d.   Newsgroups
        e.   TelNet
        Answer: e   **Reference:**   Section 11.1

4.   _____ is an Internet service that allows users to send or retrieve files from remote
        computers.
        a.   FTP
        b.   Internet mail services
        c.   MIME
        d.   Newsgroups
        e.   TelNet
        Answer: a   **Reference:**   Section 11.1

5.   _____ is the protocol that enables the sharing of documents with embedded links to
        other documents.
        a.   FTP
        b.   HTTP
        c.   HTML
        d.   TelNet
        e.   URL
        Answer: b   **Reference:**   Section 11.1

6. _____ is the language used to mark text and to indicate links to other documents.
   a.   FTP
   b.   HTTP
   c.   HTML
   d.   MIME
   e.   URL
   Answer: c   **Reference:**   Section 11.1

7. The international dynamic network of hypertext documents is called the:
   a.   Internet
   b.   TCP/IP
   c.   TelNet
   d.   URL
   e.   WWW
   Answer: e   **Reference:**   Section 11.1

8. A user's computer must have a(n) _____ to be able to read Internet documents.
   a.   browser
   b.   FTP processor
   c.   CGI processor
   d.   TelNet processor
   e.   URL
   Answer: a   **Reference:**   Section 11.1

9. Documents on the Internet are referenced or located by means of their:
   a.   FTP
   b.   HTML
   c.   HTTP
   d.   MIME
   e.   URL
   Answer: e   **Reference:**   Section 11.1

10. When an Internet server sends a file to a client, it also sends a _____ code indicating the file's type.
    a.   FTP
    b.   HTML
    c.   HTTP
    d.   MIME
    e.   URL
    Answer: d   **Reference:**   Section 11.1

11. A(n) _____ is a private network that uses TCP/IP, HTML, and related browser technology.
    a.   Internet
    b.   intranet
    c.   newsgroup
    d.   TelNet
    e.   WWW
    Answer: b   **Reference:**   Section 11.1

12.   A(n) _____ is a technique for protecting a private network from potential problems from external networks.
       a.   firewall
       b.   MIME code
       c.   password
       d.   URL
       e.   virus checker
       Answer: a   **Reference:**   Section 11.1

13.   ARPANET, the military predecessor of the Internet, was created in the:
       a.   1950s
       b.   1960s
       c.   1970s
       d.   1980s
       e.   1990s
       Answer: b   **Reference:**   Section 11.1

14.   Compared to the Internet, the typical *intranet* is:
       a.   larger and less secure
       b.   larger and more secure
       c.   about the same
       d.   smaller and less secure
       e.   smaller and more secure
       Answer: e   **Reference:**   Section 11.1

15.   Compared to the Internet, the transmission speed of the typical *intranet* is:
       a.   somewhat faster
       b.   somewhat slower
       c.   about the same
       d.   much faster
       e.   much slower
       Answer: d   **Reference:**   Section 11.1

16.   In *static report publishing*:
       a.   reports are printed by the DBMS
       b.   reports are printed by the server
       c.   the server sends data to the user
       d.   the user sends data to the server
       e.   c and d
       Answer: c   **Reference:**   Section 11.1

17.   In *DB query publishing*:
       a.   reports are printed by the DBMS
       b.   reports are printed by the server
       c.   the server sends data to the user
       d.   the user sends data to the server
       e.   c and d
       Answer: e   **Reference:**   Section 11.1

18. In the three-tier architecture, view *CRUD* is best performed by the:
     a.   HTTP client
     b.   HTTP server
     c.   database server
     d.   firewall
     e.   mainframe
     Answer: b   **Reference:**   Section 11.2

19. In the three-tier architecture, view *materialization* is best performed by the:
     a.   HTTP client
     b.   HTTP server
     c.   database server
     d.   firewall
     e.   mainframe
     Answer: a   **Reference:**   Section 11.2

20. _____ refers to an HTML standard for defining forms and sending and receiving form data.
     a.   ActiveX
     b.   CGI
     c.   Java
     d.   Perl
     e.   VBScript
     Answer: b   **Reference:**   Section 11.3

21. _____ is used to create applications that run on network servers.
     a.   ActiveX
     b.   CGI
     c.   Java
     d.   Perl
     e.   VBScript
     Answer: d   **Reference:**   Section 11.3

22. _____ is a programming language that can be embedded into an HTML page to provide programming logic.
     a.   ActiveX
     b.   CGI
     c.   Java
     d.   Perl
     e.   VBScript
     Answer: e   **Reference:**   Section 11.3

23. _____ is an object programming language that can be used to write code for processing on the client and/or server side.
     a.   ActiveX
     b.   CGI
     c.   Java
     d.   Perl
     e.   VBScript
     Answer: c   **Reference:**   Section 11.3

24.   When Java is compiled, the result is a file of Java bytecode that can be processed on:
    a.   the clients
    b.   the server
    c.   the mainframe
    d.   a and b
    e.   any computer for which a Java bytecode interpreter is available
    Answer: e   **Reference:**   Section 11.3

25.   Storing data locally on the client is called:
    a.   binding
    b.   caching
    c.   cascading
    d.   materializing
    e.   scripting
    Answer: b   **Reference:**   Section 11.4

26.   Keeping track of which client made a request is called:
    a.   data caching
    b.   declaring the document type
    c.   maintaining the session state
    d.   stylesheet publishing
    e.   view materialization
    Answer: c   **Reference:**   Section 11.5

27.   Database transaction processing requires that the Web server creates:
    a.   one application object
    b.   one session object
    c.   one application object and one or more session objects
    d.   one or more application objects and one session object
    e.   one or more application objects and one or more session objects
    Answer: c   **Reference:**   Section 11.5

FILL IN THE BLANKS

1.   A(n) __network__ is a collection of computers that communicate with one another using a standard protocol.

    Reference: Section 11.1

2.   A(n) __public__ network is one that anyone can use by paying a fee, directly or indirectly.

    Reference: Section 11.1

3.   A(n) __private__ network is one that only preauthorized users can access.

    Reference: Section 11.1

4.   The Internet uses the communications protocol called   Terminal Control Program / Internet Protocol (TCP/IP)   .

Reference: Section 11.1

5.   Any Internet user has access to   Internet mail services   for e-mail.

Reference: Section 11.1

6.   Newsgroups   allow users with common interests to conduct public discussions with one another.

Reference: Section 11.1

7.   TelNet   is an Internet service that allows a user to sign on to a remote computer.

Reference: Section 11.1

8.   FTP (File Transfer Protocol)   is an Internet service that allows users to send or retrieve files from remote computers.

Reference: Section 11.1

9.   The Internet uses   hypertext transfer protocol (HTTP)   as its protocol for sharing documents with embedded links.

Reference: Section 11.1

10.   Hypertext markup language (HTML)   is the language used to create an Internet document.

Reference: Section 11.1

11.   A user's computer must have a(n)   browser   to be able to read Internet documents.

Reference: Section 11.1

12.   The Internet has evolved into a dynamic network called the   World Wide Web (WWW)   .

Reference: Section 11.1

13.   The   universal resource locator (URL)   provides a standardized means to locate any Internet document.

Reference: Section 11.1

14.   When an Internet server sends a file to a client, it also sends a code called the multipurpose Internet mail code (MIME)   indicating the file's type.

Reference: Section 11.1

15.   A(n)   intranet   is a *private* local or wide-area network that uses the same technology as the Internet.

Reference: Section 11.1

11.   A(n) __firewall__ is a computer that serves as a security gateway to public networks.

Reference: Section 11.1

18.   __Static report publishing__ refers to applications that only display data to the client, with no means of accepting data from the client.
Reference: Section 11.1

19.   __DB query publishing__ refers to applications in which the server sends a form to the client, which enters a value for a key field that is sent to the server, and the server then sends the requested data back to the client.

Reference: Section 11.1

20.   __Application publishing__ refers to complete database applications that use the Internet or an intranet as their communication medium.

Reference: Section 11.1

21.   In the three-tier architecture, the __Web server__ is the middle tier.

Reference: Section 11.2

22.   On the client, the __browser__ is responsible for materializing views from HTML.

Reference: Section 11.2

23.   __CGI (common gateway interface)__ is an HTML standard for defining forms and sending and receiving form data.

Reference: Section 11.3

24.   __Perl (Practical Extraction and Report Language)__ is an Internet programming language used to create application programs that run on network servers.

Reference: Section 11.3

25.   __VBScript or Java Script__ is a programming language that can be embedded into an HTML page to provide programming logic.

Reference: Section 11.3

26.   __Java__ is an object programming language developed by Sun Microsystems, Inc.

Reference: Section 11.3

27.   The Remote Data Services controls available in HTML 4.0 allow data to be __cached__ (copied and stored) locally on the client machine.

Reference: Section 11.4

28.   Unlike HTML and DHTML, the _Extensible Markup Language (XML)_ provides a clear separation between document structure, content, and materialization.

   Reference: Section 11.4

29.   Each database transaction requires the Web server to create a(n) _session_ object.

   Reference: Section 11.5

30.   Every session object is tied to a(n) _application_ object.

   Reference: Section 11.5

ESSAY

1.   Describe the three fundamental Internet standards.

2.   Describe the three major functions of a Web server.

3.   Describe the languages used for Internet-technology applications.

4.   Describe the differences between HTML and DHTML.

5.   Discuss the reasons why XML is so significant for database applications.

CHAPTER 12 TEST QUESTIONS

TRUE-FALSE QUESTIONS

F 1. *Concurrency control* refers to measures needed on multi-national distributed databases where more than one monetary system is involved.
Reference: Section 12.1

T 2. If even one of the actions comprising a transaction is not completed successfully, none of the successful actions are allowed to change the database.
Reference: Section 12.1

T 3. If a transaction is completed successfully, the command *Commit Transaction* is issued by the application program.
Reference: Section 12.1

F 4. The *lost update problem* occurs when a transaction is not completed successfully.
Reference: Section 12.1

T 5. When an application program issues a *shared lock*, other application programs can read the locked item but not change it.
Reference: Section 12.1

F 6. A *deadlock* or *deadly embrace* occurs when two users are attempting to access the same item in the database.
Reference: Section 12.1

F 7. A *static cursor* is one that always points to the same row in a recordset.
Reference: Section 12.1

F 8. *Database recovery* refers to the methods and techniques that are used by application programs to retrieve data from the database.
Reference: Section 12.2

F 9. Saving a copy of the database periodically is sufficient to be able to restore it in the event of a computer or other failure.
Reference: Section 12.2

F 10. A *checkpoint* occurs when processing of the database is temporarily stopped and the database is checked for accuracy.
Reference: Section 12.2

T 11. Saving a copy of the database periodically is not sufficient to be able to restore it in the event of a computer or other failure.
Reference: Section 12.2

T 12. Database recovery using either the *rollforward* or *rollback* methods does NOT involve the original application programs.
Reference: Section 12.2

T 13. Passwords are the most commonly used technique to restrict unauthorized access to the database.
   Reference: Section 12.3

F 14. A user can only be assigned to one group at a time for security purposes.
   Reference: Section 12.3

T 15. *Pessimistic locking* assumes that a conflict will occur.
   Reference: Section 12.1

T 16. With *optimistic locking*, if a conflict occurs, one of the users must redo his or her work.
   Reference: Section 12.1

T 17. With *optimistic locking*, the locks are placed implicitly (automatically) by the DBMS.
   Reference: Section 12.1

F 18. Whenever possible, security should be built into application logic rather than relying on features contained in the DBMS.
   Reference: Section 12.3

T 19. The person in charge of one or more databases is generally called a *DBA*.
   Reference: Section 12.4

F 20. The terms *data administration* and *database administration* are synonymous.
   Reference: Section 12.4

F 21. A user is permitted to make changes to the database structure as long as the changes do not affect other users of the database.
   Reference: Section 12.4

F 22. Users are responsible for making backups of their data in the database.
   Reference: Section 12.4

T 23. A *data dictionary* is a tool for standardizing development and processing of a database.
   Reference: Section 12.4

F 24. *Tuning* refers to the responsibility of the database administrator to maximize the capacity of the database.
   Reference: Section 12.4

T 25. A *passive* data repository must be updated separately when changes are made to the structure of the database.
   Reference: Section 12.4

F 26. The database administrator is responsible for managing the *data values* in the database.
   Reference: Section 12.4

MULTIPLE CHOICE QUESTIONS

1.   A series of actions that must be completed as a unit or not at all is known as a(n):
      a.   horizontal fragment
      b.   image
      c.   lock
      d.   transaction
      e.   vertical fragment
      Answer: d   **Reference:**   Section 12.1

2.   Measures that are taken to prevent one user's work from interfering with another's are called:
      a.   concurrency control
      b.   checkpointing
      c.   database recovery
      d.   database logging
      e.   interleaving
      Answer: a   **Reference:**   Section 12.1

3.   Measures that are taken to ensure that the database can be reconstructed after a failure are called:
      a.   concurrency control
      b.   checkpointing
      c.   database recovery
      d.   database logging
      e.   interleaving
      Answer: b   **Reference:**   Section 12.1

4.   The command to change the database is:
      a.   Commit Transaction
      b.   Lock Transaction
      c.   Rollback Transaction
      d.   Save Transaction
      e.   Undo Transaction
      Answer: a   **Reference:**   Section 12.1

5.   The command NOT to change the database is:
      a.   Commit Transaction
      b.   Lock Transaction
      c.   Rollback Transaction
      d.   Save Transaction
      e.   Undo Transaction
      Answer: c   **Reference:**   Section 12.1

6.   The situation that occurs when one user's changes to the database are lost by a second user's changes to the database is known as the:
      a.   concurrent update problem
      b.   deadly embrace problem
      c.   inconsistent read problem
      d.   inconsistent write problem
      e.   serializability problem
      Answer: a   **Reference:**   Section 12.1

7. The situation which occurs when two users are each waiting for a resource that the other person has locked is known as the:
    a. concurrent update problem
    b. deadly embrace problem
    c. inconsistent read problem
    d. inconsistent write problem
    e. serializability problem
    Answer: b   **Reference:**   Section 12.1

8. A lock placed automatically by the DBMS is called a(n) _____ lock.
    a. exclusive
    b. explicit
    c. granular
    d. implicit
    e. shared
    Answer: d   **Reference:**   Section 12.1

9. A lock placed by command is called a(n) _____ lock.
    a. exclusive
    b. explicit
    c. granular
    d. implicit
    e. shared
    Answer: b   **Reference:**   Section 12.1

10. A lock that allows other users to read but not change the item is called a(n) _____ lock.
    a. exclusive
    b. explicit
    c. granular
    d. implicit
    e. shared
    Answer: e   **Reference:**   Section 12.1

11. A lock that denies other users any access to the item is called a(n) _____ lock.
    a. exclusive
    b. explicit
    c. granular
    d. implicit
    e. shared
    Answer: a   **Reference:**   Section 12.1

12. Recovering a database via rollforward involves:
    a. restoring the database from the save and reprocessing all the transactions since the save.
    b. restoring the database from the save and reapplying all the changes made by transactions since the save.
    c. undoing the changes made by erroneous or partially processed transactions, and restarting
        the valid transactions that were in process at the time of the failure.
    d. recreating the database by reentering all of the data from the beginning, and then reprocessing all of the transactions.
    e. synchronizing the database and the transaction log by checkpointing
    Answer: b   **Reference:**   Section 12.2

13.   Recovering a database via rollback involves:
    a.   restoring the database from the save and reprocessing all the transactions since the save.
    b.   restoring the database from the save and reapplying all the changes made by transactions since the save.
    c.   undoing the changes made by erroneous or partially processed transactions, and restarting
    the valid transactions that were in process at the time of the failure.
    d.   recreating the database by reentering all of the data from the beginning and, then reprocessing all of the transactions.
    e.   synchronizing the database and the transaction log by checkpointing
Answer: c   **Reference:**   Section 12.2

14.   Recovering a database via reprocessing involves:
    a.   restoring the database from the save and reprocessing all the transactions since the save.
    b.   restoring the database from the save and reapplying all the changes made by transactions since the save.
    c.   undoing the changes made by erroneous or partially processed transactions, and restarting
    the valid transactions that were in process at the time of the failure.
    d.   recreating the database by reentering all of the data from the beginning, and then reprocessing all of the transactions.
    e.   synchronizing the database and the transaction log by checkpointing
Answer: a   **Reference:**   Section 12.2

15.   With subject-oriented security:
    a.   the DBMS authorizes access permissions
    b.   each database item has an authorization matrix
    c.   the application program provides logic to enforce authorization constraints
    d.   users select their access permissions
    e.   each user or user group is allocated permissions
Answer: e   **Reference:**   Section 12.3

16.   With object-oriented security:
    a.   the DBMS authorizes access permissions
    b.   each database item has an authorization matrix
    c.   the application program provides logic to enforce authorization constraints
    d.   users select their access permissions
    e.   each user or user group is allocated permissions
Answer: b   **Reference:**   Section 12.3

17.   The size of security objects is referred to as its:
    a.   authorization
    b.   configuration
    c.   constraint
    d.   data value
    e.   granularity
Answer: e   **Reference:**   Section 12.3

18. Locks that are placed automatically by the DBMS are called:
   a.   dynamic
   b.   explicit
   c.   implicit
   d.   optimistic
   e.   pessimistic
   Answer: c   **Reference:**   Section 12.3

19. Locks that are placed automatically by the application program are called:
   a.   dynamic
   b.   explicit
   c.   implicit
   d.   optimistic
   e.   pessimistic
   Answer: b   **Reference:**   Section 12.3

20. Locks that are placed assuming that a conflict will occur are called:
   a.   dynamic
   b.   explicit
   c.   implicit
   d.   optimistic
   e.   pessimistic
   Answer: e   **Reference:**   Section 12.3

21. Locks that are placed assuming that a conflict will NOT occur are called:
   a.   dynamic
   b.   explicit
   c.   implicit
   d.   optimistic
   e.   pessimistic
   Answer: d   **Reference:**   Section 12.3

22. Which of the following levels of locking will cause the least conflict?
   a.   database
   b.   page
   c.   row
   d.   table
   e.   tablespace
   Answer: c   **Reference:**   Section 12.3

23. Which type of locking may require the user to reenter some work?
   a.   dynamic
   b.   explicit
   c.   implicit
   d.   optimistic
   e.   pessimistic
   Answer: d   **Reference:**   Section 12.3

24.   Which type of locking requires some of the data to be reread?
        a.   dynamic
        b.   explicit
        c.   implicit
        d.   optimistic
        e.   pessimistic
        Answer: d   **Reference:**   Section 12.3

25.   Which of the following is NOT a security function of the DBMS?
        a.   identifying subjects and allowing them to access the database
        b.   restricting the actions that subjects can perform
        c.   establishing policies and procedures
        d.   limiting objects that subjects can access
        e.   allowing user-developed routines to be incorporated into normal processing
        Answer: c   **Reference:**   Section 12.3

26.   The process of attempting to improve the performance of the DBMS is known as:
        a.   checkpointing
        b.   documenting
        c.   recovering
        d.   restoring
        e.   tuning
        Answer: e   **Reference:**   Section 12.4

27.   The database is most vulnerable to failure after a change in its:
        a.   authorizations
        b.   data values
        c.   documentation
        d.   performance
        e.   structure
        Answer: e   **Reference:**   Section 12.4

28.   The _____ greatly aids the database administrator in recording and tracking data
        names, formats, relationships, and cross-references.
        a.   authorization table
        b.   checkpoint table
        c.   data dictionary
        d.   log table
        e.   transaction table
        Answer: c   **Reference:**   Section 12.4

FILL IN THE BLANKS

1.   <u> Concurrency control </u> consists of measures that are taken to prevent one user's work from
        interfering with another's.

        Reference: Section 12.1

2.   __Database recovery__ refers to the methods and techniques that are used to ensure that the database can be repaired or reconstructed after a failure.

Reference: Section 12.1

3.   A *transaction* is also known as a(n) __logical unit of work (LUW)__ .

Reference: Section 12.1

4.   A *transaction* is sometimes called __atomic__ , since it is performed as a unit.

Reference: Section 12.1

5.   The situation that occurs when one user's changes to the database are lost by a second user's changes to the database is known as the __lost update or concurrent update problem__ .

Reference: Section 12.1

6.   Preventing multiple applications from obtaining copies of the same record when the record is about to be changed is called __resource locking__ .

Reference: Section 12.1

7.   Locks placed automatically by the DBMS are called __implicit__ locks.

Reference: Section 12.1

8.   Locks placed by a command from an application program are called __explicit__ locks.

Reference: Section 12.1

9.   The size or level of a lock is called the lock __granularity__ .

Reference: Section 12.1

10.   A(n) __exclusive__ lock locks the item from access of any type.

Reference: Section 12.1

11.   A(n) __shared__ lock locks the item from change but not from read.

Reference: Section 12.1

12.   The situation where two users each lock resources that the other needs is called __deadlock or deadly embrace__ .

Reference: Section 12.1

13.   A(n) __cursor__ is a pointer into a recordset.

Reference: Section 12.1

14. The method called __rollforward__ recovers the database after a failure by restoring the saved copy of the database and reapplying all valid transactions since the save.

    Reference: Section 12.2

15. The method called __rollback__ recovers the database after a failure by undoing changes made by erroneous or partially processed transactions and restarting the valid transactions that were in process at the time of the failure.

    Reference: Section 12.2

16. A(n) __checkpoint__ is a point of synchronization between the database and the transaction log.

    Reference: Section 12.2

17. __Pessimistic locking__ assumes that a conflict will occur.

    Reference: Section 12.2

18. With __optimistic locking__ , if a conflict occurs, one of the users must redo his or her work.

    Reference: Section 12.2

19. In the optimistic locking method, the data are __reread__ to see if there has been a change, before the database is updated.

    Reference: Section 12.2

20. The server computer keeps a(n) __log__ of changes made to the database, for use in recovery operations.

    Reference: Section 12.2

21. A(n) __group__ consists of one or more users.

    Reference: Section 12.3

22. When a user signs on to the database, the DBMS limits his or her actions to the defined __permissions__ for that user and for the groups to which the user has been assigned.

    Reference: Section 12.3

23. The person in charge of a database and the applications that process it, is often known as the __database administrator (DBA)__ .

    Reference: Section 12.4

24. The __data dictionary__ contains standard information about the structure of the database.

    Reference: Section 12.4

25.   The key users of a database are sometimes called __data proponents__ .

   Reference: Section 12.4

26.   The process of attempting to improve the performance of the DBMS is known as __tuning or optimizing__ the system.

   Reference: Section 12.4

27.   A *transaction* is sometimes called __atomic__ .

   Reference: Section 12.1

ESSAY

1.   Describe the concept of *concurrent processing*.

2.   Describe what is meant by *serializable transactions*.

3.   Describe the various transaction isolation levels.

4.   Describe how a database can be recovered using the original application program and using the facilities of the DBMS itself.

5.   Describe the functions of the database administrator.

CHAPTER 13 TEST QUESTIONS

TRUE-FALSE QUESTIONS

F 1. As a COM interface, OLE DB is readily accessible to all languages.
Reference: Section 13.0

T 2. Web servers are likely to obtain data from a wide variety of sources.
Reference: Section 13.1

F 3. OLE DB cannot be used as an interface to ODBC.
Reference: Section 13.1

T 4. The *open database connectivity (ODBC)* standard is an interface by which application programs can access and process SQL databases in a DBMS-independent manner.
Reference: Section 13.2

T 5. The application program, driver manager, and DBMS drivers all reside on the client computer.
Reference: Section 13.2

F 6. A *multiple-tier* driver processes both ODBC and SQL statements.
Reference: Section 13.2

F 7. The *ODBC conformance levels* are designed to ensure that all vendors meet the same standard.
Reference: Section 13.2

T 8. The *SQL-conformance levels* specify which SQL statements, expressions, and data types a driver can process.
Reference: Section 13.2

F 9. All ODBC drivers support a *scrollable cursor*.
Reference: Section 13.2

T 10. An ODBC-compliant application program does not need to be changed to run on another DBMS.
Reference: Section 13.2

F 11. The ODBC standard was developed by Microsoft.
Reference: Section 13.2

F 12. Once an ODBC data structure has been created it can be used by used by all users.
Reference: Section 13.2

T 13. An OLE DB *rowset* is a subtype of a *recordset*.
Reference: Section 13.3

F 14. A *recordset* is an object that contains a group of other objects.
Reference: Section 13.3

F 15. The actions that an object can perform are called *properties*.
Reference: Section 13.3

T   16. An *iterator* is a method that can be used to pass through or otherwise identify the objects in a collection.
   Reference: Section   13.3

F   17. An OLE DB *data provider* enters the values into the database.
   Reference: Section   13.3

F   18. An *interface* makes all of the object's properties and methods available.
   Reference: Section   13.3

T   19. An object's *implementation* can be changed without affecting users.
   Reference: Section   13.3

F   20. An object's *interface* can be changed without affecting users.
   Reference: Section   13.3

T   21. OLE DB permits a transaction to acquire data from multiple data sources on different computers.
   Reference: Section   13.3

T   22. ADO can be called from scripting languages.
   Reference: Section   13.4

T   23. An ADO <u>must</u> contain a connection object.
   Reference: Section   13.4

F   24. An ADO <u>must</u> contain a command object.
   Reference: Section   13.4

T   25. An ADO *connection* object contains a *lock type* property.
   Reference: Section   13.4

T   26. Each recordset object has a fields collection.
   Reference: Section   13.4

F   27. The contents of the fields collection is determined by the number of columns in the base table(s) of the recordset.
   Reference: Section   13.4

F   28. The *Errors Collection* must be explicitly created using code, in case an error occurs.
   Reference: Section   13.4

T   29. An ADO *command* object can be created to execute queries or stored procedures.
   Reference: Section   13.4

MULTIPLE CHOICE QUESTIONS

1.   The highest level interface that a Web server can use is:
     a.   ADO
     b.   Native Interfaces
     c.   ODBC
     d.   OLE DB
     e.   SQL
     Answer: a   **Reference:**   Section 13.1

2.   The _____ standard is an interface by which application programs can access and
     process SQL databases in a DBMS-independent manner.
     a.   ASCII
     b.   CODASYL
     c.   EBCDIC
     d.   open database connectivity
     e.   SQL
     Answer: d   **Reference:**   Section 13.2

3.   A(n) _____ processes both ODBC and SQL statements.
     a.   application program
     b.   driver manager
     c.   multi-tier driver
     d.   remote data object
     e.   single-tier driver
     Answer: e   **Reference:**   Section 13.2

4.   A(n) _____ processes ODBC calls, but passes the SQL requests directly to the data
     source.
     a.   application program
     b.   driver manager
     c.   multi-tier driver
     d.   remote data object
     e.   single-tier driver
     Answer: c   **Reference:**   Section 13.2

5.   The _____ serve(s) as an intermediary between the application and the DBMS
     drivers.
     a.   driver manager
     b.   ODBC conformance levels
     c.   operating system
     d.   remote data object
     e.   SQL conformance levels
     Answer: a   **Reference:**   Section 13.2

6.   The _____ specify(ies) which SQL statements, expressions, and data types a driver can process.
a.   driver manager
b.   ODBC conformance levels
c.   operating system
d.   remote data object
e.   SQL conformance levels
Answer: e   **Reference:**   Section 13.2

7.   The _____ concern(s) the features and functions that are made available through the driver's API.
a.   driver manager
b.   ODBC conformance levels
c.   operating system
d.   remote data object
e.   SQL conformance levels
Answer: b   **Reference:**   Section 13.2

8.   A(n) _____ is an ODBC structure that identifies a database and the DBMS that processes it.
a.   driver manager
b.   API
c.   driver
d.   data source
e.   SQL conformance level
Answer: d   **Reference:**   Section 13.2

9.   A(n) _____ is a set of functions that an application can call to receive services.
a.   driver manager
b.   API
c.   driver
d.   data source
e.   SQL conformance level
Answer: b   **Reference:**   Section 13.2

10.   The actions that an object can perform are called:
a.   classes
b.   collections
c.   methods
d.   properties
e.   procedures
Answer: c   **Reference:**   Section 13.3

11.   The characteristics of an object are called:
a.   classes
b.   collections
c.   methods
d.   properties
e.   procedures
Answer: d   **Reference:**   Section 13.3

12. The internal details of an object is(are) called the:
  a. abstract data type
  b. implementation
  c. interface
  d. methods
  e. properties
  Answer: b   **Reference:**   Section 13.3

13. The external appearance of an object is(are) called the:
  a. abstract data type
  b. implementation
  c. interface
  d. methods
  e. properties
  Answer: c   **Reference:**   Section 13.3

14. The first ADO element to be created is the:
  a. command object
  b. connection object
  c. errors collection
  d. parameters collection
  e. recordset object
  Answer: b   **Reference:**   Section 13.4

15. An ADO automatically instantiates a(n) _____ when it is needed.
  a. command object
  b. connection object
  c. errors collection
  d. parameters collection
  e. recordset object
  Answer: c   **Reference:**   Section 13.4

16. Each _____ has a *fields collection*.
  a. command object
  b. connection object
  c. errors collection
  d. parameters collection
  e. recordset object
  Answer: e   **Reference:**   Section 13.4

17. Each _____ has a *parameters collection*.
  a. command object
  b. connection object
  c. errors collection
  d. field object
  e. recordset object
  Answer: a   **Reference:**   Section 13.4

FILL IN THE BLANKS

1.   __Active Data Objects (ADO)__ enables programmers in almost any language to be able to access OLE DB functionality.

      Reference: Section 13.1

2.   The __open database connectivity__ standard is an interface by which application programs can access and process SQL databases in a DBMS-independent manner.

      Reference: Section 13.2

3.   According to the ODBC standard, a(n) __data source__ is the database, its associated DBMS, the operating system, and the network platform.

      Reference: Section 13.2

4.   The __driver manager__ serves as an intermediary between the application and the DBMS drivers.

      Reference: Section 13.2

5.   A(n) __driver__ processes ODBC requests and submits specific SQL statements to a given type of data source.

      Reference: Section 13.2

6.   A(n) __single-tier__ driver processes both ODBC calls and SQL statements.

      Reference: Section 13.2

7.   A(n) __multiple-tier__ driver processes ODBC calls, but passes the SQL requests directly to the data source.

      Reference: Section 13.2

8.   A driver __application program interface (API)__ is a set of functions that the application can call to receive services.

      Reference: Section 13.2

9.   ODBC __conformance levels__ concern the features and functions that are made available through the driver's API.

      Reference: Section 13.2

10.   __SQL conformance levels__ specify which SQL statements, expressions, and data types a driver can process.

      Reference: Section 13.2

11.   A(n) __data source__ is an ODBC data structure that identifies a database and the DBMS that processes it.

   Reference: Section 13.2

12.   __Microsoft__ was the first company to implement the ODBC standards.

   Reference: Section 13.2

13.   A(n) __rowset__ is the OLE DB abstraction of a recordset.

   Reference: Section 13.3

14.   A(n) __collection__ is an object that contains a group of other objects.

   Reference: Section 13.3

15.   The actions that an object can perform are called __methods__ .

   Reference: Section 13.3

16.   A data __provider__ is a vendor of a product that delivers OLE DB functionality.

   Reference: Section 13.3

17.   A(n) __interface__ is specified by a set of objects and the properties and methods that they expose.

   Reference: Section 13.3

18.   The internal details of an object are known as its __implementation__ .

   Reference: Section 13.3

19.   An OLE DB __tabular data provider__ presents its data via rowsets.

   Reference: Section 13.3

20.   The __connection__ object is the basis for the other ADO objects.

   Reference: Section 13.4

21.   Each command object has a(n) __parameters__ collection.

   Reference: Section 13.4

22.   Each recordset object has a(n) __fields__ collection.

   Reference: Section 13.4

23.   The ____command____ object is used to execute a query or stored procedure.

   Reference: Section 13.4

ESSAY

1.   Describe the differences between ODBC, OLE DB, and ADO.

2.   What is the reason for the development of the ODBC standard?

3.   What are the goals of OLE DB?

4.   Why is Microsoft making ADO the standard data access method?

5.   Describe the components of the ADO object model.

CHAPTER 14 TEST QUESTIONS

TRUE-FALSE QUESTIONS

F   1.   Users of a teleprocessing system can only interact with it using dumb terminals.
        Reference: 14.1

F   2.   Teleprocessing systems generally have a graphical user interface.
        Reference: 14.1

T   3.   In a client-server system, the client computer is generally a microcomputer.
        Reference: 14.1

F   4.   In a client-server system, the server processes the application programs.
        Reference: 14.1

T   5.   With a file-sharing system, each user's computer contains the DBMS.
        Reference: 14.1

T   6.   A file-sharing system generates more traffic on the communication channels than does a client-server system.
        Reference: 14.1

T   7.   In a partitioned, distributed database system, a *vertical fragment* refers to a table that is broken into two or more sets of columns.
        Reference: 14.1

T   8.   A file server on a local area network often serves as a *gateway* to a mainframe or to other networks.
        Reference: Section 14.2

T   9.   When users are allowed to upload data to the database, inconsistent data could be generated.
        Reference: Section 14.2

T   10.   Downloading data makes sense only if the users will repeatedly produce queries and reports from it.
        Reference: Section 14.2

F   11.   An OLAP cube has three dimensions.
        Reference: Section 14.3

T   12.   OLAP uses extensions to SQL to define and process its data structures.
        Reference: Section 14.3

T   13.   The role of the data warehouse is to store downloaded extracts from databases and files and make the data available to users.
        Reference: Section 14.4

F   14.   It is not necessary to store any metadata in the data warehouse.
        Reference: Section 14.4

T   15. The term *drill down* refers to the capability of seeing the data in smaller and smaller units.
Reference: Section   14.4

F   16. All data in the data warehouse are always consistent in timing and domain.
Reference: Section   14.4

T   17. Most data warehouse users are not knowledgeable about SQL.
Reference: Section   14.4

T   18. Writing software to manage the data warehouse is difficult and expensive.
Reference: Section   14.4

F   19. The term *data mart* is another name for the term *data warehouse*.
Reference: Section   14.4

T   20. An off-the-shelf DBMS product can generally be used to manage a *data mart*.
Reference: Section   14.4

F   21. Users can add their data to the warehouse.
Reference: Section   14.4

T   22. Users generally want the capability of graphical output from a data warehouse.
Reference: Section   14.4

T   23. Some of the data in a data warehouse could have been purchased from other organizations.
Reference: Section   14.4

T   24. Data are an organizational asset, as are plant, equipment, and financial assets.
Reference: Section   14.5

T   25. The data administration office must try to ensure that the organization's data are used effectively.
Reference: Section   14.5

F   26. Organizational data consists only of text and numeric data.
Reference: Section   14.5

F   27. The scope of data administration is the same as that of database administration.
Reference: Section   14.5

T   28. Data administration personnel need to be aware of the political issues when dealing with users.
Reference: Section   14.5

F   29. Data administration personnel establish the data standards without input from the users.
Reference: Section   14.5

T   30. Data administration has the authority to resolve conflicts between user groups.
Reference: Section   14.5

MULTIPLE CHOICE QUESTIONS

1. A *client-server system* is a multi-user database architecture in which:
   a.   dumb terminals transmit data to a centralized computer
   b.   one computer processes the database, and other computers in the network process application programs
   c.   the DBMS as well as the application programs are stored on the users' computers
   d.   part or all of the database is duplicated on more than one computer
   e.   parts of the database are stored on more than one computer
   Answer: b   **Reference:**   14.1

2. A *file-sharing system* is a multi-user database architecture in which:
   a.   dumb terminals transmit data to a centralized computer
   b.   one computer processes the database, and other computers in the network process application programs
   c.   the DBMS as well as the application programs are stored on the users' computers
   d.   part or all of the database is duplicated on more than one computer
   e.   parts of the database are stored on more than one computer
   Answer: c   **Reference:**   14.1

3. A *teleprocessing system* is a multi-user database architecture in which:
   a.   dumb terminals transmit data to a centralized computer
   b.   one computer processes the database, and other computers in the network process application programs
   c.   the DBMS as well as the application programs are stored on the users' computers
   d.   part or all of the database is duplicated on more than one computer
   e.   parts of the database are stored on more than one computer
   Answer: a   **Reference:**   14.1

4. A *partitioned system* is a multi-user database architecture in which:
   a.   dumb terminals transmit data to a centralized computer
   b.   one computer processes the database, and other computers in the network process application programs
   c.   the DBMS as well as the application programs are stored on the users' computers
   d.   part or all of the database is duplicated on more than one computer
   e.   parts of the database are stored on more than one computer
   Answer: e   **Reference:**   14.1

5. A *replicated system* is a multi-user database architecture in which:
   a.   dumb terminals transmit data to a centralized computer
   b.   one computer processes the database, and other computers in the network process application programs
   c.   the DBMS as well as the application programs are stored on the users' computers
   d.   part or all of the database is duplicated on more than one computer
   e.   parts of the database are stored on more than one computer
   Answer: d   **Reference:**   14.1

6.   A *vertical fragment* or *partition* refers to:
    a.   the rows of a table when they are divided into pieces
    b.   a table that is broken into two or more sets of columns
    c.   a parent-child relationship in the database
    d.   a child-child relationship in the database
    e.   a parent-parent relationship in the database
    Answer: b   **Reference:**   14.1

7.   A *horizontal fragment* or *partition* refers to:
    a.   the rows of a table when they are divided into pieces
    b.   a table that is broken into two or more sets of columns
    c.   a parent-child relationship in the database
    d.   a child-child relationship in the database
    e.   a parent-parent relationship in the database
    Answer: a   **Reference:**   14.1

8.   The greatest disadvantage of distributed databases is the:
    a.   availability
    b.   security risk
    c.   cost/complexity
    d.   difficulty of control and possible integrity problems
    e.   flexibility
    Answer: d   **Reference:**   14.1

9.   The greatest advantage of distributed databases is the:
    a.   availability
    b.   security risk
    c.   cost/complexity
    d.   difficulty of control and possible integrity problems
    e.   flexibility
    Answer: e   **Reference:**   14.1

10.   Which activity can create problems?
    a.   downloading data
    b.   merging
    c.   querying
    d.   reporting
    e.   updating downloaded data
    Answer: e   **Reference:**   Section 14.2

11.   A local area network must have a(n) _____ to connect to a mainframe or to another network.
    a.   back-end processor
    b.   front-end processor
    c.   gateway
    d.   microcomputer
    e.   modem
    Answer: c   **Reference:**   Section 14.2

12.   Downloaded databases:
    a.   increase the potential for computer crime
    b.   makes access control more difficult
    c.   makes access control easier
    d.   a and b
    e.   a and c
    Answer: d   **Reference:**   Section 14.2

13.   Which architecture(s) can be used for downloading?
    a.   client-server
    b.   file-sharing
    c.   a and b
    d.   teleprocessing and client-server
    e.   teleprocessing and file-sharing
    Answer: c   **Reference:**   Section 14.2

14.   If downloading occurs in the morning, which of the following is most likely to be true in the afternoon?
    a.   the organizational database is current and downloaded data are current
    b.   the organizational database is current and downloaded data are out of date
    c.   the organizational database is out of date and downloaded data are current
    d.   the organizational database is out of date and downloaded data are out of date
    e.   it depends on the method used for downloading
    Answer: b   **Reference:**   Section 14.2

15.   In an OLAP cube, the attributes are called:
    a.   axes
    b.   dimensions
    c.   measures
    d.   members
    e.   slices
    Answer: b   **Reference:**   Section 14.3

16.   The dimension(s) that are held constant in an OLAP cube are called:
    a.   axes
    b.   levels
    c.   measures
    d.   members
    e.   slices
    Answer: e   **Reference:**   Section 14.3

17.   The values of a dimension in an OLAP cube are called:
    a.   axes
    b.   levels
    c.   measures
    d.   members
    e.   slices
    Answer: d   **Reference:**   Section 14.3

18.   A data warehouse is a store of enterprise data that is designed for:
    a.   clerks
    b.   data administrators
    c.   database administrators
    d.   developers
    e.   managers
Answer: e   **Reference:**   Section 14.4

19.   A data warehouse is a store of enterprise data designed to:
    a.   support transaction processing
    b.   facilitate management decision making
    c.   hold backup files in case the system needs to be recovered
    d.   hold test data for developers to use when creating new applications
    e.   hold old data that may be used for long-term analysis
Answer: b   **Reference:**   Section 14.4

20.   The term *drill down* means the user wants to:
    a.   summarize data
    b.   get older data
    c.   sort
    d.   get more details
    e.   aggregate data
Answer: d   **Reference:**   Section 14.4

21.   Which operation are users permitted to perform on the data <u>in a warehouse</u>?
    a.   add new data
    b.   delete existing data
    c.   export to
    d.   import from
    e.   update
Answer: d   **Reference:**   Section 14.4

22.   Data in a data warehouse may be inconsistent because of differences in the:
    a.   attributes
    b.   domains
    c.   indexes
    d.   rows
    e.   tables
Answer: b   **Reference:**   Section 14.4

23.   A *data mart* differs from a data warehouse in that the:
    a.   domain is smaller
    b.   domain is larger
    c.   amount of data is smaller
    d.   a and c
    e.   b and c
Answer: d   **Reference:**   Section 14.4

24. Protecting and insuring effective use of the entire organization's data is the responsibility of the:
    a.   office of data administration
    b.   database administrator
    c.   developers
    d.   end users
    e.   vendors
    Answer: a   **Reference:**   Section 14.5

25. Protecting and insuring effective use of a specific database is the responsibility of the:
    a.   office of data administration
    b.   database administrator
    c.   developers
    d.   end users
    e.   vendors
    Answer: b   **Reference:**   Section 14.5

26. A *data proponent* is in charge of:
    a.   developers
    b.   data administration
    c.   data items
    d.   the database
    e.   the database administrator
    Answer: c   **Reference:**   Section 14.5

27. Who resolves conflicts about data? The:
    a.   developers
    b.   data administration
    c.   data items
    d.   users
    e.   database administrator
    Answer: b   **Reference:**   Section 14.5

28. Data administration should have a(n) _____ attitude towards information management.
    a.   ad hoc
    b.   authoritative
    c.   managerial
    d.   proactive
    e.   reactive
    Answer: d   **Reference:**   Section 14.5

FILL IN THE BLANKS

1.   A(n) __multi-user database__ is a database in which more than one user processes the database at the same time.

      Reference: Section 14.0

2.   A microcomputer can __emulate__ or act like a dumb terminal.

      Reference: Section 14.1

3.   A(n) __teleprocessing__ system uses one computer and one CPU.

      Reference: Section 14.1

4.   A system in which one computer processes the database and other computers in the network process application programs is called a(n) __client-server system__ .

      Reference: Section 14.1

5.   A system in which the DBMS as well as the application programs are stored on the users' computers is called a(n) __file-sharing system__ .

      Reference: Section 14.1

6.   A system in which part or all of the database is duplicated on more than one computer is known as a(n) __replicated__ distributed database system.

      Reference: Section 14.1

7.   A system in which parts of the database are stored on more than one computer is known as a(n) __partitioned__ distributed database system.

      Reference: Section 14.1

8.   A(n) __vertical fragment__ refers to a table that is broken into two or more sets of columns.

      Reference: Section 14.1

9.   A(n) __horizontal fragment__ refers to the rows of a table when they are divided into pieces.

      Reference: Section 14.1

10.   Retrieving data from an enterprise server so that they can be used locally is called __downloading__ .

      Reference: Section 14.2

11.   In general, users are not permitted to __update__ data that they downloaded.

      Reference: Section 14.2

12.   A file server on a local area network often serves as a(n) __gateway__ to a mainframe or to other networks.

      Reference: Section 14.2

13.   The activities of local updating and downloading must be carefully __coordinated__ .

      Reference: Section 14.2

14.   When a user changes downloaded data, the data is no longer __consistent__ with the corporate database and also with other users who have downloaded the data.

Reference: Section 14.2

15.   Downloading creates problems with __access control__ , meaning it necessitates placing restrictions on which data each employee may create, delete, read, or update.

Reference: Section 14.2

16.   Downloading data also increases the potential for __computer crime__ .

Reference: Section 14.2

17.   When data in the corporate database is extracted to a file server and users are prohibited from updating, the file server's DBMS does not need to be concerned about __concurrency__ control.

Reference: Section 14.2

18.   Both the columns and the rows of an OLAP cube are called _____axes_____ .

Reference: Section 14.3

19.   The cells of an OLAP cube represent the _____measures_____ of the cube.

Reference: Section 14.3

20.   The values of a dimension of an OLAP cube are called _____members_____ .

Reference: Section 14.3

21.   The position of a dimension in its hierarchy is called its_____level_____ .

Reference: Section 14.3

22.   Downloading moves the data __closer__ to the user.

Reference: Section 14.4

23.   A(n) __data warehouse__ is a store of enterprise data that is designed to facilitate management decision making.

Reference: Section 14.4

24.   A data warehouse needs a __DBMS__ of its own to store and process the data.

Reference: Section 14.4

25.   Getting more detailed information from a data warehouse is called __drilling down__ .

Reference: Section 14.4

26.   Summarizing or grouping data is known as data __aggregation__ .

   Reference: Section 14.4

27.   Many users of data warehouse facilities want to __import__ warehouse data into domain specific programs, such as spreadsheets.

   Reference: Section 14.4

28.   Integrating data from a data warehouse can lead to __inconsistencies__ in timing or domain.

   Reference: Section 14.4

29.   Technical support can be difficult to provide when the environment includes products from more than one __vendor__ .

   Reference: Section 14.4

30.   __Ad hoc__ queries are those that are not of a regular, recurring, pre-planned nature.

   Reference: Section 14.4

31.   The typical data warehouse user does not understand the need for __normalizing__ tables.

   Reference: Section 14.4

32.   A(n) __data mart__ is a facility like a data warehouse but for a much smaller domain.

   Reference: Section 14.4

33.   Most data warehouse users are not skilled at writing queries using __SQL__ .

   Reference: Section 14.4

34.   __Data__ are an important organizational asset, as are plant, equipment, and financial assets.

   Reference: Section 14.5

35.   In addition to protecting the data, the office of data administration must also try to increase the __utility__ of the data.

   Reference: Section 14.5

36.   The scope of the office of data administration is the __entire organization__ .

   Reference: Section 14.5

37.   A(n) __data proponent__ is the organizational unit in charge of managing a specific data item.

   Reference: Section 14.5

38.   The office of data management must have a __proactive__ attitude toward information management.

      Reference: Section   14.5

ESSAY

1.   Contrast a teleprocessing system with client-server, file-sharing, and distributed database architectures.

2.   Describe the downloading process and when it is appropriate.

3.   Contrast the structure and capabilities of relational tables and OLAP cubes.

4.   Describe data warehouses and data marts, giving the uses of both.

5.   What does the term *drill down* mean? Give an example.